Houseways in Southern Oman

This book explores how houses are created, maintained and conceptualized in southern Oman.

Based on long-term research in the Dhofar region, it draws on anthropology, sociology, urban studies and architectural history. The chapters consider physical and functional aspects, including regulations governing land use, factors in siting houses, architectural styles and norms for interior and exterior decorating. The volume also reflects on cultural expectations regarding how and when rooms are used and issues such as safety, privacy, social connectedness and ease of movement. Houses and residential areas are situated within the fabric of towns, comparison is made with housing in other countries in the Arabian Peninsula and consideration is given to notions of the "Islamic city" and the "Islamic house." The book is valuable reading for scholars interested in the Middle East and the built environment.

Marielle Risse is an Associate Professor at Dhofar University in Salalah, Oman. She has taught literature, education and cultural studies on the Arabian Peninsula for a number of years and is the author of *Foodways in Southern Oman* (Routledge, 2020).

Houseways in Southern Oman

Marielle Risse

Routledge
Taylor & Francis Group
LONDON AND NEW YORK

First published 2023
by Routledge
4 Park Square, Milton Park, Abingdon, Oxon OX14 4RN

and by Routledge
605 Third Avenue, New York, NY 10158

Routledge is an imprint of the Taylor & Francis Group, an informa business

British Library Cataloguing-in-Publication Data
A catalogue record for this book is available from the British Library

ISBN: 9781032210865 (hbk)
ISBN: 9781032218595 (pbk)
ISBN: 9781003270317 (ebk)

DOI: 10.4324/9781003270317

Typeset in Sabon
by Deanta Global Publishing Services, Chennai, India

This book is dedicated to my mom for all the flowers, to Sara for all the chats, to Anthony for all the positivity and to the people of Oman for making me feel "at home."

Contents

Preface

Marielle Risse

I once started crying because a light bulb blew out in the living room of my house in the southern Dhofar region of Oman. From long experience I knew there were even 20% chances that the problem was the bulb, the lamp, the adapter, the extension cord and the socket. And I knew that fixing the problem might be two minutes (put in new bulb) or two days (get socket rewired). I couldn't take an intellectual approach to the problem as I sobbed on the sofa, remembering the previous time a bulb blew and I put in a new one, which immediately blew out as well. Then I had to carry the lamp to another room with extra bulbs, cords and adapters to try to figure out the problem, an hour of sorting out what was wrong accompanied by a lot of cussing.

With time, I can see how each element is connected to the larger theme of housing. I had a lamp because, like most Dhofari houses, all the rooms were lit by long florescent tubes and I wanted less harsh lighting. I needed an adapter because all wall sockets are built for three-prong outlets and most appliances have only two prongs so either you stick something into the wall socket to disable safety wire (not a great idea) or you use adapters. I needed the extension cord because most rooms have only one outlet or the outlet is at shoulder height. And as for the socket, sometimes sockets stop working when the electricity goes out. This happens four to five times a year, usually because someone in the neighborhood has turned off the power to fix a problem or has accidentally cut a power line.

These are the kinds of details that I write about, which aren't found in other books about houses on the Arabian Peninsula. This isn't a fault of other writers; it's good for writers to take differing approaches, and my style is influenced by my background in travel writing, which always highlights the writer in the context of the place that is being described. When I read political science and architecture texts about the Arabian Peninsula, I always wonder: what does the author think about this and where are the opinions of the people who live here?

This book has three basic components: nuts and bolts descriptions of houses, a discussion of the cultural aspects such as who goes into which room when and how houses fit within cityscapes. These three sets of facts are interwoven with quotes from my Dhofari informants, as well as insights and anecdotes about how it feels to live in Dhofar from my expat stories. There is basic information, such as most floors are tiled, and details about what this means: it is terrifying to hear a piece of ice drop to the floor, for a small pool of water is impossible to see and water plus slippery tile equals danger.

I give some of my rules for living in Dhofar such as "during a rain-storm, don't start moving furniture until you see which windows are leaking." I made up this rule after a hurricane was moving in from the west so I moved everything out of the living room with western windows, only to have the water come in the eastern windows ruining two carpets. I include how houses are integrated with the natural world: stray camels eating their way through my garden, lizards practicing their mating calls at 2 am, ants invading my kitchen and grackles nesting in the air conditioner covers.

I also explain my informants' struggles with building and furnishing their houses: the joy of re-decorating a mother's room and the pain of realizing your new husband has decorated the bedroom in your least favorite color. The joy of buying good quality frankincense for your mom to burn every morning and the pain of carpenters who aren't ready with the furniture on time.

By chance, I have lived in all four basic types of housing in Salalah, the main city in the Dhofar region: an apartment and a house built for expats, as well as an apartment and a house built for Dhofaris so I talk about the joy of knowing a good plumber and the pain of house builders who start drilling at 6 am. The joys of living in rooms with high ceilings and graceful arches; the pain of having paint thinner disposed of by being poured under my car. There is the thrill of correctly doing an exchange of Ramadan treats with a neighbor and the sorrow of hearing a marriage end in a series of 1 am fights outside their kitchen door because the couple had nowhere else to argue as all the rooms in their house had people in them.

My first book on the Dhofar region, *Community and Autonomy in Southern Oman* (2019), focused on the lifeways of informants who come from one group of tribes, known as *hakli* or *qara*, who speak the unwritten Southern Arabian language of Gibali (Jibbali, also known as Shahri/Shehret) as their first language. The second, *Foodways in Southern Oman* (2021), widened my scope to include information about other Dhofaris.[1] As I often can't tell who owns the house, my focus in this book is again more generally about Dhofari-Omanis rather than just one group of tribes. As in the other books, I try to be clear which level I am talking about, e.g. *hakli*, Dhofaris who live in the mountains, Dhofaris who live in the main city of Salalah etc.[2]

I would like to acknowledge that there is an occasional repetition of facts and citations, as well as the notices of "I will discuss this point further in Chapter X." As this book will be sold online by chapter, I needed to mention important references more than once and point out where further information could be found for readers who will only have one chapter.

For more information about me and my research, please see *Come From Away*, https://mariellerisse.com.

Notes

1 I like the construction of putting "-ways" after a noun (lifeways, foodways, houseways) because the compound word then encompasses objects, actions and beliefs.

When I write "Dhofaris," I mean Omanis who were born, raised and live in this region, i.e. not including Omanis who come from other regions and live temporarily in Dhofar for work or to study.

2 Comments such as "it's usual in Dhofar ..." do not imply that this point is unique to Dhofar. If there is a cultural construct that is exclusive/exceptional, I will make that clear.

Acknowledgments

Marielle Risse

With great happiness, I showed one of the research guys the dedication of my second book: "This book is dedicated to all the Omanis who trusted me with their stories and shared their lives." He tilted his head, stuck his chin out a little, narrowed his eyes and asked, "We trust you?" Ah, the charming *hakli* sense of humor. These types of exchanges still bring on heart palpitations, but I now know better than to show it. I said, "Yes, you trust me. As well you should." He shrugged.

Sometimes doing research is like dancing *Swan Lake* blindfolded in a small room as someone constantly rearranges the furniture; sometimes it's a thing of beauty and a joy forever. I am never on an even keel. My car once broke down, and two research guys came to help. This was during the pandemic, and the time of curfew was approaching so one commandeered a younger brother's car for me to get back home. As I left he told me, "I put some fish in the trunk for you." I got home ten minutes before the curfew to find that "some fish" meant eight lobsters and several kilos of tuna. So I spent an hour finding plastic bags and repacking the freezer and fridge to get everything to fit. The tuna leaked blood overnight so the next morning was spent washing out the fridge and giving all the seafood away. Then the research guy called to say my car was okay, and I started to drive thinking we would meet in a town where I could refill the gas tank. But as I got close, they told me that they wanted to meet in another place so I had to give the car back with only a little fuel and received a lecture on the necessity of planning ahead of time and not being thoughtless. They are generous and I am clueless sums up most of our encounters.

I would like to thank my research assistants who have done amazing work to help with my projects: Onaiza Shaikh, who took beautiful photographs to illustrate housing details; Maria Cristina Hidalgo, who drew helpful architectural plans of houses, buildings and picnic/campsites to help illustrate how space was used; and Arooba Al Mashikhi, who translated the fishing and some housing essays.

I would also like to thank the photographers Salwa Hubais, Hussein BaOmar, M.A. Al Awaid and S.B. who kindly allowed me to use their photos on my website.

I would like to thank my family for a lot of discussions about how people should live and the ruins. The house without walls and the Miss Todmans' house made me realize what a house could be, how it fits into the landscape and how it functions. I also want to thank Paul Malo for his kindness and designing the house without walls, Frank and Sandy for opening their house and their hearts, June and Peter for introducing me to a real English house and Shelia (finally, someone who agrees with me about how to decorate a living room!).

I was in Salalah from July 2019 until the beginning of June 2021 with a lot of lockdowns/curfews and much-delayed mail service. It was a little funny and a little grueling to be writing about houses when, because of online teaching, I left my house only once a week to go grocery shopping for several months at a time. A huge thank you to my home crew for all your support: Sara, Anthony, Barby, Becky, Isadora, Joe, Michael, Mouse, Patty, Teresa, Traci and Yash, and to Keye, who was here in spirit and sent articles.

Thanks to Trygve, Sandrine and her family and Fran for friendship through the pandemic and quarantines: boxes on the bus, avocados by my door, talks in the garden and "there's chocolate at the grocery store."

My gratitude to Steve Cass who always spoke truth to power; his kindness and friendship are missed by many people.

For helping me create a happy home, I want to thank Ali, world's best landlord, and Dr Elke.

At work, I would like to thank Dr Julius Irudayasamy, Dr Ali Algryani, Dr Amer Ahmed, Dr Hussain Al Dheeb, Dr Iryna Lenchuk, Dr Osman Yapar, Dr Sani Yantandu, Dr Said Bait Mubarak, Mr Said Al Maashani and Dr Yasser Sabtan for their kindness and collegiality. I want to especially thank Dr Hedi Haddad and Dr Zied Bouyahia, who stood by me in difficult times; your encouragement and friendship brightened many dark days.

I would like to thank Stephen Kite, Toni Kotnik and Gabriele vom Bruck for sending me copies of their work and Sandrine Sjolund for useful comments on an early draft of Chapter 1. I would like to express my appreciation to Laurent Bonnefoy, Steve Caton and Anne Meneley for their support of my work. I am grateful to Vincent Charpentier for reviewing the sections on pre-historic lifeways in Chapter 2; any mistakes that remain are mine.

I would also like to thank the anonymous reviewers of various articles and books who gave encouraging and pertinent suggestions; it was a blessing to have comments from people who did not think I should imitate their research interests.

I am grateful for *Aida* (Broadway and concept albums); "Mama Knows the Highway," Hal Ketchum; "Unwritten," Natasha Bedingfield; "La Vie Boheme," *Rent*; "Drunk Americans," Toby Keith; "American Rock 'n Roll," Kid Rock, "Let the River Run," Carly Simon, as well as Jimmy Buffet, Pink, Prince, Bob Seger, Shaggy and Tina Turner.

For more information about me and my research, please see *Come From Away*, https://mariellerisse.com.

1 Overview

Introduction

When I was elected to the Board of Governors of a small expat school in Salalah, a friend whose child attended the school told me, "Everyone wants a good education for their children and everyone has a different idea of what 'a good education' means." The same holds true for houses; everyone wants a safe house and a comfortable house, but the definition of what is "safe" and "comfortable" changes widely across cultures.

Most houses in Salalah, the main city in the region of Dhofar, have barred windows on the ground floor. I look at the bars and think "to keep thieves out" and a fire safety hazard; Dhofaris think "to keep children safe" because with bars, children can't jump out of the window. I keep my front door locked when I am at home; the Dhofari men in my research group think this is ridiculous because Dhofar is "safe."

In this book, I will talk about how houses are constructed and what they look like, but the heart of this work is the discussion about the beliefs linked to houses: how do Dhofaris create a house that is "safe" and "comfortable"? What does it mean to be a "good neighbor"? Where do people feel "at home" outside of their own home? How do houses here compare to houses I have lived and/or visited in Egypt, Jordan, the United Arab Emirates, Australia, Denmark, Germany, Greece, Italy, the Netherlands, the United Kingdom and India?

In exploring Dhofari concepts of home use, I use interviews with local informants and examples from other countries on the Arabian Peninsula, such as work on Qatar, Yemen, the Emirates and Saudi Arabia.[1] I also explain the pragmatics of maintaining privacy in middle-class houses by drawing on over 15 years of living in and visiting Dhofari-designed houses. I discuss texts on architectural history and design on the Arabian Peninsula, the use of the *salle* and *majlis*, "Islamic city," the "Islamic house" and Arab Urbanism.

Research focus: culture, space and privacy

My previous books are *Community and Autonomy in Southern Oman* (2019) and *Foodways in Southern Oman* (2021). Most of my work has been with

DOI: 10.4324/9781003270317-1

informants who come from one group of tribes, *qara* or *hakli*, who speak an unwritten Southern Arabian language called Gibali (Jebbali/Shahri) as their first language with family and friends; they speak Arabic in educational, business, government and religious settings. This book will include a larger sample of the Dhofari population groups because when looking at houses it is not always possible to know which tribe the owner belongs to.

As with my first two books, I focus here on middle-class Dhofari life, meaning people who do not have food scarcity and can afford their own house and a car. As health care is subsidized, high school graduates with good grades are given university scholarships and there are several types of monthly government aid for people who are unable to work, the majority of Dhofaris are middle class, a social level about which there is not a lot of research on the Arabian Peninsula.

I found a lot of information about "starchitects" and historic buildings, but nothing about camping and having picnics, something most Dhofaris do every week. Although social media from the Arabian Peninsula is full of images of cups of tea next to campfires, there is no academic work on the when, where, why and how of camping, much less what camping signifies, what role it plays in creating and passing on knowledge, solidifying friendship groups etc.

I also use comparisons with Western texts, for example, Speck's ideas about a "useful, safe, comfortable, and interesting" city in *Walkable City: How Downtown Can Save America One Step at a Time* (2013 11) are very different from Dhofari concepts. In *Happy City: Transforming Our Lives Through Urban Design* (2014) Montgomery argues that a "meaningful life" encompasses "getting up every day and working very hard towards goals that make your life meaningful … [the] realization of talent and potential, and the feeling that you are able to make the most of your abilities in life" (36).[2] For these two authors, a good civic life means little or no commute, access to nature, shops and friends nearby, feeling safe in your dooryard, etc. Most Dhofaris would instead emphasize nearness to extended family and a mosque. One informant told me that the good house was located "500 meters from mosque"; a second told me "three plots [i.e. three houses] from mosque."

This chapter sets out my methodology, gives a general description of the area discussed and includes a literature review. Chapter 2 covers the physical setting and the history of housing in Dhofar. Chapter 3 explains how houses are sited, built, decorated and repaired. Chapter 4 walks through each of the different elements of a house including doors, windows, walls and each of the types of room, as well as a section on apartments.

Once these basics are explained, the next four chapters focus on the topics of cultures and space.[3] In Chapter 5 I focus on questions such as: who controls the house (and what does "control" mean)? How and when do people move between and within houses? Looking at a house from the outside, how can you tell what is happening inside? What are sights, sounds, smells and textures within a house? What is the connection between animals and houses? Between religion and houses? How is housing different for Dhofaris and expats?

A second theme is: how are the spaces within a house used? For example, the fact that Dhofari women wear long, loose housedresses with a light, cotton headscarf at all times inside the house makes their conception of private and public spaces within houses much different than the rest of the Arabian Peninsula. A lot of writing about privacy within houses centers on the idea that women need to always be kept out of sight because she is not modestly dressed. For example in Saudi, women might remove hair covering and wear sleeveless shirts and/or mini-skirts in the *salle* (female/family living room). This would not happen in Dhofar, and by taking their privacy with them from room to room, so to speak, there is less worry about blocking off parts of the house from women.

Chapter 6 concentrates on how spaces outside of a house are created to be and treated as a home, for example while living in a rented space, picnicking and camping. Chapter 7 begins with a discussion of the "Islamic city" using Abu-Lughod's (1987) and Bianca's (2000) texts as starting points. It then examines how various types of places, such as stores and public parks, are placed and used in relation to houses. Next, I discuss how house design and usage in Dhofar differs from other Arabian Peninsula countries including Yemen, Qatar and Kuwait.

The final chapter centers on the concept of privacy, beginning with a discussion of the term "Islamic" houses. I then explore in detail not only who goes where within a house but who sees what; for example, how houses are planned to have both long sightlines, e.g. the main corridor, and limited viewsheds, e.g. never being able to see the upper floors. I give several illustrations of how Dhofaris create pockets of seclusion within the public spaces in houses, the necessity of not observing neighbors, how to cover windows, what types of noises are acceptable and what is photographed within a house.

Lastly, a theme that developed during my research that I had not foreseen was the disparity between how most Dhofaris live in houses that they have designed but move through many spaces (cafes, restaurants, shops, malls, institutes of higher learning etc.) which were planned by people who have never lived in Oman and/or have no conception of everyday lifeways. This is combined with a cultural understanding of not publicly announcing information so that many buildings, including where I work, do not have maps or lists of room numbers in the lobby. The result is a lot of time spent wandering around looking for a specific place.[4]

Tribes

As all Omanis belong to a tribe and tribal identity impacts how and where Dhofaris live, I would like to briefly engage with the term. As Brandt explains

> During the period of the Euro-American colonial expansions, the term "tribe" served as a term for societies that were considered "primitive,"

> "uncivilized," or "underdeveloped." During the postcolonial era, the concept of "tribe" and the evolutionist world view behind it were critically discussed. as a consequence, the term tribe was widely discredited and abandoned as an analytical term.
>
> (2021 11)

But Dhofari cultures can't be understood without not only using the word but using it in a positive way. In America the adjective "tribal" is often used meaning either unthinking loyalty or as signaling an object was made in the periphery of the first world, such as a dress or handbag that is or looks handmade.

It is heartening to read Brandt because, even though she is writing about Yemen, her work reflects the reality in Dhofar in that the term here means "locally specific notions of belonging, genealogy and descent, territory, collective agency and interaction with the wider world" (12). Further,

> rather than being anachronisms or expressions of nostalgia for the past, tribes and tribalism are phenomena that are able to cope with and respond to changing circumstances in their social, political, economic and ecological environments … [also] despite its ability to change and the impossibility of a concluding definition, tribalness or *qabyalah* remains an organizing principle, mostly in the sense of giving priority to kinship loyalties and common action with those who are considered fellow tribesmen.
>
> (16, 17)

"Giving priority" is a very important concept as, from the outside, belonging to a tribe is sometimes seen as the necessity of lock-step behavior. As William and Fidelity Lancaster rightly point out

> tribes, and the series of named sets that make up a tribe are not corporate, solidary, or legal bodies. Tribes and their series of named sections cannot and do not act as one, and are not jointly responsible for each other … The unnamed and indeterminate groups that comprise the named sets are made up of autonomous individuals living in a moral balance expressed as a balance of honour and equated with right behaviour.[5]
>
> (2020 177)

Rather than the common, negative connotation of tribes being dangerous, the Lancasters explain

> As men [I would say "people" when referring to *hakli* tribes] should live in a personal peace of behaving rightly, so should tribes. Keeping the peace is the purpose of tribal leaders, who become leaders because tribesmen gather around them for particular enterprises and in certain situations. They are regarded to be more able to judge events and

> personalities, to be experienced and well-informed, to have shown courage, integrity, and generosity, to be skilled in negotiations.
>
> (177)

An additional point is that while tribe is an important factor in a person's life, it is not an all-defining attribute. An older quote from Eickelman is helpful in understanding this point:

> Persons achieve social honor on the basis of varying, experimental combinations of their attributes – wealth, political office, residence in a quarter ... or descent from the Prophet, etc. – in no case can the social honor of an individual be determined from the abstract knowledge of his attributes or statuses alone.
>
> (1974 281)

In other words, the tribe name, as well as what section of Dhofar a person lives in, will assist you in creating an image of that person. Job title might also give information, but there are many factors at play in creating a person's reputation. Someone with a high-status job might, by their behavior, have a terrible reputation.

Methodology

In my other two books, *Community and Autonomy in Southern Oman* (2019) and *Foodways in Southern Oman* (2021), I have written long explanations about my methods; for more details, please see Chapter 1 of each book. In brief, I have worked with three separate groups of Gibali-speaking Dhofari men who I refer to as "research guys" as to call a man a "friend" would imply a romantic relationship. None of these men are associated with the university where I work. I am also friends with several Dhofari women. "Informants" means I did formal interviews for this book; not all Dhofari friends are informants and not all informants are friends. When I mention house visits, camping trips, weddings, etc., I have coded Excel charts with documentation such as the date, place, who I was with and what happened.

I started research on houses in the summer of 2019 as I was working on my book about foodways.[6] I had to write about how kitchens are situated, designed, decorated and used in Dhofari houses, and as I found this work so interesting, I started taking notes and asking questions about other rooms in houses, as well as collecting photographs. When the food book was sent to the publisher, I began working on houses full time by finding and reading texts about houses on the Arabian Peninsula. I did targeted interviews and went back through my research notes to compile charts about which houses I had been in and for what reason.

There are Dhofari houses I have been in more than 25 times, while some I have only visited once. I have done many social visits as well as visits to give condolences, for doing my make-up for a party, *Eid* visits, *iftar* meals at sunset during Ramadan, to meet a new baby, a formal dinner party, birthday parties and to see a new house. With the men in my research group, I have been on almost 400 picnics, more than 30 camping trips and over a dozen boat trips. I have been invited to see several houses that were being built by friends and snuck into more than a dozen houses that were being built in the neighborhood where I have lived.

In the spring of 2021, I hired Maria Cristina Hidalgo and Onaiza Shaikh to help with documentation; both have lived in Dhofar for more than 20 years. From information I gave her, Ms Hidalgo created floor plans from Dhofari-planned houses to show how rooms are organized and the placement of furniture. She also created maps of picnic and camping sites. Ms Shaikh took photographs of the exterior of houses to show design details (such as windows) and the steps of house construction. As it is too expensive to include these images in this book, they are all available on my website. In the spring of 2022, I hired Arooba Al Mashikhi to translate some of the essays on the topics of housing and fishing on my website into Arabic.

All of my work circles around the question: how do middle-class, Arab, Muslim, tribal, Dhofari people live day to day? The limitation I see in myself is that I cannot get to the research guys' level of instinctive kindness and generosity. If you imagine a person coming to your house and asking, "Why did you put that sofa there? Is this the usual temperature of this room? How many times a day do you sit in the living room? May I take a photo of your kitchen? How much did it cost to decorate your brother's room when he got married? Where do you eat breakfast? Do you lock your door when you sleep? How many houses have you lived in? Do you have a particular place in the house where you pray? How long did it take you to build this house? Why did you choose this color for the walls? Do you have a regular repair person for the ACs?" etc., you have a sense of what my informants are up against.[7]

The limitations to my research that others see are language, historical knowledge and writing style. I do not speak Gibali and am not fluent in academic Arabic. The people who believe that it's impossible to write about a culture without speaking the language have made their position perfectly clear to me. My area of interest is not linguistics, and I am happy Dr Miranda Morris and Dr Janet Watson have created a research group to focus on linguistics and cultures.[8]

This book does not go deeply into historical knowledge of houses. I would love to know about the mountain lifestyles of living in caves and practicing transhumance, but this would require interviews with older Dhofaris on sensitive subjects such as lifeways before and during the Dhofar War (1965–75), information which would not be readily shared with an outsider. That is a topic for someone local or fluent in Gibali and able to win the trust of older people in order to learn about how caves were chosen for habitation and the placement of objects/arrangement of eating, sleeping and sitting spaces.

My writing style has been called "accessible" (not as a compliment) and "a sort of laundry-list description, without ethnographic experiences." Given how few texts have been written by expats who have lived in Oman for more than 15 years, I am pleased my books are understandable to non-specialist audiences.

The issue of carefully choosing ethnographic examples and making general statements is a result of living in the place I am describing. My life is very different than people who do fieldwork and then return to a home institution. I am one of very few North Americans in Dhofar; every time I leave my house, I see people who know who I am, including my students and their parents.

Few Dhofari women are close friends with Christian, expat women and covering my informants is extremely important because if I am too specific, for example saying, an informant "with this number of children" or "who works at this place," many Dhofaris would know exactly who I was talking about.[9]

With men, part of my research is trying to fit the oddity of an American woman sitting alone with a Dhofari man into an acceptable cultural framework. To give one example of the complexities I navigate: one evening I set up a meeting with one of the *hakli* research guys (X). I had thought we were, as usual, going to sit in an open area away from the nearest town, so I brought supplies to make tea including firewood. After an hour's drive, I arrived to find that he had been sick, so he decided we would sit in an outside café out of the wind. After 20 minutes, a *hakli* friend of his (Y) arrived. X talked to Y for a few moments, and then Y went to sit at another table. X told me that when I was finished asking questions, he would invite Y to sit with us.

I was disappointed as I had been trying to catch X for over a month, and now our conversation time would be cut short. But I also realized that I had not seen him because he was sick, and, as usual among *haklis*, he had not told me as he did not want me to worry. Meeting at the café meant I could finally ask questions, but also that I would have to spend at least an hour chatting with X and Y so that Y could learn who I was and what I was doing. *Hakli* male friends do not usually ask questions of each other. X has known me for more than ten years but never mentioned me to Y and, as a good friend, Y would not ask who I was. Thus X and I would need to spend time with Y so that Y could fit me into an explicable framework. The cost, so to speak, of X meeting me in a café was the time and effort needed to explain why X was in a café with a woman.

So I reevaluated which questions to ask, and after half an hour, X went to Y's table and asked Y and two other friends to join us. They declined out of politeness and X insisted. The three men and X came over to the table where I was sitting and there was a short conversation about me; then, the four men talked to each other while I sat quietly for half an hour. Now that the preliminaries were over, the talk opened up to include me again for about ten minutes and then the men talked to each other. After another 20 minutes, I left. Leaving quickly, i.e. as soon as Y joined us, would have been read as my being angry or trying to hide something. This would mean that X would not bring me to that café or to meet those men again.

As an example of asking questions when I wanted to get information about the party given when people move into a new house, I asked a *hakli* man (Z) who I knew had moved into a new house within the last two years, "Did you give a party when you moved to your house? Is that common?" His answer, like most I am given, started with the religious context, moved to his specific circumstances and then to general statements.

He began by reminding me that in Islam, there were only two celebrations (*Eid al Adha* and *Eid at Fitr*) and that other parties (*hafla*) were "not good" but that some people had parties when they moved to a new house. In his opinion, it was "not necessary to have a party." Then he said more specifically that in Islam the best is "to do something the people not to see it, hidden" and that it is "better to help the people" than have a party. His suggestion was to kill an animal and give the meat to people to celebrate the good fortune of having a new house.

Then he said that maybe the people spent all their money on the house, so they would not have enough for a party. Also, he said that people should "look at your family" to see what others have done. It is important to be "thinking from all sides." For example, one of his older brothers had moved into a new house less than a year before, and as that brother did not have a party, he decided it was better to also not have a party. His brother did not have money for a party and Z did not want people to wonder why Z invited people but not his brother. Thus Z felt he had respected his religion and his family by not having a party.

However, if a person wanted to, it was fine. He had been to several housewarmings (my term, not his), and when I asked him about how they were organized, he explained who was invited and what food was served.

Everything I am told that I can't verify from experience, I re-check with others. For example, I asked a *hakli* informant (A) for information about when he started camping and for stories about camping as a teenager. Two months later, I was sitting with two other *hakli* informants (B and C) talking about fishing for a different project. I asked them if I could check something, and when they agreed, I said that I would tell them some details about camping and could they please think if this information was similar or different to what they had experienced. Then I ran through the information that A had given me without mentioning his name or tribe. B and C reflected and concurred that A's description of camping was similar to their own and then mentioned a few funny situations that they had faced while camping as young teenagers.

General description of Dhofar and Salalah

To help orient the reader, the following is a brief description of Dhofar and its main city, Salalah.[10] There is a more detailed description in Chapter 2.

Dhofar

Dhofar is 99,300 square km and is the southernmost of the 11 governorates in Oman. The coast of the Indian Ocean is south, Yemen lies to the west, Saudi Arabia is north and the other Omani governorates are to the east/north-east.

There are two main roads which connect Dhofar to the rest of Oman. One starts on the coast at Salalah (the main town), goes north through the mountains and then north-east across the desert plains through the towns of Thumrait, Dauka/Dawkah and Muqshin, the furthest north town in Dhofar (350 km N of Salalah).

The other road starts at Sarfait in the south-west corner of Dhofar and the southern of the two border-crossings with Yemen. The road follows east through the coastal towns of Dhalkut/Dalkut, Rakhyut, Mughsayl, Salalah, Taqa, Mirbat, Sudah, Hadbeen/Hadbin and Hasik. Then the road turns inland though dry mountains and returns to the coast at Shuwaymiyah after which the road again turns inland to Shalim and then back to the coast at Sharbithat (369 km E of Salalah).

Dhofar has ten provinces (*wilayat*) seven of which are along the southern coast and have the same name as the principle town, from west to east: Dhalkut, Rakhyut, Salalalh, Mirabt, Taqa, Sudah and Shalim, which includes the seven Hallaniyat Islands.

The province of Thumreit/Thumrait is centered on the town of Thumreit (86 km N of Salalah), on the far side of the mountains which surround Salalah's coastal plain. The province of Muqshin is the northernmost area, and Mazyona/Mazyunah is the western province. The town of Mazyona is the northern border crossing with Yemen. All of the 300 km western border is with Yemen, but there are only two crossing points, and, given the current unrest in Yemen, there is now a strong military presence at the Oman-Yemen border and, along part of the border, a technologically enhanced fence.[11]

Dhofar has five distinct geographic regions: beach/coast, coastal plains, mountains, *nejd* and desert. The southern border is the Indian Ocean. There is a straight, sandy beach running from the port of Raysut (the western part of the city of Salalah) 40 km east to the coastal town of Taqa.

North of the beach close to Salalah, there is a flat plain that extends north for about 15 km miles and east for 30 km. Along the coast to the east and west, the mountains come down to the ocean so there is usually either no beach or sheltered bays that are used for fishing but have no permanent structures. In the places where there is a small coastal plain, there are towns such as Hadbin and Hasik.

North of Salalah's coastal plain is a semi-circle of three sets of mountains: Jebel al Qamar (*jebel* is "mountain" in Arabic, *qamar* is "moon" in Arabic) to the east of Salalah, Jebel al Qara behind Salalah and Jebel Samhan to the west of Salalah. They are referred to by their name or as one entity ("the mountain"). Jebel al Qamar continues west to the Hadhramaut region in Yemen; Samhan is the highest, over 2,000 meters (see Zarins 2001 23).

The *nejd* is the area on the far side of the mountains as they slope down to the desert (to the north and north-east of Salalah) with fewer people, settlements and plants. North-east of Thumreit is the archeological site of Shisur which is on the edge of the true desert, the Empty Quarter. This area, the north-east section of Dhofar, has another small town, Hashman, which is the most common jumping-off place for desert adventures.

Salalah

The southern edge of Salalah is the beach of the Indian Ocean. The area closest to the beach is neighborhoods of houses and (on the eastern side) small, walled farms. The central area, Haffa, has Al Husn/Hosn palace and used to hold the main traditional souq. The souq has been closed, and the surrounding neighborhood's houses have been destroyed to ready the area for a coming multi-purpose development.

The northern edge of the city is the Salalah Bypass Road which runs east/west. It has the access to the airport and several roundabouts, from which one can go south into town, north into the mountains, west towards Yemen or east towards several coastal towns and, eventually, to Muscat. There is car traffic, but this road is heavily used by construction and cargo trucks.[12]

The section to the north of the Salalah Bypass Road has some housing areas but is mostly left open. In *khareef* (the monsoon season, June–September) it is inhabited by camel herders who build make-shift corrals and tents, usually a metal frame covered with a water-proof tarp.

The western edge of Salalah is the Raysut section where there is a small harbor for fishing boats, the Hilton, the free zone and the large, commercial port for cargo ships. Further west past Raysut, the mountains come down to the sea and the road turns inland continuing past a few villages and two coastal towns, ending at the border with Yemen.

To the east, the town ends at open, flat, sandy/rocky land. There is a clear break between Salalah, a coastal development with hotels and condominiums, and then the coastal town of Taqa. From Taqa, the road continues along the coast (with a few roundabout with roads leading north up into the mountains) through four coastal towns, then a long stretch through high rocky, barren mountains, eventually ending up in the coastal town of Shuwaymiyah, where the road turns inland and connects to the main road to Muscat.

Thus, from Salalah there are three roadways: west to Raysut then along to Yemen, north to Thumreit then onwards across the desert to Muscat or east to the coastal towns and uninhabited areas on the coastal road to Muscat.

Literature review

This section is not meant to be an exhaustive list of works on architecture on the Arabian Peninsula. I focus on texts which helped me put Dhofari houses into the larger context of international work on houses, as well as Arabic and Islamic cultures.

Thinking about a "house" in different cultural contexts: *Patterns of Home*

I like Alexander et al.'s *A Pattern Language: Towns, Buildings, Construction* (1977) for the same reason I like *Architectural Digest*. Some people want to read realistic suggestions about how to create a home; I like to see photos of living spaces that are well planned down to the last detail. For me, the fact that the book is unrealistic (the only group who create houses which follow its principles are Hobbits) does not take away from the impressive collection of information.

Two architects who worked on *A Pattern Language* and their business partner later wrote *Patterns of Home: The Ten Essentials of Enduring Design* (Jacobson, Silverstein and Winslow 2002). This book helped me reflect on how Dhofari houses are built and lived in following different cultural understandings than in North America.

It would be easy to say that the basic difference is that *A Pattern Language* and *Patterns of Home* take for granted that all members of the house will have equal access to the common rooms so there is an emphasis on flow and connection which does not translate to Dhofari homes which are designed to keep certain people in specific locations. For example, the *majlis* (male/male guest sitting room) needs to have an external door and attached bathroom so guests will never see the main part of the house, as well as an internal door so people can bring in food and drink. Also, the maid's bedroom should be away from public rooms and family bedrooms, hence it is usually located next to the kitchen or on the roof.

But I think it is more interesting to look at the design elements, given that *Patterns of Home*'s recommendations for planning homes do not hold up cross-culturally. I am not pointing this out as a mistake or error on the part of the authors. Their houses are beautiful and they do not make any claim for universal application. But seeing their photos of houses designed following their patterns made me look at Dhofari houses in a new way.

For example, one pattern they recommend is a "sheltering roof" which, in their examples, is always sloped. They even address the topic directly with a side-bar: "Can a flat roof be a sheltering roof?" (93). The answer is an implicit "no" with the example of how homeowners transformed flat-roofed, Le Corbusier-designed houses in Pessac, France, by adding pitched roofs.

Dhofari houses have emphatically flat roofs with many horizontal elements such as a cornice with only level, parallel lines on the decorative molding. By law, all roofs have some sort of wall around the edge for safety, and the most common type is plastered cement blocks up to waist height with a smooth, level top.[13] Some houses have a more traditional style in which rooflines look like battlements with the edge wall as a parapet with stepped crenellations, sometimes fashioned to look like the distinctive local style of incense burners, *majmar*.

The roof could still be seen as "sheltering," but in a militaristic way in that most Dhofaris houses look eminently defendable. Storming a Dhofari house would require climbing over the surrounding wall and running across the open *hosh* (courtyard) while being vulnerable to attack from people on the roof.

Similarly, the discussions about "composing with light" and "composing with materials" made it easier for me to articulate how rooms are designed and decorated in Dhofari houses. First, the view is rarely if ever taken into account. Dhofaris don't sit and look out of windows; seats are placed around the perimeter of the room facing in. Except for small, opaque windows in kitchens and bathrooms which are connected to extractor fans, all windows have elaborate treatments usually including a sheer chiffon underlayer and two or three heavy, lined, light-blocking layers with fringes and beading, as well as a valance or pelmet/cornice with swags. *Patterns of Home*'s designs in which windows are places to catch sunlight throughout the day make no sense in Dhofar, where everyone is trying to avoid the sun as much as possible.

Reading "composing with materials" made me realize that wood is only used for doors and doorframes, never floors, and stone is not used as a design element. Sitting rooms and bedrooms are usually made with the contrasting elements of hard (white tile floors, concrete block walls, sofas and chairs which are usually firm to the point of uncomfortable) and soft (rugs, cushions, curtains made of silk, velvet, tulle, chiffon etc.). Courtyards have a paving brick (interlock) floor and are surrounded by six-foot or taller concrete block walls. There might be a tree (usually with a metal fence around the base to protect it from cars and hungry camels) or plants in pots, but no other greenery.

Also *Patterns of Home* raises the question: who can have a house built to their specifications? The gorgeous photos make me remember that such living spaces are now and will forever be out of my budget. There are three non-Omanis I know well who have hired an architect to plan and builders to make a house: two are American millionaires and the other is an Indian man who works as a low-level clerk. That sentence encapsulates a fundamental issue of house construction. In places where hired labor is expensive, only the very rich can live in a house they have designed; in places where hired labor is inexpensive, like Dhofar and India, great wealth is not needed. In Salalah, I know a taxi driver who, with his brothers who have similar low-paying jobs, built a large, three-story house.

Thinking about a house in different cultural contexts: *"The Kabyle House" and "A House Turned Inside Out"*

Another text that helped me think about how to explain Dhofari houses is Bourdieu's "The Kabyle House or the World Reversed" (1972). I read it several times and thought often about his series of oppositions, e.g.

> between the house and the men's assembly, between private life and public life, or, if you will, between the full light of day and the secrecy

> of night, corresponds exactly to the opposition between the dark, nocturnal, lower part of the house and the noble, brightly lit, upper part. (142)

I agree that

> the special position of the house within the system of magical representations and ritual practices justifies the initial abstraction by which it is taken out of the larger system so as to be treated as a system in its own right. (footnote 3, 134)

Most of the chapters in this book are an argument for looking at houses in and of themselves. However, Bourdieu's point of view, like most writing about the Arabian Peninsula, is focused on male/female separation, whereas in Dhofar segregation and privacy within houses are based on relationships and age as well as gender.

For example, the *majlis* is usually described as the male sitting room, but in daily life, a middle-aged woman will use the room more than a ten-year-old boy. When I go to a female informant's house to ask questions, we almost always sit in the *majlis* because the door can be locked to keep children out. My female interlocutor wants to talk without being interrupted, and the *salle* is open to the main hallway. For weddings and parties, the *majlis* becomes female territory.

The *salle* is usually described as the female or family sitting room, but men who live in the house and the fathers, brothers, sons, uncles and nephews of female inhabitants, as well as male neighbors, use it. An older man with limited mobility may spend his days in the *salle*, as there is visual access to the main hallway so he can be more integrated into the life of the house and people are easier to call for/hear.

It was useful to read vom Bruck's response to "The Kabyle House" in her article "A House Turned Inside Out: Inhabiting Space in a Yemeni City" (1997). Although her work is based in Yemen, many points correspond closely to Dhofar in that gender is not the only or, in some cases, the most important indicator of where a person might go in the house. For example,

> The attributes of the body – inherited substance, gender, age – are taken by Yemenis as indices of inner moral states and used to place persons into diverse categories. What is read into space depends on what is read into their bodies. For example, Yemeni prepubescent boys are permitted to enter into space occupied by unrelated women because their gaze does not yet indicate carnal desire. (142)

In the same manner there are "spatial divisions in accordance with asymmetrical same-gender relationships such as those between unmarried sisters and wives" (152). In Dhofar there are also subtle hierarchy differences between girls of the same age if one is the daughter and the other is the granddaughter of the senior man.

Further, vom Bruck explains

> On the one hand, the house is the inviolable, sacred patrimony of its owners. On the other hand, to a significant extent ... Both men and women can hardly ever be at ease when they leave one space in order to pass into another ... Crossing the threshold from the entrance hall to the various rooms, or from one room to another, requires knowledge about the people who occupy the space they might wish to enter. (167)

I will go into detail about this aspect of movement within houses in Chapter 5, but I would like to highlight here that where a person goes within a house is more dependent on who is in that space than which space it is.

Feeling "at home" in public: *Global Dreams*

A theme that I had not considered when I started working on this topic was how Dhofaris feel, or did not feel, "at home" in public. Reading De Koning's *Global Dreams: Class, Gender, and Public Space in Cosmopolitan Cairo* (2009) made me realize that I needed to ask my informants, for example, about how they made choices as to where they would have coffee and eat in public.

Ammann's article "Islam in Public Space" (2002) and his book co-authored with Göle, *Islam in Public: Turkey, Iran and Europe* (2006), helped me think more deeply about these issues, especially Komecoglu's chapter, "New Sociabilities: Islamic Cafes in Istanbul." AlMutawa examines similar questions from an insider's perspective in her series of short articles about the United Arab Emirates for the *London School of Economics Middle East Blog* (2019a, b, 2018, 2017). The insights elicited by these texts are discussed in Chapter 6.

Key Arabic and/or Islamic architecture texts: Hakim, Ragette and Maneval

Hakim's *Arabic-Islamic Cities: Building and Planning* (2008, originally published 1986) centers on the city of Tunis with many photos and maps to explain the religious and cultural rules which underpinned the city's expansion. Hakim and I are interested in different topics, but we are kindred spirits in our love of exhaustive explanations with lots of details. There are many writers who talk about "Islamic cities" or "Arab cities," but Hakim writes out the sections from the holy Qu'ran and the *Sunnah* (the sayings of the Prophet Mohammed) that he thinks are relevant to how a Muslim should live. He documents the smallest architectural elements such as windows and door placement to explain how sightlines are blocked to create privacy at the doorstep, as well as larger components such as markets and mosques.

Ragette's *Traditional Domestic Architecture of the Arab Region* (2003) starts with the origins of architecture and then explains traditional materials and construction techniques such as post-beam and building with palm fronds, as well as issues relating to water and waste management. Like most authors, he focuses on courtyard houses, designs for creating privacy from strangers and the segregation of genders using examples from Morocco, Algeria, Tunisia, Libya, Egypt, Syria, Lebanon, Jordan/Palestine, Iraq, Saudi Arabia, United Arab Emirates, Yemen and Oman. Of his 15 Omani examples, six are from Dhofar: two each from the towns of Salalah, Mirbat and Sadh. His interest is in the architectural details, so there is no information about when the houses were built, only detailed drawings of the exterior and floor plans with room types marked.

I read Maneval's *New Islamic Urbanism* (2019) at the very start of my work on this topic, and it helped shape my thinking about cities, houses, space and privacy. I am grateful that the author addresses issues on the Arabian Peninsula from an academic, as well as personal, point of view. Maneval has a thorough understanding of the architectural history of Jeddah, but, to me, the best aspect is his musings on what "it's like" to walk down the streets and through the buildings. I have read many discussions of Arabian Peninsula cities, but he is the only author who talks in the first person about the difficulty of everyday actions such as crossing a street or finding the entrance to a building.[14]

In this work he wants to reframe the concepts of public and private to

> conceive of these spaces as variable products of social practice involving both people and artefacts ... [e.g.] walls, doors, curtains etc. are not enough to turn a building into a private space. It could just as well be used as an office or for the assembly of a political party. In order for it to become a private space, whether continuously or temporarily, people have to use it as such, that is, keep other people out to remain undisturbed, screen certain bodily appearances and activities from view, do what they only want to do alone or with a limited number of persons with whom they share an intimate bond.
>
> (63)

A sub-theme is how gender separation displaces both women and men with examples of how he was not being able to enter an art exhibit or sit in a café with a group of men. His opening example, of being guided/guarded through a female-only university, is the only time I have read a male author explaining how it feels to be "othered" on the Arabian Peninsula.

I will discuss his findings in greater detail in sections on the "Islamic city" (Chapter 7) and privacy (Chapter 8), but here I would like to look closely at his term "New Islamic Urbanism." This means buildings "characterised by screens, metal blinds, walled enclosures, tinted windows, shutters etc." which disconnect interior spaces and residents from the outside world (222). The result of this type of architecture is to

> enable a wide range of activities which are prohibited in public. At home, away from the public eye, people do not have to follow the rules of conduct derived from Wahhabi theological exegesis that govern public urban spaces. The architecture of seclusion thus enables different conceptions of privacy: one centres on concealing the body and avoiding contact between unrelated men and women; another emphasises the non-interference of outsiders in personal affairs and the freedom of the individual. My assumption is that New Islamic Urbanism was so successful because it served different needs and even contrary desires.
> (222–3)[15]

Further, Maneval emphasizes that houses with barriers "that are supposed to protect potential targets of militant Islamists in Saudi Arabia actually make these targets much more identifiable ... [as] they become reminders of the fact that something needs to be hidden, shut in and defended" (162). What is "hidden" is the disconnect between behavior inside and outside of home spaces, e.g.

> Just as airtight sealing of rooms enables air conditioners to generate an indoor climate that contrasts with outdoors weather, the architectural insulation of domestic space permits social practices that deviate completely from the rules governing behaviour in public. Headscarf, veil and *ʿabāya* have to be worn only outside the home ... Thus the walls and screens of residential homes offer a refuge for otherwise forbidden practices, heterogeneous identities and divergent worldviews, as well as platforms of exchange for dissident political opinions.
> (162, 165)

This is crucial because it clarifies the difference between Dhofar and other places on the Arabian Peninsula. Although the houses in Maneval's book, as well as imagines in books about Qatar, the Emirates, Bahrain and Kuwait, are similar to Dhofar with large cement-block houses surrounded by a high wall, the actions of Dhofaris make the use of the house quite different.

Reading Maneval made me understand how houses are not necessarily "a refuge for otherwise forbidden practices" in Dhofar where homes are more permeable in that there are often people coming to the house unexpectedly. For example, family members often drop off foodstuffs and prepared food such as fish, limes, honey and desserts. Family members visit without prior warning, and it is normal for unknown men to show up in the *majlis*.[16] Many of my male informants have told me about going to visit houses in which they didn't know anyone. Specifically on the point of clothes, Dhofaris are always fully dressed whenever they are not in the bedroom; a woman would not walk into the *salle* without a headscarf.

Arabian Peninsula architecture: historical and present day

Potts' "Trends and Patterns in the Archaeology and Pre-Modern History of the Gulf Region" (2016) gives an overview of research done on early dwellings in the eastern Arabian Peninsula. There are also a few texts about creating traditional houses on the Arabian Peninsula, such as Kay and Zandi's *Architectural Heritage of the Gulf* (1991), Yarwood's chapter "Essay on Traditional Building Construction in the Gulf" in his *Urban Planning in the Middle East: Case Studies* (2012) and Remali, Salama, Wiedmann and Ibrahim's "A Chronological Exploration of the Evolution of Housing Typologies in Gulf Cities" (2016).

Hawker's *Traditional Architecture of the Arabian Gulf: Building on Desert Tides* (2008) has 29 pages about Oman and four on the Dhofar region including drawings of two undated houses and photos of the traditional round house made of store courses topped with wood (*strayt*), a cave dwelling and forts. The drawings are based on houses explained in Damluji's *The Architecture of Oman* (1988).[17]

Salama's "A Century of Architecture in the Arabian Peninsula: Evolving Isms and Multiple Architectural Identities in a Growing Region" (2014) sets out three architectural periods for the Arabian Peninsula, noting that "such an approach is less pertinent to the case of Oman and Yemen, it is highly relevant to Bahrain, Kuwait, Qatar, Saudi Arabia, and United Arab Emirates" (138).[18] The first is the pre-oil era from 1914 to the 1930s, during which "the desert climate and tribal tradition are the most prominent constituents" (138).

As Hakim (above) argued, Salama states that

> Islamic traditions regarding male and female privacy prescribed stringent building rules. Privacy was ensured by following certain building practices such as a designated minimum building height, or constructing curved entrances, making it impossible for passers-by to look inside a dwelling. (139)

However, specifically for the Arabian Peninsula, "The typical pre-oil settlement was characterized by a core that constituted an ensemble of the Friday mosque, the courthouse, and the ruler's house" (139). The predominate type of dwelling in towns was a courtyard house made of coral stone and gypsum with crenulated roofs.

The second era, 1930s to 1960s, is termed "Oil Architecture" during which

> new building industry started to boom and required vast investments from the state, as well as ambitious local entrepreneurs and shareholders.

> At first, major infrastructure projects such as streets, energy infrastructure, desalination plants, airports and harbors were the main focus of public investment; eventually, however, after this first stage of industrial and infrastructural development, investment became more directed toward establishing industries designed to help decrease the need for the import of basic commodities such as food, furniture and building materials. The industrial production of other non-essential consumer goods, such as plastics and fertilizers, was the last stage in the so-called industrial revolution.
>
> (141)

The third phase, 1990s to the present, is "Post-Oil Architecture: Global Flows and Service Hubs" in which cities have more expat workers than locals and governments seek to create statement buildings such as Burj Khalifa in Dubai, Doha Tower and the King Fahd National Library in Riyadh (142). Salama argues that Arabian Peninsula cities are now examples of Appadurai's mediascapes, finanscapes, technoscapes and ideascapes because of media enterprises such as Al-Jazeera and Al-Arabiya, the role of Dubai in creating and moving currencies, as well as the rise of free trade zones and universities.

Salama expands his argument in "Urban Traditions in the Contemporary Lived Space of Cities on the Arabian Peninsula" (2015) which has a darker tone than his previous article. In discussing the pre-oil era, he says that buildings were constructed using local laws and local knowledge of building materials and techniques. In particular, the laws

> helped clarify issues related to streets and their use [such as] noise, or environmental concerns such as pollution, that might cause disturbance or harm. Laws also covered such areas as overlooking building elements (roofs or balconies), walls between neighbors and rights of ownership to them, and the use (and even the drainage) of rain and wastewater.
>
> (24)

The growth of cities has led to government regulations superseding local laws and drastic changes in how buildings look, for example "the spread of architectural or urban elements such as balconies, terraces, plazas, and other public spaces that originated in one context – the northern Mediterranean – became the norm in parts of the Arabian Peninsula" (23). Further,

> segregation between nationals and expatriates is zealously maintained. The development of a less anonymous and more integrated society is further constrained by the temporary nature of labor contracts, with a large percentage of the workforce being exchanged on a regular basis ... [and] little effort has been made to develop more integrated

> environments as platforms for an emerging society ... In part this pattern is due to a lack of public transport.
>
> (30)

He ends by arguing, "A principal urban tradition today would seem to be the maintenance of very different, parallel communities that are not necessarily bound by, or rooted in, place or locality" (37). This is problematic because buildings in pre-oil communities were rooted in place by linages of agreed upon or locally adjudicated laws pertaining to structures, local building materials and local architecture practices. All of these grounding behaviors have disappeared so that cities are now fragmented and will eventually consist of "multiple manifestations and multiple socio-spatial practices" (37).

Molotch and Ponzini's article "The New Arab Urban: Test Beds, Workarounds, and the Limits of Enacted Cities" (2019)[19] reviews various theories of how and why cities develop and explain why these don't fit in the context of the Arabian Peninsula, focusing on Abu Dhabi, Dubai, and Doha. They try to "avoid thinking in terms of any single 'Gulf City model.' We do not want to repeat the historically common essentializing error of treating cities, variously 'Islamic' or 'Arab' or 'Middle East,' as the same" (10).

They state that "Gulf cities need to be explained in terms of their complexities, and part of that complexity is represented by the limits of what has been said and not said" (14). For example, "Markets are not open and free; information is held close to the chest on vastly unequal playing fields ... Investments, in real estate or in other sectors, are detached from so-called market discipline" (11). Another example is that "Elites sometimes construct buildings that will remain mostly (or completely) empty" (17).

One negative aspect of urban spaces on the Arabian Peninsula is the "spatial separation" in terms of creating places

> that permit exception for activities like Western-style education (allowing a high degree of academic freedom) as well as easy social mixing, particularly across genders. Tourist service zones also cater to special tastes and pleasures—providing, in effect, a kind of "morality zoning."
>
> (18)

These zones and "modes of inclusion and exclusion" are negative because the authors state that

> enclaves and spaces of exception – we persist in believing – run counter to urbanism's generative potential. They do not leverage the buzzing complementarities of the city. Ongoing accomplishment—which can have legs to carry it into the future and across space—depends on energy and daring from life *in situ*. There also needs to be social trust and tolerance.
>
> (19)

They call the cities "an archipelago of special districts" which "may help in implementing individual megaprojects, but such a tactic does not portend synergy" (19).

A second problem is that having so many expats "militates against the building up of knowledge empathies, especially across groups, professions, and institutions" (19). The result is urban areas in which people don't always know what is being/going to be built when (as there is little public information about city planning), buildings stand empty and there are a variety of non-integrated areas for different purposes and populations. Further, accumulated knowledge isn't always shared as architects and urban planners are brought in for specific projects and are not part of the warp and weft of daily urban life.

Another aspect of research on Arabian Peninsula architecture is the need to use air conditioning (AC), for example Winter's "Urban Sustainability in the Arabian Gulf: Air Conditioning and Its Alternative" (2015). Winter's focus is on how the indigenous use of cooling wind towers has changed so that while "these towers are reproduced constantly across hotels, shopping malls, indoor souqs and residential properties," they are merely ornamental (4). For cities such as Doha which are currently working towards sustainability, Winter wonders if the "urban sociality and every-day habits that formed under non-AC conditions can also be upheld or reinstated" or pre-AC lifeways will be irreversibly lost (12).

I have also looked at texts that are country specific such as Stephenson's "Women and the Malleability of the Kuwaiti Dīwāniyya" (2011), Le Renard's *A Society of Young Women: Opportunities of Place, Power and Reform in Saudi Arabia* (2014), Kanafani's *Aesthetics and Ritual in the United Arab Emirates* (1979) and Alkhalidi "Sustainable Application of Interior Spaces in Traditional Houses of the United Arab Emirates" (2013).

The two countries with the most research about houses are Qatar and Yemen. Qatar's government has put large amounts of research money into play, resulting in work on all aspects of Qatari buildings. Yemen's ancient cities have long attracted archeologists and, unlike any other country on the Arabian Peninsula, there are many texts by researchers who have lived with Yemeni families so there is a lot of information about daily life within houses.

Jaidah and Bourennane have written an overview of Qatari buildings in *The History of Qatari Architecture from 1800 to 1950* (2009). Eddisford and Carter have done another overview in "The Vernacular Architecture of Doha, Qatar" (2017), while Eddisford and Morgan's *The Radwani House: Architecture, Archaeology and Social History* (2013) is a detailed look at one building.

Fletcher and Stepney look at the changes in houses in "Morphologies of Housing in Doha: from Bayt Sha'bi to Suburban Villa" (n.d.). Nagy also focuses on houses with "Social Diversity and Changes in the Form and Appearance of the Qatari House" (1998) and "Keeping Families Together: Housing Policy, Social Strategies and Family in Qatar" (2004).

More recently Sobh and Belk have published several articles which focus on Qatari houses: "Domains of Privacy and Hospitality in Arab Gulf Homes" (2011a) and "Privacy and Gendered Spaces in Arab Gulf Homes" (2011b). Asmi discusses how female gatherings in houses are a source of power and influence in "Finding a Place to Sit How Qatari Women Combine Cultural and Kinship Capital in the Home Majlis" (2016).

Al-Mohannadi, Saleh and Furlan's "Socio-cultural Patterns Embedded into the Built Form of Qatari Houses: Regenerating Architectural Identity in Qatar" (2019) uses the theory of space syntax to examine how people move through Qatari houses, a framework I used when looking at Dhofari houses.

I cannot write a complete list of all researchers who lived in and/or have written about Yemeni houses, but a few I have consulted include Stark's *A Winter in Arabia: A Journey through Yemen* (1940), Maclagan's "Food and Gender in a Yemeni Community" (1994), Makhlouf's *Changing Veils: Women and Modernisation in North Yemen* (1979), Dorsky's *Women of 'Amran: A Middle Eastern Ethnographic Study* (1986), Meneley's *Tournaments of Value: Sociability and Hierarchy in a Yemeni Town* (1996), Caton's *Yemen Chronicle: Anthropology of War and Mediation* (2005), Kotnik's "The Mirrored Public Architecture and Gender Relationship in Yemen" (2005) and Weir's brilliant *A Tribal Order: Politics and Law in the Mountains of Yemen* (2007).[20]

More recent works include De Regt's "Preferences and Prejudices: Employers' Views on Domestic Workers in the Republic of Yemen" (2009) and "Ways to Come, Ways to Leave: Gender, Mobility, and Il/legality among Ethiopian Domestic Workers in Yemen" (2010), as well as vom Bruck's *Mirrored Loss: A Yemeni Woman's Life Story* (2018).

Marchand edited a marvelous book, *Architectural Heritage of Yemen: Buildings That Fill My Eye* (2017), with many excellent chapters which are full of details about how Yemeni houses are built and lived in. Of particular use for comparisons to Dhofar were Dorman's "A *Nasraniyya* in Sanaa, 1988–99," Meneley's "The Zabidi House," Varanda's "The Domestic Architecture of the Northern Plateaux and Eastern Slopes of Yemen: Building Attitudes and Formal Identities" and vom Bruck's "Bodies on the Move: Gender Dynamics on a Sanaani Minibus."

Oman: architectural and anthropological sources

This section looks at texts which discuss architectural, including pre-modern, structures in the other regions of Oman; texts which discuss only Dhofar are in the section below. De Cardi gives an overview of the beginnings of historical research in "British Archeology in Oman: The Early Years" (2002), a more recent text is Cleuziou and Tosi's *In the Shadow of the Ancestors: The Prehistoric Foundations of the Early Arabian Civilization in Oman* (2020).

Costa, who worked extensively in different areas of Oman wrote several important texts including "Notes on Settlement Patterns in Traditional Oman" (1983), *Musandam: Architecture and Material Culture of a Little Known Region of Oman* (1991), *Studies in Arabian Architecture* (1994) and *Historic Mosques and Shrines of Oman* (2001).

Other works on architecture include Al Harthy's *The Traditional Architecture of Oman: A Critical Perspective* (1992), Al Hinai, Batty and Probert's "Vernacular Architecture of Oman: Features that Enhance Thermal Comfort Achieved within Buildings" (1993), Biancifiori's *Works of Architectural Restoration in Oman* (1994), Damluji's *The Architecture of Oman* (1998) and Kite's "The Poetics of Oman's Traditional Architecture: Towards an Aesthetic Interpretation" (2002).

Texts which focus on one area in Oman include Hegazy's "Conservation of Omani Archaeological Sites, Harat Al Bilad – A Case Study" (2014), Mershen's "Settlement Space and Architecture in South-Arabian Oases: Preliminary Remarks on the Use and Division of Space in Omani Oasis Settlements" (1999) and Nagieb, Siebert, Luedelin et al.'s "Settlement History of a Mountain Oasis in Northern Oman – Evidence from Land-use and Archaeological Studies" (2004).

Bandyopadhyay has written several texts about buildings in Oman, including "The Deconstructed Courtyard: Dwellings of Central Oman" (2006). The key text is *Manah: An Omani Oasis, an Arabian Legacy Architecture and Social History of an Omani Settlement* (2011), noteworthy for its exhaustive survey of the buildings.

There has not been much anthropological work done in Oman, and almost all of the texts concentrate on areas north of Dhofar. The main anthropology/ethnography studies are Wikan (Sohar – 1982), Barth (Sohar – 1983), Dale Eickelman (1983), Christine Eickelman (Hamra – 1984, 1988), Limbert (Bahla – 2010) and Breteau (Muscat – 2020).

Chatty has written extensively on the Jiddat il Harasiis, the area directly north of Dhofar. Notable texts include "From Camel to Truck" (1976), *Mobile Pastoralists: Development Planning and Social Change in Oman* (1997), "Integrating Participation into Research and Consultancy: A Conservation Example from Arabia" (2000a), "Women Working in Oman: Individual Choice and Cultural Constraints" (2000b) and "Negotiating Authenticity and Translocality in Oman: The 'Desertscapes' of the Harasiis Tribe" (2013).

Muscat: architecture and urban studies' sources

Most of the work about architecture and urban design in Oman focuses on Muscat. Smith has two helpful, early texts. "The Islamic Garden in Oman: Sanctuary and Paradise" (1991) looks at garden design and "Desert Developments" (1983) covers which firms were designing which areas in Muscat in the early 1980s. Of particular interest is how he describes Western influences on apartment design, for example having only one, open-plan living room rather than separate areas for men and women.

Bontenbal has several texts on districts near Muscat such as "Place Attachment and Sense of Belonging in Oasis Villages in the Capital Area of Muscat, Oman" (2013) and "Residential Satisfaction and Place Identity in a Traditional Neighborhood: The Case of Mutrah, Oman" (2015). She has also spoken about women's lives within the context of a changing geographical and economic landscape in "Policy Brief – Opportunities and Constraints of Female Labour Participation in Oman's Private Sector" (2017).

Hegazy's "Cultural Sustainability between Traditional and Contemporary Omani Residences – A Comparative Case Study" (2015) concentrates on examples from northern Oman. There is an excellent overview of building regulations, for example, "The architectural design of facades/elevations of residential and residential/commercial buildings shall be according to the local, Arabic, or Islamic style ... [and] restricting height of buildings to a maximum of three stories for residential buildings" (191).

However, general statements such as "In the traditional Omani architecture, the main apparent principle which affects the house design relates to Islamic conventions of privacy" are followed by details which do not obtain in Dhofar such as "the bent entrance (*majaz*), the exterior screened windows and the combination of the covered interior courtyard and the wind catcher (*malqaf*) are all distinctive characteristics of the Omani house" (190). There is one example from Salalah of a house built in 2011; the discussion is limited to a brief description, floor plans and three photos (193).

Heim, Joosten, Richthofen and Rupp's "Land-allocation and Clan-formation in Modern Residential Developments in Oman" (2018) explains

> To regulate housing for a growing population and to manage spatial resources the Omani government installed a particular land-allocation process *by lottery* in the 1980s granting every Omani citizen, first male and since 2003 female, the right to enter this lottery and eventually receive a plot.

They see the lottery system as negative as

> The absence of a land management system and taxes further aggravates the situation and encourages land-grabbing and land-speculation. Since plots are in short demand and the list of applicants is getting longer, the government allocates plots in regions further away from established economic centres ... . The ministry of housing zones large districts of 2000 and more plots. These plots form a pool for the lottery system before the planning process has been completed and any infrastructure such as asphalted roads or electricity has been installed.

Also, they point out, "Technically, the allocated plot remains state property and the citizens are granted a right to usufruct their plot, similar to the Anglo-Saxon land lease."[21] Given that, as discussed above, tribes are an important factor in Omani life, the author's research question is whether "Omanis in urban and rural areas choose to regroup their clan members by arranging plots of land in the vicinity of the tribe members, could the governmental land-allocation system by lottery really counter this effect?" Their result is that "Oman is closer to the metaphorical 'salad bowl' ... where tribal groups might get relocated but not dissolved, than the 'melting pot'."

In "Co-designing the Pedestrian Revolution in Muscat" (2020) De Siqueira and Al Balush believe that the lottery system did create more tribally diverse neighborhoods but, like Heim et al., also created disorganized growth: "The greatest legal change to the city structure was a land allocation system introduced in the 1980s, that aided in tribe mixing and led to the sprawl we see today."

They review the beginning of the lottery system with "*Royal Decree 81/84—the Government Land Entitlement System* effective since 1984 stated that all Omani male citizens could apply for and receive free 600 sqm housing plots at the age of 23" and then explain that Muscat is

> under pressure to catch up with the development of the public spaces, because landowners began building their homes before the implementation of infrastructure and basic services such as roads, water, gas, electricity lines, streetlights, phone lines and any sort of public gathering space.

The result is that

> three generations of residents have grown up in isolated conditions with cars as the main access to most functions in their everyday life. The dependence of cars to move around the city is high, with public bus transportation not beginning until late 2014 and still not connecting neighborhoods well.[22]

Thus, "Having already established that the large monofunctional residential neighborhoods of Muscat are unpleasant to walk through, we set out to understand to what degree residents are nevertheless walking within their areas." De Siqueira, Al Balush and their assistants created spaces and methods for their 236 participants to give feedback about how they view the positive and negative aspects of the neighborhood in terms of ease of movement. For example, "Preliminary results yielded the mosque as a walkable core exclusively for males, and the attached stores include the use of space possible for the female residents." Also, "Through the activity of placing pedestrian infrastructure, sidewalks were almost always regarded as an infringement of privacy when placed too close to a house's boundary wall."

Similar to Bontenbal (above), the focus is on how the inhabitants experience the area surrounding their house which gives a fascinating and rarely seen perspective on daily life.

As De Siqueira and Al Balush had both male and female informants, they were able to break down viewpoints by gender, for example:

> Altogether commerce and education (34%), mosques (26%), and neighborhood gardens (18%), were highly appreciated. Male residents of Muscat were most likely to point at the nearby services and mosques in their neighborhood as a "Good" detail, while women instead perceived educational facilities and gardens in the area as a positive.

Lastly, Benkari has several articles on Muscat, including "Urban Development in Oman: An Overview" (2017) which traces the expansion of Muscat over several decades.[23] She mentions that "urbanization in Oman has been increasing ... From approximately 30% in 1970 and around 50% a decade later, it grew to reach 80% today and is expected to range around 85% by 2040" (147). Thus, "29.1% of the total population is congested in 5.3% of the total area of the country [i.e. the greater Muscat area]" (147).

She notes that while "Like its neighbors, though in a more restrained fashion, Oman invested in transportation (roads, highways, airports and ports) ... the urbanization in Oman was slower, less drastic and more controlled" (148, 154). Yet, there have also been problems in the development of infrastructure and housing. Specifically,

> The key planning authorities are not coordinating their efforts at the different levels (national, regional, local, private consultants). The multitude of well-thought-out and thoroughly documented plans and proposals are lost in the implementation process due to the heavy bureaucracy.
>
> (152)

Benkari's other articles change the focus from government to community, for example "Community-led Initiatives for the Rehabilitation and Management of Vernacular Settlements in Oman: A Phenomenon in the Making" (2021). In "Local Community Involvement in the Adaptive Reuse of Vernacular Settlements in Oman" (2019) she mentions that "some privately funded initiatives or house restorations have been recorded over the past decade in different locations with varying levels of importance," including Bait Al-Sail Al-Ghassani in Salalah (8).

Dhofar: historical sources

This section is organized chronologically by the time period discussed and then by publication date. I begin by listing texts about pre-historic and early modern Dhofar and then review travelers to Dhofar. Some of these texts will be examined in more detail in Chapter 2.

Vitaly Usik, Yamandu Hilbert and Jeff Rose, working with each other and others, have also written several articles about traces left by the early inhabitants of Dhofar.[24] Articles include Rose, Usik, Marks et al.'s "The Nubian Complex of Dhofar, Oman: An African Middle Stone Age Industry in Southern Arabia" (2011); Hilbert, Rose and Roberts's "Late Paleolithic Core Reduction Strategies in Dhofar, Oman" (2012); Hilbert's "Khamseen Rock Shelter and the Late Palaeolithic-Neolithic Transition in Dhofar" (2013); Usik, Rose, Hilbert, et al.'s "Nubian Complex Reduction Strategies in Dhofar, Southern Oman" (2013); Rose and Hilbert's "New Paleolithic Sites in the Southern Rub' Al Khali Desert, Oman" (2014); Hilbert, Parton, Morley et al.'s "Terminal Pleistocene and Early Holocene Archaeology and Stratigraphy of the Southern Nejd, Oman" (2015); Hilbert, Usik, Galletti et al.'s "Archaeological Evidence for Indigenous Human Occupation of Southern Arabia at the Pleistocene/Holocene Transition: The Case of al-Hatab Dhofar, Southern Oman" (2015) and Rose, Hilbert, Marks and Usik's *The First People of Oman: Palaeolithic Archaeology of the Nejd Plateau* (2018).[25]

Other texts about pre-historic lifeways in Dhofar include McCorriston, Harrower, Steimer et al.'s "Monuments and Landscape of Mobile Pastoralists in Dhofar: The Arabian Human Social Dynamics (AHSD) Project 2009-2011" (2014); Cremaschi, Zerboni, Charpentier et al.'s "Early-Middle Holocene Environmental Changes and pre-Neolithic Human Occupations as Recorded in the Cavities of Jebel Qara" (2015); Zimmerle's *Cultural Treasures from the Cave Shelters of Dhofar: Photographs of the Painted Rock Art Heritage of Southern Oman* (2017) and Garba, Danielisová, Maiorano et al.'s "TSMO (Trilith Stone Monuments of Oman) Research Project Expedition Report of the 2nd Season 2019-2020" (2020). Garba and Farrington also did the poster exhibit "Walled Structures and Settlement Patterns in the South-western Part of Dhofar, Oman" at the 2010 *Seminar for Arabian Studies* (2011).

Archeological studies in Dhofar started in the 1950s but were disrupted by the war and resumed in the late 1970s. The focus has always been on two main sites: the fortified city of Sumhuram, located at the bay of Khor Rori/Ruwi, and the ancient city of Al Balid/Baleed on the coast in the south-east sector of Salalah. Both sites will be discussed in Chapter 2.

Articles about the early archeological work include Cleveland's "The Sacred Stone Circle of Khor Rori" (1959) and "The 1960 American Archaeological Expedition to Dhofar" (1960), as well as Pirenne's "The Incense Port of Moscha (Khor Rori) in Dhofar" (1975), Beeston's "The Settlement at Khor Rori" (1976), Albright's *The American Archaeological Expedition in Dhofar, Oman, 1952-1953* (1982) and Costa's "The Study of the City of Zafar (Al-Balid)" (1982).

Juris Zarins played an important role in the start of archeological work in Dhofar and has written texts on both sites including *The Land of Incense: Archaeological Work in the Governorate of Dhofar, Sultanate of Oman,*

1990-1995 (2001) and "Aspects of Recent Archaeological Work at al-Balid" (2007). After these earlier texts, he co-wrote several works with Lynne Newton including "Al Balid: Ancient Zafar, Sultanate of Oman. Report of Excavations, 2005–2011 and Salalah Survey" (2012). He is the second author on Newton's "A Possible Indian Quarter at al-Baleed in the Fourteenth-seventeenth Centuries AD?" (2014) and *The Archaeological Heritage of Oman. Dhofar Through the Ages. An Ecological, Archaeological and Historical Landscape* (2017). Newton has also published single-author texts, including "Shrines in Dhofar" (2010).

More recent work on Al Baleed has been done by Alexia Pavan with articles such as "Husn Al Baleed: Civil and Military Architecture along the Indian Ocean in Medieval Times" (2018) and "The Port of Al Baleed (southern Oman), the Trade in Frankincense and Its Coveted Treasures" (2020). She has also worked with several co-authors such as with Fusaro, Visconti, Ghidoni and Annucci on "New Researches at The Port of Al Balid and Its Castle (Husn): Interim Report (2016-2018)" (2020); with Laurenza and Valentini on "Masonry and Building Techniques in a Medieval City Port of the Sultanate of Oman: Preliminary Typological Atlas at al-Balīd" (2020); and with Visconti on "Trade and Contacts between Southern Arabia and East Asia: The Evidence from al-Balīd (southern Oman)" (2020).

Other research on Al Baleed includes Ibrahim and ElMahi's "A Report on Two Seasons of Sultan Qaboos University Excavations at Al-Balid, Dhofar 1996-7" (1997); Belfioretti and Vosmer's "Al-Balīd Ship Timbers: Preliminary Overview and Comparisons" (2010); Jansen's edited work "The Archaeological Park of Al-Baleed, Sultanate of Oman. Site Atlas along with selected Technical Reports 1995-2001" (2015) and Fusaro's "The Islamic Port of al-Balīd (Oman), between Land and Sea: Place of Trade, Exchange, Diversity, and Coexistence" (2021).

Avanzini has written extensively on Sumhuram including "Incense Routes and Pre-Islamic South Arabian Kingdoms" (2002); "Sumhuram: A Hadrami Port on the Indian Ocean," in *The Indian Ocean in the Ancient Period: Definite Places, Translocal Exchange* (2007); *A Port in Arabia between Rome and the Indian Ocean (3rd C.BC. – 5th C.AD) Khor Rori Report 2* (2008) which she edited; and "The Stratigraphy of Sumhuram: New Evidences" (2005) co-authored with Sedov.

Other research on Sumhuram includes Orazi's "The Harbour and City of Khor Rawri" (2002) and Buffa and Sedov's "The Residential Quarter" in *A Port in Arabia between Rome and the Indian Ocean (3rd C. BC – 5th C. AD);* (2008); Pavan and Degli Esposti's *The Urban Shrine in Quarter A at Sumhuram: Stratigraphy, Architecture, Material Culture* (2016) and Degli Esposti and Pavan's "Water and Power in South Arabia: The Excavation of 'Monumental Building 1' (MB1) at Sumhuram" (2020).

There are two texts about Dhofar in the early modern time periods: Guest's "Zufar in the Middle Ages" (1935) and Smith and Porter's "The Rasulids in Dhofar in the VIIth-VIIIth/XIII-XIVth Centuries" (1988) which updates guest's article with more recent discoveries.

Cruttenden gives a brief view of the Dhofar coast in the 1830s with "Journal of an Excursion from Morbat to Dyreez, the Principal Town of Dhofar" (1838). Haines and Saunders were given the same task of surveying the southern coast of the Arabian Peninsula for the British government in the late 1830s using the same ship, the *Palinurus*. They both published their captain's logs: Haines' "Memoir to Accompany a Chart of the South Coast of Arabia from the Entrance of the Red Sea to Misenat, in 50, 43, 25 E. Part I" (1839), Haines' "Memoir of the South and East Coasts of Arabia: Part II" (1845) and Saunders' "A Short Memoir of the Proceedings of the Honorable Company's Surveying Brig 'Palinurus,' during Her Late Examination of the Coast between Ras Morbat and Ras Seger, and between Ras Fartak and the Ruins of Mesinah" (1846). Carter accompanied both captains and wrote several articles about Dhofar which include brief mentions of structures including "Notes on the Gara Tribe" (1845) and "The Ruins of El Balad" (1846).

The next set of travelers who wrote about Dhofar were Theodore and Mabel Bent who visited in 1893–4; Mabel wrote an account of their visit in *Southern Arabia* (1900). Thomas, famous for being the first Western person to cross the Empty Quarter, published his account of the journey which started in Dhofar in *Arabia Felix: Across the Empty Quarter of Arabia* in 1932. Thesiger made himself and southern Arabia famous with his classic *Arabian Sands* (1959).

There are several accounts of the Dhofar War (1965–75). The first one to be publicly approved by the Omani government was Gardiner's excellent *In the Service of the Sultan: A First-hand Account of the Dhofar Insurgency* (2007) which was widely displayed in bookstores when it was first published.

After the war, research started on the current lifeways of Dhofaris, particularly in terms of their connection to the terrain. Examples include Clements' "The Islands of Kuria Muria: A Civil Aid Project in the Sultanate of Oman Administered from Salalah, Regional Capital of Dhofar" (1977); Cordes and Scholz's "Changes in the Nomad Region of Oman" and "Settlement Projects in Inner Oman, and Other Measures to Develop the Rural/Nomad Region" (1980), Sale's "The Ecology of the Mountain Region of Dhofar" (1980), Janzen's *Nomads in the Sultanate of Oman: Tradition and Development in Dhofar* (1986, see also Janzen 2000) and Morris' "Dhofar – What Made It Different" (1987). Tabook's unpublished PhD thesis, *Tribal Practices and Folklore of Dhofar, Sultanate of Oman* (1997), is a comprehensive look at local cultures written by a Dhofari. A more recent text is Ball, MacMillan, Tzanopoulos et al.'s "Contemporary Pastoralism in the Dhofar Mountains of Oman" (2020).

Dhofar: architectural sources

There are very few sources about buildings in Dhofar.[26] Costa and Kite wrote the early text "The Architecture of Salalah and the Dhofar Littoral" (1985). More recent works include Singh's newspaper article "A Saga of

Legacy at Bait al Ghassani" (2018) and among Bandyopadhyay's (mentioned above) several texts about buildings in Oman is "The Bait as-Sail Rehabilitation and Restoration Project, Salalah, Oman" (2019).

Cazacova, who was an architecture professor in Dhofar, has written several texts on Dhofari buildings, including "Islamic Architecture Features and Modern Housing: A Case Study of the North Awqad District in Salalah, Oman" (Al Kathiri and Cazacova 2014), "The Building as a Statement of an Artefact: The Mijmara" (Yapicioglu and Cazacova 2016) and "'Omani Burqa' vs. Decorated Facade of Modern Omani House: The Case of Salalah, Dhofar Region, Oman" (Yapicioglu and Cazacova 2018). There are also printed copies of two presentations which are helpful: "The Round Dhofari House Popularity Uniting the Past and the Present" (Adam and Cazacova 2012) and "Culture Embedded in City's Architecture; Incense Burning Custom and Its Effects on Modern Buildings' Features of Salalah, Oman" (Yapicioglu and Cazacova 2016). All of these texts will be discussed in Chapter 2.

Note: I would like to acknowledge that there is an occasional repetition of facts and citations, as well as the notices of "I also discuss this point in Chapter X." As this book will be sold online by chapter, I needed to mention important references more than once and point out where further information could be found for readers who will only have one chapter.

Notes

1 "Dhofari" here means Omanis who are born/live/culturally identify as Dhofari, not Omanis from other areas who are in Dhofar for work (usually in rented or government housing), non-GCC expats (in rental housing or housing arranged by employer), or GCC expats who allowed to buy land so they might be in a private house or rental, but usually only during *khareef*, the monsoon season of June–September. Further, stating that an action is common in Dhofar does not imply that it is unique to Dhofar.

2 Another similarity is that both texts make the arguments that detached houses and long commutes, which are bad for the home owner and the environment, only benefit foreign interests; see Montgomery's *Happy City* (2014 49) and Speck's *Walkable City* (2013) gas money is "bound for the pockets of Middle Eastern princes" (29, see also 30, 52, 60).

3 In other words, the book is set up to explain the physical details of a house, then the cultural aspects, and then expand outward to examine the concept of home spaces away from home and within the context of towns. If you prefer to approach topics from a macro- to micro-level, read the chapters in this order: 1, 2, 7, 6, 5, 8, 3 and 4.

4 And a frantic dependence on friends to explain where something is. One international shipping company's storefront is covered with advertisements for dresses. Unless you have been specifically told to open the door with a photo of children sitting in a garden, you would never know you were at the right place.

5 The Lancasters' article, "Some Relations between 'Tribes' and 'Territory' in the Arabian Peninsula in the Recent Past," begins with a general statement (below) which agrees with what I have seen in my fieldwork:

> Arab thought is descriptive, *bi-'l-waṣf*, not determinative. When a tribesperson talks about processes, groups, situations, relations, he or she is describing,

> not defining, these actions in terms of tribal moral premises in which all are equal and answerable before God, where no-one can command another, each must be generous, and protect those? all? who ask. The emphasis is on equal and autonomous individuals leads to a language that describes but cannot define. An individual cannot impose his description of "whatever" on his fellows. They may agree with his words and so there is a consensus, but a consensus is not a definition. With a consensus, each participant knows that each, in some particular, would not agree totally, but overall and in general, and depending on the audience, an agreement on meaning can be reached.
>
> (2020 177)

6 "Foodways" means the objects, practices and beliefs relating to producing, obtaining, cooking, eating and disposing of food. This includes food preparation, who makes what kind of food and how and when meals are eaten, as well as topics such as catching fish, herding camels, growing fruits, designing kitchens, cooking meals and setting leftovers out for animals.

7 Although I am not local, I have found articles such as Anderson's "Positionality, Privilege, and Possibility: The Ethnographer 'at Home' as an Uncomfortable Insider" (2021) very helpful for thinking about how to do fieldwork in the place where you live.

8 Janet Watson, Miranda Morris, Alex Bellem, Domenyk Eades, Alec Moore and Saeed al-Mahri, see https://ahc.leeds.ac.uk/modern-south-arabian-languages.

9 An example of the way in which I am observed and remarked on, even by Dhofaris who don't know me: I wore a dress a few times before deciding it was a little too short. I set it aside and eventually asked a friend in the States to send me a few yards of lace edging to add to the hem; after she did this, I brought the dress and lace to my tailor who sewed it on. This whole process took over six months. I then started to wear the dress again. An expat friend told me that a Dhofari woman she knew, who I had never met, had mentioned how it was "good" that I had added the trim. This means the Dhofari woman saw me wearing the dress, remembered that more than six months previously there wasn't a lace trim and thought this change was important enough to comment on.

10 Many place names have stayed stable for over a century, for example Cruttenden states that

> Dofar is a district extending from Morebat [Mirbat] to Ras-el Ahhmar, or Bunder Resoot [Raysut], and contains several villages ... of these Dyreez [Dhariz] is the principal. It is ... surrounded by well cultivated lands like Thagah [Taqa] ... The next in consequence is Solahlah [Salalah] rather more inland than Dyreez, and distant from it three of four miles. Between Solahlah and the sea lies the town of El Hafeh [Haffa], between which and Dyreez, are the remains of an old town called El Bellut [Al Baleed].
>
> (1838 187)

Dhofar is now the name of the region, and Mirbat is a town to the east of Salalah. Raysut (west) and Dhariz (south-east) are now sections of the city of Salalah; Taqa is a separate town to the east. Haffa (south-central) is part of Salalah; Al Baleed (south-central on the coast) is an archeological site with a museum.

11 The Dhofar region has a long border with Saudi Arabia to the north-west, but there is no crossing point. The only open border crossing is at Ramlat Khaliya (Rub Al-Khali entry point in Saudi Arabia) in the Dhahirah region in the north of Oman.

12 It is very easy to navigate in Salalah as the mountains are almost always in view and are due north. The main roads run east/west with the Salalah Bypass Road northernmost and then Robat Street; both streets have at least two lanes in each direction, divided down the center with roundabouts. In Salalah itself, the east/west streets are 23rd July (two lanes each direction, divided with stoplights), As Salam Street (one lane each direction, stoplights), Al Muntazah (one lane each direction, stop/yield signs, eastern part has plantations to the south) and As Sultan Qaboos Street (one lane each direction, stop/yield signs, eastern part has plantations to the north and beach views to the south).

13 Some newer houses have a flat roof that is smaller than the footprint, a wall at the edge, then a slope of three to five courses of clay tile which meet the wall of the upper story and/or closely spaced decorated balusters, glass inserts, metal railings, etc.

14 An article that also discusses "what it's like" to walk in Arabian Peninsula cities is Nastasi's excellent "A Gulf of Images: Photography and the Circulation of Spectacular Architecture" (2019), but this text concentrates on urbanscapes, not houses.

15 Explained another way, although New Islamic Urbanism is

> embedded in a discourse of piety and religious renewal, this architectural trend was also embraced by people who do not share the conservative view and lifestyle of its proponents … [because it] facilitated the creation of 'bubbles' of alternative lifestyles.
>
> (Maneval 2019 166)

16 As happens frequently when writing, the topic that I am trying to explain suddenly comes to life. At 8 pm on the same day I wrote this, I got a phone call from one of the research guys. He asked if I was free, and when I said I was, he told me that was in the parking lot of my house with two other men. I closed the phone, ran to the living room to turn on the lights and AC, ran to get into a *thobe* (long, loose, house dress) and *lossi* (simple cotton head scarf) then ran to the kitchen and tossed various sodas and bottles of water onto a tray. After I put the drinks in the living room, I quickly unlocked and opened the front door then back to the kitchen to put snacks on a tray. Knowing that I live alone and my *majlis* is not always set up for visitors, they took several minutes to walk the short distance to my house. Once they were settled and we started to talk, I had no idea if they were going to stay a few moments or four hours.

17 I would have loved to read Damluji's *The Architecture of Oman* (1998), but all the texts I reference I have found online have been given as a gift or paid for myself, and I was not able to purchase a copy.

18 Specifically, "With the exception of Yemen and the Sultanate of Oman, the new Gulf coastal nation-states were founded as oligarchies, based on the tribal hierarchy of ruling families in each country" (Salama 2014 141).

19 They are also the editors of *The New Arab Urban: Gulf Cities of Wealth, Ambition and Distress* (2019).

20 I cannot read academic French but would like to mention Arnaud's "La Formation de l'Architecture Contemporaine à Sanaa" (1995).

21 I will discuss this in more detail in Chapter 2, but the concept of usufruct means that a person is allowed to live on, develop and use a piece of land not in their possession, i.e. the government of Oman continues to own the land given to a citizen in the lottery. In practice, Omanis discuss their land using terms of complete ownership.

22 Another aspect of neighborhood design is that

> planning practices dictate that a mosque needs to be present, and specifically that all residents should have a "neighborhood" mosque within a

> 400–500 m radius of their home. This radius, equivalent to a 5-min walk, also coincides with the pedestrian shed, i.e. the average distance in which walkable interactions are most likely.
>
> (De Siqueira and Al Balush 2020)

23 I would like to note that she, like many other writers, discusses the effect of "British and American oil companies" which "began building new towns for their employees working on the site" (Benkari 2017 146). One result was

> The right of decision-making was gradually shifted from the traditional community and tribes representatives to be conveyed to specialized ministries, executive directorates and foreign consultants. This is how firms like Llewellyn-Davies Weeks and Weidleplan & Muamir have largely influenced the development strategies, and urban planning policies in Oman.

However, she clarifies that "a higher proportion of local population, less important oil resources and a more restrained and social oriented transformation have kept a close control on the progressive urbanization in Oman" (146). In Chapter 2 I will argue that there was little outside influence in Dhofar.

24 To help understand the articles' titles: in the system of dating geological data across continents the Pleistocene is the time period from c. 2.588 million years ago until c. 11.7 thousand years ago; the Holocene is c. 11.7 thousand years ago until today. The Paleolithic is the time period from when archaic human species started to use stone tools to the end of the Pleistocene. The Paleolithic is followed by the Neolithic period which starts c. 12,000 years ago and lasted until 6,500 years ago (4500 BC) in some areas, much later in others.

25 Rose's *An Introduction to Human Prehistory in Arabia: The Lost World of the Southern Crescent* (2022) has just been published so I have not been able to read it, but I assume the text is relevant to this discussion.

26 There is a brief mention of urbanization in Salalah in Richthofen's unpublished dissertation *Spatial Diversity and Sustainable Urbanisation in Oman* (2019 225).

References

For photos and a full bibliography, please see: *Come From Away*, https://mariellerisse.com

Abu-Lughod, Janet. 1987. "The Islamic City: Historical Myth, Islamic Essence and Contemporary Relevance." *International Journal of Middle East Studies* 19.2: 155–76.

Adam, Khalid and Liudmila Cazacova, 2012. "The Round Dhofari House Popularity Uniting the Past and the Present." Proceedings of the 6th International Seminar on Vernacular Settlements. Famagusta, North Cyprus: Eastern Mediterranean University. 365–74.

Al Harthy, Sultan. 1992. *The Traditional Architecture of Oman: A Critical Perspective.* Unpublished M.Arch. thesis. The University of Arizona. https://repository.arizona.edu/bitstream/handle/10150/555398/AZU_TD_BOX353_YARP_1120.pdf?sequence=1 – https://repository.arizona.edu/handle/10150/555398

Al Hinai, H., W. J. Batty and S. D. Probert. 1993. "Vernacular Architecture of Oman: Features that Enhance Thermal Comfort Achieved within Buildings." *Applied Energy* 44.3: 233–244. 10.1016/0306-2619(93)90019-L

Al Kathiri, Muna Salim and Liudmila Cazacova. 2014. "Islamic Architecture Features and Modern Housing: A Case Study of the North Awqad District in Salalah, Oman." *The International Journal of the Constructed Environment* 4: 1–18.

Al Mohannadi, Asmaa Saleh and Raffaello Furlan. 2019. "Socio-cultural Patterns Embedded into the Built Form of Qatari Houses: Regenerating Architectural Identity in Qatar." *Journal of Urban Regeneration and Renewal* 12.4: 1–23.

Al Mohannadi, Asmaa Saleh, Raffaelo Furlan and Mark David Major. 2019. "Socio-Cultural Factors Shaping the Spatial Form of Traditional and Contemporary Housing in Qatar: A Comparative Analysis based on Space Syntax." Proceedings of the 12th Space Syntax Symposium.

Albright, Franklin. 1982. *The American Archaeological Expedition in Dhofar, Oman, 1952–1953*. Washington, DC: American Foundation for the Study of Man.

Alexander, Christopher, Sara Ishikawa, Murray Silverstein, Max Jacobson, Ingrid Fiksdahl-King and Shlomo Angel. 1977. *A Pattern Language: Towns, Buildings, Construction*. Oxford: Oxford University Press (Center for Environmental Structure Series).

Alkhalidi, Abdulsamad. 2013. "Sustainable Application of Interior Spaces in Traditional Houses of the United Arab Emirates." *Procedia: Social and Behavioral Sciences* 102: 288–99.

AlMutawa, Rana. 2019a, Nov 8. "Dubai Mall or Souq Naif? The Quest for "Authenticity" and Social Distinction." *London School of Economics Middle East Blog Posts*. https://blogs.lse.ac.uk/mec/2019/11/08/dubai-mall-or-souq-naif-the-quest-for-authenticity-and-social-distinction/

———. 2019b. "The Mall Isn't Authentic!: Dubai's Creative Class And The Construction of Social Distinction." *Urban Anthropology and Studies of Cultural Systems and World Economic Development* 48, 1–2: 183–223.

———. 2018, Dec. 4. "Challenging Concepts of "Authenticity": Dubai and Urban Spaces in the Gulf." *London School of Economics Middle East Blog Posts*. https://blogs.lse.ac.uk/mec/2018/12/04/challenging-concepts-of-authenticity-dubai-and-urban-spaces-in-the-gulf/

———. 2017. "Women and Restrictive Campus Environments: A Comparative Analysis Between Public Universities and International Branch Campuses in the UAE." *Higher Education in the Gulf States: Present and Future*. 17–9.

Ammann, Ludwig. 2002."Islam in Public Space." *Public Culture* 14.1: 277–79.

Anderson, Esther. 2021. "Positionality, Privilege, and Possibility: The Ethnographer 'at Home' as an Uncomfortable Insider." *Anthropology and Humanism* 46.2: 212–25.

Arnaud, Jean-Luc. 1995. "La Formation de l'Architecture Contemporaine à Sanaa," in *Sanaa hors les Murs, une Ville Arabe Contemporaine*. Franck Mermier and Gilbert Grandguillaume, eds. Urbama – CFEY: Tours: 165–226. halshs-01225119

Asmi, Rehenuma. 2016. "Finding a Place to Sit How Qatari Women Combine Cultural and Kinship Capital in the Home Majlis." *Anthropology of the Middle East* 11.2: 18–38.

Avanzini, Alessandra, ed. 2008. *A Port in Arabia between Rome and the Indian Ocean (3rd C.BC. – 5th C.AD) Khor Rori Report* 2. Rome: L'Erma di Bretschneider.

———. 2007."Sumhuram: A Hadrami Port on the Indian Ocean," in *The Indian Ocean in the Ancient Period: Definite Places, Translocal Exchange BAR*

International Series 1593. Eivind Heldaas Seland, ed. Oxford: Archaeopress. 23–31.

———. 2002. "Incense Routes and Pre-Islamic South Arabian Kingdoms." *Journal of Oman Studies* 12: 17–24.

Avanzini, Alessandra and Alexander Sedov. 2005. "The Stratigraphy of Sumhuram: New Evidences." *Proceedings of the Seminar for Arabian Studies* 35: 11–7.

Ball, Lawrence, Douglas MacMillan, Joseph Tzanopoulos, Andrew Spalton, Hadi Al Hikmani and Mark Moritz. 2020. "Contemporary Pastoralism in the Dhofar Mountains of Oman." *Human Ecology*. https://doi.org/10.1007/s10745-020-00153-5

Bandyopadhyay, Soumyen. 2019. "The Bait as-Sail Rehabilitation and Restoration Project, Salalah, Oman." *Architecture and Cultural Heritage of India, Arabia and the Maghreb*. https://www.archiam.co.uk/ghassani-house-adaptive-reuse-project/

———. 2011. *Manah: An Omani Oasis, an Arabian Legacy Architecture and Social History of an Omani Settlement*. Liverpool: Liverpool University Press.

———. 2006. "The Deconstructed Courtyard: Dwellings of Central Oman," in *Courtyard Housing: Past, Present and Future*. B. Edwards, M. Sibley, M. Hakmi and P. Land. eds. New York: Taylor & Francis. 109–21.

Barth, Fredrik. 1983. *Sohar: Culture and Society in an Omani Town*. Baltimore: Johns Hopkins University Press.

Belfioretti, Luca. and Tom Vosmer. 2010. "Al-Balīd Ship Timbers: Preliminary Overview and Comparisons." *Proceedings of the Seminar for Arabian Studies* 40: 111–18.

Benkari, Naima. 2021. "Community-led Initiatives for the Rehabilitation and Management of Vernacular Settlements in Oman: A Phenomenon in the Making." *Built Heritage* 5.1: 1–20.

———. 2019. "Local Community Involvement in the Adaptive Reuse of Vernacular Settlements in Oman," in *Vernacular and Earthen Architecture: Towards Local Development*. Miles Lewis, Shao Yong, Gisle Jakhelln and Mariana Correia, eds. Shanghai: Tongji University Press. 557–64.

———. 2017. "Urban Development in Oman: An Overview." *Transactions on Ecology and the Environment* 226.1: 143–56.

Beeston, Alfred. 1976. "The Settlement at Khor Rori." *The Journal of Oman Studies* 2: 39–41.

Bent, Theodore and Mabel. 2005/1900. *Southern Arabia*. London: Elibron.

Bianca, Stefano. 2000. "Basic Principles of Islam and Their Social, Spatial and Artistic Implications" in *Urban Form in the Arab World*. London: Thames & Hudson. 23–48.

Biancifiori, M. 1994. *Works of Architectural Restoration in Oman*. Rome: Edizioni De luca.

Bontenbal, Marike. 2017. "Policy Brief: Opportunities and Constraints of Female Labour Participation in Oman's Private Sector." Economic Research Forum – German University of Technology in Oman. 1–8.

———. 2015. "Residential Satisfaction and Place Identity in a Traditional Neighborhood: The Case of Mutrah, Oman," in *Gateways to the World: Port Cities in the Gulf: Working Group Summary Report*. Doha: Center for International and Regional Studies at the Georgetown University School of Foreign Service in Qatar. 189–215.

———. 2013. "Place Attachment and Sense of Belonging in Oasis Villages in the Capital Area of Muscat, Oman." *Trialog: A Journal for Planning and Building in the Global Context* 3. 16–20.

Bourdieu, Pierre. 1972. "The Kabyle House or the World Reversed," in *Algeria 1960*. Cambridge: Cambridge University Press. 133–54.

Brandt, Marieke. 2021. "Introduction: The Concept of Tribe in the Anthropology of Yemen," in *Tribes in Modern Yemen: An Anthology (Denkschriften Der Philosophisch-historischen Klasse 531)*. Najwa Adra, Marieke Brandt, Steven C. Caton, Paul Dresch and Andre Gingrich, eds. Vienna: Institut für Sozialanthropologie der Österreichischen Akademie der Wissenschaften. 11–8.

Breteau, Marion. 2020. *Amours à Mascate: Espaces, Rôles de Genre et Représentations Intimes chez les Jeunes (Sultanat d'Oman). Anthropologie Sociale et Ethnologie*. Aix-Marseille Université.

Buffa, Vittoria and Alexander Sedov. 2008. "The Residential Quarter" in *A Port in Arabia between Rome and the Indian Ocean (3rd C. BC – 5th C. AD)*. A. Avanzini, ed. Khor Rori Report 2, Roma: L'Erma di Bretschneider: 15–59.

Carter, Henry. 1846. "The Ruins of El Balad." *Journal of the Royal Geographical Society of London* 16: 187–99.

———. 1845. "Notes on the Gara Tribe." *Journal of the Bombay Branch of the Royal Asiatic Society* 2: 195–201.

Carter, Robert and Daniel Eddisford. 2017. "The Vernacular Architecture of Doha, Qatar." *Post-Medieval Archaeology*: 1–26. https://doi.org/10.1080/00794236.2017.1320918

Caton, Steve. 2005. *Yemen Chronicle: Anthropology of War and Mediation*. New York: Hill and Wang.

Cazacova, Liudmila and Balkiz Yapicioglu. 2014. "Fertile Crescent Defensive Cities Architectural Features Influenced by the Land of Incense Culture." Proceedings of the CAUMME II International Symposium: Architectural and Urban, Architectural and Urban Research, Education, and Practice in the Era of Post-Professionalism. Girne, North Cyprus: Girne American University. 322–46.

Cazacova, Liudmila, M. Hidalgo, M. Farhan, F. Al-Masikhi, F. Al-Hafidh, H. Qatan, J. Hubais, L. Ghafoor, M. Al-Marhoon, M. Darwish, M. Al-Amri, S. Al-Baraami, S. Al-Shanfari and S. Al-Rawas, 2014. "Recognition of Mirbat Town's Old Area as Historical Environment." Proceedings of REHAB. Tomar, Portugal. 581–91. https://doi.org/10.14575/gl/rehab2014

Chatty, Dawn. 2013. "Negotiating Authenticity and Translocality in Oman: The 'Desertscapes' of the Harasiis Tribe," in *Regionalizing Oman: Political, Economic and Social Dynamics*. Steffen Wippel, ed. Heidelberg: Springer. 129–45.

———. 2000a. "Women Working in Oman: Individual Choice and Cultural Constraints." *International Journal of Middle Eastern Studies* 32: 241–54.

———. 2000b. "Integrating Participation into Research and Consultancy: A Conservation Example from Arabia." *Social Policy and Administration* 34.4: 408–18.

———. 1997. *Mobile Pastoralists: Development Planning and Social Change in Oman*. New York: Columbia University Press.

———. 1976. "From Camel to Truck." *Folk* 18: 114–28.

Clements, Frank. 1977. "The Islands of Kuria Muria: A Civil Aid Project in the Sultanate of Oman Administered from Salalah, Regional Capital of Dhofar." *Bulletin* (British Society for Middle Eastern Studies) 4.1: 37–9.

Cleuziou, Serge and Maurizio Tosi. 2020. *In the Shadow of the Ancestors: The Prehistoric Foundations of the Early Arabian Civilization in Oman*, second edition. Dennys Frenez and Roman Garba, eds. Muscat: Ministry of Heritage and Tourism.
Cleveland, R. L. 1960. "The 1960 American Archaeological Expedition to Dhofar." *Bulletin of the American Schools of Oriental Research* 159: 14–26.
———. 1959. "The Sacred Stone Circle of Khor Rori (Dhofar)." *Bulletin of the American Schools of Oriental Research* 155: 29–31.
Cordes, Rainer and Fred Scholz. 1980. "'Changes in the Nomad Region of Oman' and 'Settlement Projects in Inner Oman, and Other Measures to Develop the Rural/Nomad Region,'" in *Bedouins, Wealth, and Change: A Study of Rural Development in the United Arab Emirates and the Sultanate of Oman*. Tokyo: United Nations University. https://archive.unu.edu/unupress/unupbooks/80143e/80143E00.htm
Costa, Paulo. 2001. *Historic Mosques and Shrines of Oman*. Oxford: British Archaeological Reports.
———. 1994. *Studies in Arabian Architecture (Variorum Collected Studies)*. London: Routledge.
———. 1991. *Musandam: Architecture and Material Culture of a Little Known Region of Oman*. London: Immel.
———. 1983. "Notes on Settlement Patterns in Traditional Oman." *Journal of Oman Studies* 6.2: 247–68.
———. 1982. "The Study of the City of Zafar (Al-Balid)." *Journal of Oman Studies* 5: 111–50.
Costa, Paulo and Stephen Kite. 1985. "The Architecture of Salalah and the Dhofar Littoral." *Journal of Oman Studies* 7: 131–58.
Cremaschi, Mauro, Andrea Zerboni, Vincent Charpentier, Remy Crassard, Ilaria Isola, Eleonora Regattieri and Giovanni Zanchetta. 2015. "Early-Middle Holocene Environmental Changes and pre-Neolithic Human Occupations as Recorded in the Cavities of Jebel Qara (Dhofar, southern Sultanate of Oman)." *Quaternary International* 382. 264–76.
Cruttenden, Charles. 1838. "Journal of an Excursion from Morbat to Dyreez, the Principal Town of Dhofar." *Transactions of the Bombay Geographical Society* 1: 184–88.
Damluji, Salma Samar. 1998. *The Architecture of Oman*. Reading: Ithaca Press.
de Cardi, Beatrice. 2002. "British Archeology in Oman: The Early Years." *Journal of Oman Studies* 12. 11–15.
De Koning, Anouk. 2009. *Global Dreams: Class, Gender, and Public Space in Cosmopolitan Cairo*. Cairo: American University in Cairo Press.
De Regt, Marina. 2010. "Ways to Come, Ways to Leave: Gender, Mobility, and Il/legality among Ethiopian Domestic Workers in Yemen." *Gender and Society* 24.2: 237–60.
———. 2009. "Preferences and Prejudices: Employers' Views on Domestic Workers in the Republic of Yemen." *Signs* 34.3: 559–81.
De Siqueira, Gustavo and Amal Al Balush. 2020. "Co-designing the Pedestrian Revolution in Muscat." *City, Territory and Architecture* 7.11: 1–15. https://doi.org/10.1186/s40410-020-00119-6
Degli Esposti, Michele and Alexia Pavan. 2020. "Water and Power in South Arabia: The Excavation of 'Monumental Building 1' (MB1) at Sumhuram (Sultanate of

Oman)." *Arabian Archeology and Epigraphy*. 1–29. https://doi.org/10.1111/aae.12159

Dorman, Deborah. 2017. "A *Nasraniyya* in Sanaa, 1988–99," in *Architectural Heritage of Yemen: Buildings that Fill my Eye*. Trevor Marchand, ed. London: Ginko. 179–86.

Dorsky, Susan. 1986. *Women of 'Amran: A Middle Eastern Ethnographic Study*. Salt Lake City: University of Utah Press.

Eddisford, Daniel and Colleen Morgan, 2013. *The Radwani House: Architecture, Archaeology and Social History*. 1–92. https://www.academia.edu/33365222/The_Radwani_House_Architecture_Archaeology_and_Social_History

Eddisford, Daniel and Robert Carter. 2017. "The Vernacular Architecture of Doha, Qatar." *Post-Medieval Archaeology* 51.1: 81–107.

Eickelman, Christine. 1988. "Women and Politics in an Arabian Oasis," in A Way *Prepared: Essays on Islamic Culture in Honor of Richard Bayly Winder*. New York: New York University Press. 199–215.

———. 1984. *Women and Community in Oman*. New York: New York University Press.

Eickelman, Dale. 1983."Omani Village: The Meaning of Oil," in *The Politics of Middle Eastern Oil*. J. E. Peterson, ed. Washington, DC: The Middle East Institute, 1983, 211–19.

———. 1974. "Is There an Islamic City? The Making of a Quarter in a Moroccan Town." *International Journal of Middle East Studies* 5.3: 274–94.

Fletcher, Richard and Erin Stepney. "Morphologies of Housing in Doha: from Bayt Sha'bi to Suburban Villa." 1–23. https://www.academia.edu/41429399/Morphologies_of_Housing_in_Doha_from_bayt_shabi_to_suburban_villa

Fusaro, Agnese. 2021. "The Islamic Port of al-Balīd (Oman), between Land and Sea: Place of Trade, Exchange, Diversity, and Coexistence." *Journal of Material Cultures in the Muslim World* 1.1–2: 67–95. https://doi.org/10.1163/26666286-12340003

Garba, Roman and Peter Farrington. 2011. "Walled Structures and Settlement Patterns in the South-western Part of Dhofar, Oman (poster)." *Proceedings of the Seminar for Arabian Studies* 41: 95–100.

Garba, Roman, Alžběta Danielisová, Maria Pia Maiorano, Mahmoud Abbas, Dominik Chlachula, David Daněček, W. Al-Ghafri, Stephanie Neuhuber, Denis Štefanisko and Jakub Trubač. n.d. *TSMO (Trilith Stone Monuments of Oman) Research Project Expedition Report of the 2nd Season 2019–2020 (campaigns TSMO 2A & 2B)*. Muscat: Ministry of Heritage and Culture, Sultanate of Oman. https://www.researchgate.net/publication/341193620_TSMO_EXPEDITION_REPORT_OF_THE_2nd_SEASON_2019-2020_campaigns_TSMO_2A_2B_Ministry_of_Heritage_and_Culture_Sultanate_of_Oman

Gardiner, Ian. 2007. *In the Service of the Sultan: A First-hand Account of the Dhofar Insurgency*. South Yorkshire: Pen and Sword Military.

Göle, Nilüfer and Ludwig Ammann, eds. 2006. *Islam in Public: Turkey, Iran and Europe*. Istanbul: Istanbul Bilgi University Press.

Guest, R. 1935. "Zufar in the Middle Ages." *Islamic Culture* 9: 402–10.

Haines, Stafford. 1839. "Memoir to Accompany a Chart of the South Coast of Arabia from the Entrance of the Red Sea to Misenat, in 50, 43, 25 E. Part I." *Journal of the Royal Geographical Society of London* 9: 125–56.

———. 1845. "Memoir of the South and East Coasts of Arabia: Part II." *Journal of the Royal Geographical Society of London* 15: 104–60.

Hakim, Besim. 2008. *Arabic-Islamic Cities: Building and Planning Principles*. London: Kegan Paul.

Hawker, Ronald. 2008. *Traditional Architecture of the Arabian Gulf: Building on Desert Tides*. Southampton: WIT Press.

Hegazy, Soheir. 2015. "Cultural Sustainability between Traditional and Contemporary Omani Residences – A Comparative Case Study." *European Journal of Sustainable Development* 42: 185–194.

———. 2014. "Conservation of Omani Archaeological Sites, Harat Al Bilad – A Case Study." International Journal of Arts & Sciences 7.4: 435–48.

Heim, Bernhard, Marc Joosten, Aurel v. Richthofen and Florian Rupp. 2018. "Land-allocation and Clan-formation in Modern Residential Developments in Oman." *City Territory and Architecture* 5.8: 1–9. https://doi.org/10.1186/s40410-018-0084-6

Hilbert, Yamandu. 2013. "Khamseen Rock Shelter and the Late Palaeolithic-Neolithic Transition in Dhofar." *Arabian Archeology and Epigraphy* 24: 51–58.

Hilbert, Yamandu, A. Parton, M. Morley, L.P. Linnenlucke, Z. Jacobs, L. Clark-Balzan, R. Roberts, Chris Galletti J.-L. Schwenninger and Jeff Rose. 2015a. "Terminal Pleistocene and Early Holocene Archaeology and Stratigraphy of the Southern Nejd, Oman." *Quaternary International* 282: 250–263. https://www.sciencedirect.com/science/article/abs/pii/S1040618215001603

Hilbert, Yamandu,Vitaly Usik, Chris Galletti, M. Morley, A. Parton, L. Clark-Balzan, J-L Schwenninger, L. Linnenlucke, R. Roberts, Z. Jacobs and Jeff Rose. 2015b. "Archaeological Evidence for Indigenous Human Occupation of Southern Arabia at the Pleistocene/Holocene Transition: The Case of al-Hatab Dhofar, Southern Oman." *Paléorient* 41.2: 31–49.

Hilbert, Yamandu, Jeff Rose and R. Roberts. 2012. "Late Paleolithic Core Reduction Strategies in Dhofar, Oman." *Proceedings of the Seminar for Arabian Studies* 42: 1–18.

Ibrahim, Moawiyah and Ali Tigani ElMahi. 1997. "A Report on Two Seasons of Sultan Qaboos University Excavations at Al-Balid, Dhofar 1996–7." Unpublished MS. Office of the Advisor to HM the Sultan for Cultural Affairs: Muscat- Salalah.

Jaidah, I. and M. Bourennane. 2009. *The History of Qatari Architecture from 1800 to 1950*. Milano: Skira.

Jacobson, Max, Murray Silverstein and Barbara Winslow. 2002. *Patterns of Home: The Ten Essentials of Enduring Design*. Newtown: Taunton Press.

Jansen, Michael, ed. 2015. *The Archaeological Park of Al-Baleed, Sultanate of Oman. Site Atlas along with selected Technical Reports 1995–2001*. Muscat: Office of the Adviser to His Majesty the Sultan for Cultural Affairs.

Janzen, Jorg. 2000. "The Destruction of Resources among the Mountain Nomads of Dhofar," in T*he Transformation of Nomadic Society in the Arab East,* University of Cambridge Oriental Publications 58. Martha Mundy and Basim Musallam, eds. Cambridge: Cambridge University Press. 160–175.

———. 1986. *Nomads in the Sultanate of Oman: Tradition and Development in Dhofar*. London: Westview Press.

Kanafani, Aida Sami. 1979. *Aesthetics and Ritual in the United Arab Emirates*. unpublished dissertation, University of Texas at Austin.

Kay, Shirley and Dariush Zandi. 1991. *Architectural Heritage of the Gulf*. Dubai: Motivate Publishing.

Kite, Stephen. 2002. "The Poetics of Oman's Traditional Architecture: Towards an Aesthetic Interpretation." *The Journal of Oman Studies* 12: 133–55.

Komecoglu, Ugur. 2006. "New Sociabilities: Islamic Cafes in Istanbul," in *Islam in Public: Turkey, Iran and Europe*. Nilüfer Göle and Ludwig Ammann, eds. Istanbul: Istanbul Bilgi University Press. 163–89.

Kotnik, Toni. 2005. "The Mirrored Public Architecture and Gender Relationship in Yemen." *Space and Culture* 8.4: 472–83.

Lancaster, William and Fidelity. 2020. "Some Relations between "Tribes' and 'Territory" in the Arabian Peninsula in the Recent Past." *Semitica et Classica: International Journal of Oriental and Mediterranean Studies* 13. 177–87. https://doi.org/10.1484/J.SEC.5.122987

Le Renard, Amélie. 2014. *A Society of Young Women: Opportunities of Place, Power and Reform in Saudi Arabia*. Stanford: Stanford University Press.

Limbert, Mandana. 2010. *In the Time of Oil: Piety, Memory and Social Life in an Omani Town*. Stanford: Stanford University Press.

Maclagan, Ianthe. 1994. "Food and Gender in a Yemeni Community," in *Culinary Cultures of the Middle East*. Sami Zubaida and Richard Tapper, eds. New York: I. B. Tauris Publishers. http://food.oregonstate.edu/ref/culture/middleeast/yemen_zubaida.html

Makhlouf, Carla. 1979. *Changing Veils: Women and Modernisation in North Yemen*. London: Croom Helm.

Maneval, Stefan. 2019. *New Islamic Urbanism: The Architecture of Public and Private Space in Jeddah, Saudi Arabia*. London: University College London Press.

Marchand, Trevor, ed. 2017. *Architectural Heritage of Yemen: Buildings that Fill my Eye*. London: Ginko.

McCorriston, Joy, Michael Harrower, Tara Steimer, Kimberly D. Williams, Matthew Senn, Mas'ūd Al Hādhari, Mas'ūd Al Kathīrī, 'Ali Ahmad Al Kathīrī, Jean-François Saliège and Jennifer Everhart. 2014. "Monuments and Landscape of Mobile Pastoralists in Dhofar: the Arabian Human Social Dynamics (AHSD) Project 2009–2011." *Journal of Oman Studies* 12: 117–44.

Meneley, Anne. 2017. "The Zabidi House," in *Architectural Heritage of Yemen: Buildings that Fill my Eye*. Trevor Marchand, ed. London: Gingko Library. 195–203.

———. 1996. *Tournaments of Value: Sociability and Hierarchy in a Yemeni Town*. Toronto: University of Toronto Press.

Mershen, Birgit. 1999. "Settlement Space and Architecture in South-Arabian Oases: Preliminary Remarks on the Use and Division of Space in Omani Oasis Settlements." *Proceedings of the Seminar* for Arabian Studies 29: 103–10.

Molotch, Harvey and Davide Ponzini. 2019a. "The New Arab Urban: Test Beds, Work-arounds, and the Limits of Enacted Cities." *AlMuntaqa* 2.1: 9–23. https://www.jstor.org/stable/10.31430/almuntaqa.2.1.0009

——— eds. 2019b. *The New Arab Urban: Gulf Cities of Wealth, Ambition and Distress*. New York: New York University Press.

Montgomery, Charles. 2014. *Happy City: Transforming Our Lives Through Urban Design*. New York: Farrar, Strauss and Giroux.

Morris, Miranda. 1987. "Dhofar: What Made it Different" in *Oman: Economic, Social and Strategic Development*. B.R. Pridham, ed. London: Croom Helm. 51–78.

Nagieb, Maher, Stefan Siebert, Eike Luedeling, Andreas Buerkert and Jutta Haser. 2004. "Settlement History of a Mountain Oasis in Northern Oman – Evidence from Land-use and Archaeological Studies." *Die Erde* 135.1: 81–106.

Nagy, Sharon. 2004. "Keeping Families Together: Housing Policy, Social Strategies and Family in Qatar." *The MIT Electronic Journal of Middle East Studies* 4: 42–58.

———. 1998. "Social Diversity and Changes in the Form and Appearance of the Qatari House." *Visual Anthropology* 10.2: 281–304.

Nastasi, Michele. 2019. "A Gulf of Images: Photography and the Circulation of Spectacular Architecture," in *The New Arab Urban: Gulf Cities of Wealth, Ambition and Distress*. Molotch, Harvey and Davide Ponzini, eds. New York: New York University Press. 99–129.

Newton, Lynne. 2010. "Shrines in Dhofar," in *Death and Burial in Arabia and Beyond: Multidisciplinary Perspectives, Society for Arabian Studies Monographs 10*. Lloyd Week, ed. Muscat: Ministry of Heritage and Culture Sultanate of Oman 329–40.

Newton, Lynne and Juris Zarins. 2017. *The Archaeological Heritage of Oman. Dhofar Through the Ages. An Ecological, Archaeological and Historical Landscape*. Muscat: Ministry of Heritage and Culture Sultanate of Oman.

———. 2014. "A Possible Indian Quarter at al-Baleed in the Fourteenth-Seventeenth Centuries AD?" *Proceedings of the Seminar for Arabian Studies* 44: 257–76.

Orazi, Roberto. 2002. "The Harbour and City of Khor Rawri." *Journal of Oman Studies* 12: 210–22.

Othaman, Zulkeplee, Rosemary Aird and Laurie Buys. 2015. "Privacy, Modesty, Hospitality, and the design of Muslim Homes: A Literature Review." *Frontiers of Architectural Research* 4: 12–23. http://dx.doi.org/10.1016/j.foar.2014.12.001

Pavan, Alexia. 2020. "The Port of Al Baleed (southern Oman), the Trade in Frankincense and Its Coveted Treasures." *Polish Archaeology in the Mediterranean* 29.1. https://doi.org/10.31338/uw.2083-537X.pam29.1.13

———. 2017–2018. "Husn Al Baleed: Civil and Military Architecture along the Indian Ocean in Medieval Times." *Journal of Indian Ocean Archaeology* 13–14: 28–41.

Pavan, Alexia and Chiara Visconti. 2020. "Trade and Contacts between Southern Arabia and East Asia: The Evidence from al-Balīd (southern Oman)." *Proceedings of the Seminar for Arabian Studies* 50: 243–57.

Pavan, Alexia and Michele Degli Esposti. 2016. *The Urban Shrine in Quarter A at Sumhuram: Stratigraphy, Architecture, Material Culture*. Quaderni di Arabia Antica, Roma: L'Erma di Bretschneider.

Pavan, Alexia, Agnese Fusaro, Chiara Visconti, Alessandro Ghidoni and Arturo Annucci. 2020a. "New Researches at The Port of Al Balid and Its Castle (Husn): Interim Report (2016–2018)." *The Journal of Oman Studies* 21: 172–99.

Pavan, Alexia, S. Laurenza and R. Valentini, 2020b. "Masonry and Building Techniques in a Medieval City Port of the Sultanate of Oman: Preliminary Typological Atlas at al-Balīd." *Newsletter Archeologia* 10. 321–46.

Pirenne, J. 1975. "The Incense Port of Moscha (Khor Rori) in Dhofar." *Journal of Oman Studies* 1: 81–96.

Potts, Daniel. 2016. "Trends and Patterns in the Archaeology and Pre-Modern History of the Gulf Region," in *The Emergence of the Gulf States: Studies in Modern History*. J.E. Peterson (ed.). London: Bloomsbury. 19–42.

Ragette, Friedrich. 2003. *Traditional Domestic Architecture of the Arab Region*. Felbach: Edition Axel Menges.

Remali, Adel, Ashraf Salama, Florian Wiedmann and Hatem G. Ibrahim. 2016. "A Chronological Exploration of the Evolution of Housing Typologies in Gulf Cities." *City, Territory and Architecture* 3.14: 1–15. https://doi.org/10.1186/s40410-016-0043-z

Richthofen, Aurel von. 2019. *Spatial Diversity and Sustainable Urbanisation in Oman*. unpublished dissertation. Technische Universitaet Carolo-Wilhelmina zu Braunschweig. https://doi.org/10.24355/dbbs.084-201901220928-0

Risse, Marielle. 2021. *Foodways in Southern Oman*. London: Routledge.

———. 2019. *Community and Autonomy in Southern Oman*. Cham, Switzerland: Palgrave Macmillan.

Rose, Jeff. 2022. *An Introduction to Human Prehistory in Arabia: The Lost World of the Southern Crescent*. New York: Springer.

Rose, Jeff and Yamandu Hilbert. 2014. "New Paleolithic Sites in the Southern Rub' Al Khali Desert, Oman." *Antiquity* 88.381. https://antiquity.ac.uk/projgall/rose341

Rose, Jeffery, Yamandu Hilbert, Anthony Marks and Vitaly Usik. 2018. *The First People of Oman: Palaeolithic Archaeology of the Nejd Plateau*. Sultanate. Muscat: Ministry of Heritage and Culture.

Rose, Jeff, Vitaly Usik, A. Marks, Yamandu Hilbert, Chris Galletti, A. Parton, V. Černý, J. Geiling, M. Morley and R. Roberts. 2011. "The Nubian Complex of Dhofar, Oman: An African Middle Stone Age Industry in Southern Arabia." *PLoS ONE* 6(11) e28239.

Salama, Ashraf. 2015. "Urban Traditions in the Contemporary Lived Space of Cities on the Arabian Peninsula." *Traditional Dwellings and Settlements Review* 27.1: 27–39.

———. 2014. "A Century of Architecture in the Arabian Peninsula: Evolving Isms and Multiple Architectural Identities in a Growing Region." in *Architecture from the Arab World (1914–2014): A Selection: Bahrain Catalogue in Biennale Venice*. G. George Arbid (ed.). Manama: Bahrain Ministry of Culture. 137–43.

Sale, J. 1980. "The Ecology of the Mountain Region of Dhofar." In *The Journal of Oman Studies: Special Report 2: The Oman Flora and Fauna Survey 1975*. Muscat: Diwan of H. M. for Protocol. 25–54.

Saunders, J. P. 1846. "A Short Memoir of the Proceedings of the Honorable Company's Surveying Brig 'Palinurus,' during Her Late Examination of the Coast between Ras Morbat and Ras Seger, and between Ras Fartak and the Ruins of Mesinah." *Journal of the Royal Geographical Society of London* 16: 169–86.

Singh, Kaushalendra. 2018, Jan 12. "A Saga of Legacy at Bait al Ghassani." *Oman Observer*. https://www.omanobserver.om/article/64672/Front Stories/a-saga-of-legacy-at-bait-al-ghassani

Smith, G. Rex and Venetia Porter. 1988. "The Rasulids in Dhofar in the VIIth-VIIIth/XIII-XIVth Centuries." *The Journal of the Royal Asiatic Society of Great Britain and Ireland* 1: 26–44.

Smith, John Alexander. 1991."The Islamic Garden in Oman: Sanctuary and Paradise." *Garden History* 19: 187–208.

———. 1983. "Desert Developments." *Building Design* 11: 18–21.

Sobh, Rana and Russell Belk. 2011a. "Domains of Privacy and Hospitality in Arab Gulf Homes." *Journal of Islamic Marketing* 2.2: 125–37.

———. 2011b. "Privacy and Gendered Spaces in Arab Gulf Homes." *Home Cultures* 8.3: 317–40.

Speck, Jeff. 2013. *Walkable City: How Downtown Can Save America One Step at a Time*. New York: North Point Press.

Stark, Freya. 2002/1940 *A Winter in Arabia: A Journey through Yemen*. New York: Overlook Press.

Stephenson, Lindsey. 2011. "Women and the Malleability of the Kuwaiti Dīwāniyya." *Journal of Arabian Studies* 1.2: 183–99.

Tabook, Salim Bakhit. 1997. *Tribal Practices and Folklore of Dhofar, Sultanate of Oman*. Unpublished PhD thesis, Faculty of Arts, Exeter University.

Thesiger, Wilfred. 1991/1959. *Arabian Sands*. New York: Penguin.

Thomas, Bertram. 1932, reprint. *Arabia Felix: Across the Empty Quarter of Arabia*. London: Jonathan Cape.

Usik, V., J. Rose, Y. Hilbert, P. Van Peer and A. Marks. 2013. "Nubian Complex Reduction Strategies in Dhofar, Southern Oman." *Quaternary International* 300: 244–266.

Varanda, Frenando. 2017. "The Domestic Architecture of the Northern Plateaux and Eastern Slopes of Yemen: Building Attitudes and Formal Identities." in *Architectural Heritage of Yemen: Buildings that Fill my Eye*. Trevor Marchand, ed. London: Gingko Library. 89–99.

vom Bruck, Gabriele. 2018. *Mirrored Loss: A Yemeni Woman's Life Story*. New York: Hurst.

———. 2017. "Bodies on the Move: Gender Dynamics on a Sanaani Minibus." in *Architectural Heritage of Yemen: Buildings that Fill my Eye*. Trevor Marchand, ed. London: Gingko Library. 187–93.

———. 1997. "A House Turned Inside Out: Inhabiting Space in a Yemeni City." *Journal of Material Culture* 2.2: 139–72.

Weir, Shelagh. 2007. *A Tribal Order: Politics and Law in the Mountains of Yemen*. Austin: University of Texas Press.

Wikan, Unni. 1982. *Behind the Veil in Arabia: Women in Oman*. Chicago: University of Chicago Press.

Winter, Tim. 2015. "Urban Sustainability in the Arabian Gulf: Air Conditioning and its Alternatives." *Urban Studies*. 1–15. DOI: 10.1177/0042098015608782

Yapicioglu, Balkiz and Liudmila Cazacova. 2018. ""Omani Burqa" vs. Decorated Facade of Modern Omani House: The Case of Salalah, Dhofar Region, Oman." *The Academic Research Community Publication* 101–111. ISSN online: 2537–0162

———. 2016a. "The Building as a Statement of an Artefact: The Mijmara." *International Journal of Ecology & Development* 31.3: 99–116.

———. 2016b. "Culture Embedded in City's Architecture; Incense Burning Custom and Its Effects on Modern Buildings' Features of Salalah, Oman." In Proceedings of the 5th International Conference on Sustainable Tourism and Cultural Heritage. Istanbul, Turkey.

Yarwood, John. 2012. *Urban Planning in the Middle East: Case Studies*. Newcastle upon Tyne: Cambridge Scholars Publishing.

Zarins, Juris. 2007. "Aspects of Recent Archaeological Work at al-Balid (Zafar), Sultanate of Oman." *Proceedings of the Seminar of Arabian Studies* 37: 309–24.

———. 2001. *The Land of Incense: Archaeological Work in the Governorate of Dhofar, Sultanate of Oman, 1990–1995*. Muscat, Oman: Sultan Qaboos University Publications.

Zarins, Juris and Newton, Lynne. 2012 "Al Balid: Ancient Zafar, Sultanate of Oman. Report of Excavations, 2005–2011 and Salalah Survey." Unpublished MS. Muscat-Salalah.

Zimmerle, William. 2017. *Cultural Treasures from the Cave Shelters of Dhofar: Photographs of the Painted Rock Art Heritage of Southern Oman*. Washington: Sultan Qaboos Cultural Center/Liberty Press.

2 Geographical and historical considerations

Setting: location, climate, geography

The Dhofar region covers 99,300 square km with a population of about 4,357,000.[1] Salalah, the main city in Dhofar, is located at 13 m above sea level on the coast of the Arabian Sea/Indian Ocean, 17°00′54″ N/54°05′32″ E. Thumrait, a town 86 km north of Salalah on the far side of the mountains, is at 454 m above sea level on the edge of the Empty Quarter/*Rub al Khali*, 17°38′25″ N/54°1′59″ E.

The area is considered BWh (arid-desert-hot) in the Köppen-Geiger climate classification. But it is often described in non-scientific texts, especially tourist brochures, as tropical or subtropical. Zerboni, Perego, Mariani et al. state that "the southern Arabian Peninsula is tectonically dynamic, and where local deserts meet the sea their evolution is controlled by the interplay between climate change, tectonics (uplift, faulting, and folding), and relative sea level change" (2020 187).

The average yearly temperature is 27°C, cooler in the winter months and warmer from March to May. When the weather changes from warmer to cooler (November) and cooler to warmer (April and May), there are sometimes strong storms or hurricanes. On May 25, 2018, category 3 hurricane Mekunu hit Dhofar with estimated maximum sustained winds of 185 kph.

There are frequent, strong, sand-bearing, north winds from December to March. In the middle of June, temperatures drop as clouds move in for the South-East monsoon season. From the end of June until the beginning of September there is frequent drizzle, occasional rain storms and high seas. The monsoon, *khareef*, effects only the south-western part of Dhofar and rarely reaches the far (north) side of the mountains or as far west as the coastal town of Hasik. Because of the *khareef*, rainfall in Dhofar is on average greater than in other parts of the Arabian Peninsula with 100 mm to over 300 mm per year. Some areas may have a greater rainfall total in one year because of a storm, but Dhofar's monsoon means that Salalah and the southern-facing mountains are green with growing grasses, bushes and trees every year (see Galletti, Turner and Myint 2016).

In a detailed study of the region, Hilbert, Parton, Morley et al. discuss the "six distinct ecological zones: the coastal plain; the summit grasslands;

DOI: 10.4324/9781003270317-2

the seaward slopes and the southern draining wadis; the northern draining wadis on the northern face of the escarpment; the dry plateau; and the interior desert" (2015 252). I will quote this work in detail as geology is not my area of expertise. In summary:

> Northern Dhofar is classified as open desert, comprising flat gravel plains and the *Rub' al-Khali* sand sea, where sand dunes rise over 100 m in height and are superimposed over limestone plateau landscape features ... The dry plateau, also known as the *Nejd*, is a rocky, medium relief landscape ... Northward draining wadis have carved long, river valleys that debouch from the Dhofar Mountains to the open desert in the north. Although these valleys today are highly ephemeral and largely dry, the relict fluvial geomorphology suggests former perennial flows and wide, meandering channels.
>
> (2)

In terms of geology, "The dry plateau is composed of two horizontally bedded, Paleocene to Late Eocene, shallow-marine carbonate shelf units, the Upper and the Lower Hadhramaut Group. These consist of alternating limestone and dolomitic chalk beds, containing several chert-bearing layers" (2).

Further,

> The summit grasslands and seaward slopes form a partition between the monsoon-affected areas and the dry plateau. Grasses are the most common land cover on the summit, but trees and shrubs of the Somali-Masai phytogeographic zone are also found ... The seaward slopes are situated at the northern extent of summer monsoon rainfall and as a result are heavily vegetated. Forests are common on the seaward slopes and include characteristic tree species such as Anogeissus dhofarica and Commiphora spp.
>
> (2)

Lastly,

> The coastal plain is mostly flat and covered by fluvial/alluvial sediment coming from the slopes of the Dhofar Mountains. In areas where the basement geology is exposed carbonate and conglomeratic deposits (Fars Group) are found, whilst to the east between Mirbat and Hasik, crystalline basement rocks are apparent.
>
> (2)

In a more specialized study which just looks at the southern section of the Dhofar region Zerboni, Perego, Mariani et al. explain that

> the large coastal plain of Salalah abruptly end[s] against the step escarpment of the Jebel Qara limestone plateau. The massif is the natural watershed

> separating the coastal plain and the Arabian Sea from the Nejd Desert. Late Cretaceous to Neogene limestone strata form the Jebel Qara.[2]
>
> (2020 188)

Historical considerations of dwellings

Pre-historic[3]

Zerboni, Perego, Mariani et al. explain, "Evidence of Pleistocene human occupation in the coastal Dhofar is sparse. The Jebel and the Arabian seashore and coastline were more intensely settled since the Early Holocene by late Palaeolithic groups" (2020 188).

One very early dwelling site is discussed by Charpentier, Berger, Crassard et al.

> a glimpse of these 9th and 8th millennium BCE communities living on the Omani shores of the Arabian Sea has recently been possible thanks to data from the Natif 2 cave. These hunter-gatherers were selectively foraging the shallow waters of the coast, where small pelagic fish (anchovies and sardines) are abundant and easily captured. Sharks, sometimes up to two metres long, were also taken. This scenario of fishing in shallow waters ... appears to be unusual and original in Arabia.
>
> (2016 345)

However, later sites are more common, as Hilbert, Parton, Morley et al. clarify

> Numerous surface and buried Late Palaeolithic sites have been documented throughout every region of Dhofar over the past decades ... Buried sites are most often found in Dhofar in close proximity to fluvial and erosion gully systems, rocks shelters and close to piedmont situations ... These sites share similar geomorphological settings: a low limestone rockshelter, a pronounced talus slope, and a sheltered location conducive to the preservation of sediments from erosion.
>
> (2015 5)

Cremaschi, Zerboni, Charpentier et al.'s article "Early-Middle Holocene Environmental Changes and Pre-Neolithic Human Occupations as Recorded in the Cavities of Jebel Qara" discusses the contrasting evidence between pre-historic cave- and coast-dwellers in Dhofar:

> The caves and the rock shelters that dot the wadis cutting the southern part of Jebel Qara, a massif facing the coast of Dhofar ... provide an important opportunity to fill this gap as they include anthropogenic sediments of the Early Holocene hunter-gatherers.[4]
>
> (2015 2)

In contrast,

> The more recent sites dated to the Neolithic period (from c. 8000 cal BP [calibrated years before the present]) are mostly shell middens along the Omani coasts, with rich and consistent cultural material ... and frequently linked to mangroves and lagoons.
>
> (3)

Thus, the two types of sites (caves and coastal) may not be related to each other as

> we have no evidence for any kind of connection between the Early Holocene sites of Jebel Qara and the coastal area, as for example no marine shell has been found in the inland sites. Along the coast, sites of that age are extremely rare, as one single cave site has been discovered so far dated to the Early Holocene.
>
> (11)

Further, Hilbert's "Khamseen Rock Shelter and the Late Palaeolithic-Neolithic Transition in Dhofar" (2013) considers two types of evidence of human occupation in a rock shelter

> The Late Palaeolithic assemblage recovered from the basal layer is marked by direct hard-hammer blade production using a *semi-tournant* strategy and a toolkit composed of burins, diverse cutting and scraping implements and tanged projectile points. It is attributed to the Khashabian industry, which is part of the apparently long-standing Nejd Leptolithic tradition ... [while] The Neolithic assemblage is marked by the production of bifacial implements using both hard- and soft-hammer technique and pressure-retouched projectile points. Blank production is primarily flake-oriented and based on multiple platform cores. Analogous assemblages have been reported across Yemen, Oman and the Emirates.
>
> (56–57)

This difference between the two types of rock tools might point to a difference in population. Hilbert argues

> Based on the lithic evidence the transition from the LP [Late Palaeolithic] to the Neolithic in Dhofar was not a linear process through which the Khashabian changed into the Neolithic. This discontinuity may represent either population replacement or admixture and subsequent acculturation ... Provided that the connection between the Khashabian and the Nejd Leptolithic proposed here holds, it may be argued that Dhofar was populated prior to the onset of the Holocene and was therefore

> inhabited by an older population that has no descendants among modern populations.[5]
>
> (2013 57)

Although there might have been a "replacement" event, i.e. the previous population which inhabited Dhofar disappeared and the region was reoccupied by an unrelated group of people, there has been continual habitation from the Bronze Age until the present day. This means that while perhaps two unrelated groups lived in the Dhofar region, there have always been occupants: "A microlithic industry which shows evident comparisons with Iron Age sites located along the coast of Dhofar ... has enabled archaeologists to identify a continuity in the exploitation of the territory from the first millennium BC to the Islamic period" (Pavan and Visconti 2020 246).

Pre-modern[6]

Most of the archeological work in Dhofar has concentrated on two sites: Sumhuram and Al Baleed/Al Balid.[7] Zerboni, Perego, Mariani et al. explain

> Thanks to the trade of frankincense the city of Khor Rorī (also known as Sumhuram) flourished in the first centuries BCE and CE along the shoreline, becoming one of the main maritime centres of that time...In Medieval times, the Dhofarian shoreline was a crucial node in the maritime commercial routes across the Indian Ocean between the Horn of Africa, the Arabian Peninsula, and India. In this phase, the city of Al-Balīd (ancient Salalah) grew and became one of the main harbours of southern Arabia.
>
> (2020 189)

Sumhuram was a heavily fortified small city used as a collection point for incense with a military output first established at the end of the 2nd century BCE and then developed into a city in the first half of the 1st century CE by the kingdom of Hadramawt (see Pavan and Degli Esposti 2016).[8] Zarins states, "It would appear major formal construction at the site commenced ca. 20-15 B.C. and ended by A.D. 350 ... [and] continued to be occupied without interruption well past the fifth century" (2009 668, 670). In "Incense Routes and Pre-Islamic South Arabian Kingdoms" (2002) Avanzini mentions that when Sumhuram was functioning, there were "settlements of fishermen-shepherds on the coast, occupied on a periodical basis," as well as "permanent agricultural villages" with "irrigated agriculture and animal raising" (23; see also Avanzini 2007 and 2008).

In "Water and Power in South Arabia: The Excavation of 'Monumental Building 1'" Degli Esposti and Pavan explain and clarify that the main reason Sumhuram was built by power over 800 km to the west is

> the location of the town is close to the semi-arid Nejd region where the best quality of frankincense (Boswellia sacra Flueck.) grows. At

> the same time, it constitutes an ideal and well-protected port-of-call along the naval routes connecting Arabia with India... Later on, with the involvement of Roman traders, these routes will become part of a complex "triangular network" [Mediterranean – west coast of India – Red Sea – Arabian Gulf].
>
> (2020)

The town was abandoned because the natural harbor in the bay of Khor Ruwi silted up, but there is evidence of "ephemeral dwellings dated to the Late Antiquity and the Early Islamic period" (2020).

The ruins of the second site, Al Baleed, are located along the coast in the south-east section of Salalah. The area was the site of "a long occupation dating back to the Bronze Age as evidenced by a number of stone tools found in the area" (Pavan and Visconti 2020 246; see also Zarins 2007). The city flourished as a trading center from the 10th to the 18th century CE when trading patterns changed and it fell into disrepair.

Pavan, Fusaro, Visconti et al. (2020) explain the various people and entities who have excavated there and then set out details of recent finds in one of its main buildings, the *husn* (castle). Phase VI (1600–800) is the "last occupational phase of Husn Al Balid ... represented by rather poor structures unearthed below the surface or slightly emerging from it" (175). Phase V (1500–600) is

> characterized by noticeable changes in the layout of the Husn, which provides evidence of an evolution of the traditional architecture in the post-gunpowder period. Circular towers were placed at three of the corners of the building, and one at protection of the monumental gate. (177)
>
> Phase IV (1279–500)

> represents the most splendid phase at the site. The amount, variety and quality of the pottery found in layers dated to this period, confirms a large circulation of items, including high-quality artefacts especially from China, Iran and Egypt ... [which] highlight the pivotal role of Ẓafār [Dhofar] in the international trade of that time
>
> (178)[9]

Specifically

> Ẓafār was one of the destinations of the voyages of Zheng He (c .1371–1435), the famous Chinese Muslim admiral who travelled across the Indian Ocean on behalf of the Ming emperors Yongle (1402–1424) and Xuande (1425–1435) ... A number of different sources of information were provided about ... about the goods traded between the two

> countries – frankincense, dragon's blood, aloes, myrrh, benzoin, liquid storax, camels, and ostriches were exchanged for silk and porcelains.
> (Pavan and Visconti 2020 243)

During this time, "the region of Dhofar was under the control of the Rasūlid dynasty (1279–420) which had conquered the port of al-Shiḥr in 1277 and the port of al-Balīd in 1279, while enjoying productive diplomatic and commercial relations with the Chinese world" (248). The "the final abandonment" of the city occurred "between 1660 and 1700" (247).[10]

A third site of interest is Shisr, the ruins of an ancient trading post at the edge of the Empty Quarter, north-west of Salalah. In 1991, Nicholas Clapp put together the Trans-Arabian Expedition looking for a fabled city, Ubar, which is mentioned in the Holy Quran. The search is recounted in *The Road to Ubar: Finding the Atlantis of the Sands* (1999) which includes an extended discussion of what was known about pre-historic and pre-modern southern Oman at the time the book was written. The team originally thought they might have found Ubar, but the site is now referred to as Shisr.

The locations of both the pre-historic and pre-modern sites are listed in the *Atlas of Archaeological Survey in the Governorate of Dhofar Sultanate of Oman* (2013). This book is in English and Arabic and includes maps of the sites with photos of the places as well as satellite images. There are maps for each time period, as well as one map showing all sites so it is clear how groups of people settled in various places at various times; for example, the earlier sites are scattered throughout the mountains and *nejd*[11], and later sites are clustered on the coast.

Descriptions of pre-1970s dwellings

In the two sections above, I have briefly explained the types of Dhofari dwellings which have been well researched: pre-historic caves, coastal sites and the archeological sites of Sumhuram and Al Baleed. From writings in the early 1800s, it is clear that from the desertion of Al Baleed to when the historical records start again, most Dhofaris lived in vernacular structures[12]: caves, stone-built houses or temporary structures made from plant material in the mountain regions and palm-frond and plaster, limestone, coral or mudbrick houses along the coast.[13]

Information about Dhofar in modern times in English begins with the first English explorers in the Dhofar region: Captain Haines and his crew from the Indian Navy who surveyed and explored the Dhofar coast in the Brig *Palinurus* in 1834, 1835 and 1836. Commander J.P. Saunders, with the same ship and some of the same crew, continued this surveying work in 1844–46. Haines (1839, 1845), Saunders (1846) and several officers published articles about the trip in general or Dhofar in detail including Carter (1845, 1846, 1847, 1851, 1852) and Cruttenden (1838). Two sailors, Hulton and Smith, wrote about inscriptions they had found (1835 and

1839); Hulton's journal was published by his brother in 1844. These texts include information about weather patterns, proving that Dhofar had more rainfall in the past, e.g. "Dyreez [Dhariz] is ... surrounded by well cultivated lands like Thagah [Taqa]" (Cruttenden 1838). Wild animals mentioned include hyenas, wolves, ibex, rabbits, foxes and partridges; trees mentioned include frankincense, fig, tamarind, henna, lime and coconut, as well as sugar cane, aloes, tobacco, corn and onions.

Theodore and Mabel Bent arrived in Dhofar, at the town of Mirbat, on December 20, 1893, and left from Al Hafa (part of modern-day Salalah) on January 23, 1894. During their short stay, they traveled along the coast and a short distance in the mountains; I believe they are the first Westerners to visit the Dhofar mountains to write a description of it. In *Southern Arabia* (1900/2005), they describe Mirbat as having "some fifty houses and a few Bedu huts, with about two hundred inhabitants" with a "fort built of mud bricks" (230, 231). Then they moved to Al Hafa in the "castle" of the *Wali* (governor). In their tours of the coastal plain, they found the sites of seven "ruined towns" of which two in particular Al Balad (now Al Baleed) on the coast, and Robat, "two miles inland" (240).

On December 29, they left for a trip through the mountains, observing the "Gara" (now Qara) "know no home save their ancestral caves" but make "reed huts" to stay in when they come "down to the plain in Dhofar in the rainy season for pasturage" (246). It might be expected that Victorian travelers would make fun of or disparage the cave dwellings, but the description is quite positive: "the floor of their caves is soft and springy" and "we found them cool and refreshing" (259).

They discuss the ruins of an "extensive" town in Wadi Nahast (now Nahiz), but their most important achievement is concluding that Khor Ruwi, the location of the ancient fort/town of Sumhuram discussed above, is the site known as "Abyssapolis" in Ptolemy and "Moscha" in the Periplus of the Erythraean Sea, a Greek document which lists directions to/between coastal cities in present-day India, South Arabia, West Africa, Egypt and the Mediterranean written in the middle of the 1st century by an unknown author. The Bents did not see the ruins of Sumhuram but explored the flat floodplain leading to the sheer cliff (waterfall after heavy rain) which is just inland from the ruins (see also Bent 1895).

The next visitor is Craufurd, who stopped in Dhofar for one day in April, year unspecified. He makes clear in his essay that he had not read the Bent's book when his boat "After five years' continuous service off the bleak Arabian coast" landed in Dhofar (1919 100). As a naval officer, his primary interest is the boats and the method of maneuvering past the breaking swell; he states that "their manner of working through the surf was exceedingly clever" (100). He notes that

> in the Dhofar district there lies a fertile land of some 40 miles from Bander Reisut to Merbat, with an average depth of 12 miles. The whole

> of this presumably fertile region is practically virgin soil uncultivated for lack of incentive.
>
> (103)

Unusually for an early 1900s traveler, he also gives the local point of view

> The Sheikh's son pointed out to us that the inhabitants of Dhofar are perfectly satisfied with the smaller means of life. They have the powerful Sultan of Maskat to the eastward, The British protectorate lies westwards. There is therefore no anxiety from the restless tribes of the interior. If they began to trade they would merely be exciting cupidity.
>
> (102)

In *Arabia Felix* (1932) Thomas recounts his journey across the *Rub al Kahli* (Empty Quarter) in the fall/winter of 1930. His trip started in Salalah, so there are a few mentions of houses, buildings and lifeways.[14] For example he leaves the fort of the *Wali* where he is staying to visit the town of Salala and describes the "lofty many-storyed houses of dazzling whiteness – the stone hewn from the plain where they stand – the ornamentation giving the semblance of dignified age" (16).[15] He details the house of his host, the merchant Sa'ad bin Abdul'Aziz: "the narrowest of steps led thence to the guest-chamber at the top of the house a large room with a fine central beam of Malabar teak" (17).

In the mountains, he describes "the straw thatch of beehive shape" that one man was living in, as well as structures made of "stone, rough, undressed and uncemented" but that in "summer rains and winter cold" people and herds stayed in caves (58).

A geologist who traveled with Bertram Thomas on a short visit to Dhofar in the 1920s writes

> Regarding the interesting non-Arab tribes, the Mahri and the Gara … They are entirely nomad, and live under the shelter of trees or caves. They have no cultivation, but live on the produce of large herds of cattle and some camels. I found them always very friendly, and on several occasions I was persuaded to partake of a meal with them … Their diet consists exclusively of meat and milk products.
>
> (Lees 1928 456, 457)

Thomas's *Arabia Felix* (1932) and the next important text about Dhofar, Thesiger's *Arabian Sands* (1959), are divided by the Second World War. Thesiger traveled through present-day Oman, Yemen and the United Arab Emirates between 1946 and 1950; like Thomas, he crossed the *Rub al Khali*, but he spent more time with his guides and was far more interested in their lives than Thomas. However, he spent little time in Salalah, nor was he interested in buildings, so his descriptions of lifeways are concentrated on camping.

After Thesiger, the next travel writer is Jan (then James) Morris' journey with Sultan Said bin Taymur from Salalah to the north of Oman in 1956 as described in *Sultan in Oman* (1957/2008). Whereas Dhofaris are discussed with accuracy and respect by Thesiger, Morris lets loose with insults as demeaning as the Bents. They have "shaggy," "strange" and "fuzzy" hair and practice "obscure rituals, taboos, and prejudices" (30, 39, 31). In keeping with the general tone of relegating the inhabitants to pre-historic times, there is no mention of guns. The people "hurl in the general direction of their neighbors the heavy throwing sticks (less scientific than boomerangs) with which they were sometimes quaintly armed" (40). It is clear in both Thomas' and Thesiger's accounts that the men of this region had access to and knowledge of guns.

A similar tone is found in St Alban's *Where Time Stood Still: Portrait of Oman* (1980) which describes her visit to Dhofar in the late 1970s. She states that there are "nine illiterate tribes of primitive aborigines" in the Qara [Mountains]" and these "grand, pastoral, cave-dwelling noblemen have never worked with their hands" (152). How would "primitive" people living in caves and herding flocks have survived if they had "never worked with their hands"? And these "primitive aborigines" had just waged a ten-year war with the Omani government during which they had close contact with not only the People's Democratic Republic of Yemen but Russia, China, Cuba and various Arab countries. Further, St Albans only describes the life of those Dhofaris who were living in caves and rough stone and wood dwellings in the mountains. At the time she was there, there was an airport, Holiday Inn, "shops and offices and ultra-modern television centre" and a hospital (180), but she never shows Omanis interacting in/working in these modern surroundings. Thus, immediately after the Dhofar War, there was a time in which some Dhofaris were living traditionally in caves and round houses, while others were transitioning to modern life-ways with cement block houses with electricity and running water.

Adam and Cazacova's presentation "The Round Dhofari House Popularity Uniting the Past and the Present" (2012) explains the types of vernacular dwellings made with stones, palm fronds, fabric, wood, mud and mudbricks. It has helpful photographs and drawings of how the round houses were constructed; there is also an illustration of the placement of items inside a round house. Cazacova, Hidalgo, Farhan, Al-Masikhi et al.'s "Recognition of Mirbat Town's Old Area as Historical Environment" (2014) has information about undated, traditionally built (i.e. limestone, plaster, palm tree trunk and palm fronds, not cement block) houses in one of the coastal towns.

One type of house that was common on the Arabian Peninsula but found less frequently in Dhofar is the courtyard house. Alkhalidi explains

> The traditional courtyard house, a low rise and inward-looking building, was developed as a perfect solution to account for climate, available building material and techniques, and socio-cultural requirement

> such as privacy. The compactness of the housing materials was and still is suitable for the climate as well as the culture by allowing social interaction in the private areas. Usually the courtyard is the core of the house due to its centrality and all the family's spaces are organized around it. (2013 290)

Writing about Qatar, Al Mohanndi, Furlan and Major (2019) describe that the interior of the house had "an open-air courtyard that resembles the core of the housing unit, physically and socially."

Because of the *khareef* (June–September monsoon season) having an open courtyard surrounded by rooms was less practical in Dhofar than in other areas which typically have year-round sun. Some of the 1800s- and 1900s-built limestone houses have courtyards, but from the illustrations found, for example in Rageete (2003), most had small light wells instead of an extensive space surrounded by rooms. Some courtyard houses were built in Salalah after the war, as discussed below, but these were a series of small rooms around an open area, not a house with an open space in the middle. This type of house was used because it was easy to build and easy to add more rooms if needed, and they were eventually replaced by conventional houses.

In the past 15 years, I have seen a few courtyard dwellings in Dhofar, but they were either in areas at the edge of or outside the *khareef* zone and consisted of a walled area with a cement floor with rooms along one or two walls. There is also an older style of building that is not a typical courtyard style but an area surrounded by a low wall with several rooms placed throughout the space, not in a row and/or with doors facing one central space but almost like a mini-village with tiny alleys/mini-courtyards to give privacy at the threshold.

Housing themes

I had wanted to do a straight chronological discussion of housing in Dhofar, but two issues came up which span decades. I examine pastoralism and the scarcity of outside architectural influences in this section, then return to a chronological approach below. These topics are pulled out as both cover the time before and after the war (1965–75) which was a watershed in terms of development and change in Dhofar.

The first topic, pastoralism, was the main way of life in the mountains for centuries and, although modified, still persists among some sectors of the population. The second theme, the effect of external influences on architecture, is important for most regions on the Arabian Peninsula, but not Dhofar which modernized later than other areas.

Pastoralism

Zerboni, Perego, Mariani et al. explain that "the spreading of pastoralism started in the Bronze Age (~3500–1000 BCE), and included the Jebel Qara and the Salalah coastal plain. Pastoral land-use is attested also in the Iron

Age and Islamic times, up to recent years" (2020 189). Pastoralism refers to a lifestyle which is supported by keeping domesticated animals which are fed primarily by grazing; in Dhofar, this means goats, cows and camels. Usually pastoralism is used as a description in opposition to farming, but in the mountains, inhabitants did and continue to farm small enclosed fields which were watered by the *khareef*.

The specific form of pastoralism in Dhofar is seasonal transhumance, i.e. stock owners and herders, both expat and local, move animals to different areas throughout the year. In each area, the animals are released during the day; goats are almost always with a herder, while cows and camels are often left on their own and rounded up before sunset.[16] For the purpose of this discussion, the two important aspects of these seasonal movements are that Dhofaris live/lived in different types of dwellings depending on the topography and that this pastoralism continues into the present day.

Janzen's *Nomads in the Sultanate of Oman: Tradition and Development in Dhofar* (1986), based on field work from January to August 1977 and January to May 1978 (xxi), gives a helpful snapshot of Dhofar during a time of immense change at the end of the Dhofar War. At that time (1977), "Dhofar had a total population of about 65,000 inhabitants, of whom about 26,000, or 40%, lived in a nomadic-peasant environment" (39).

Janzen's many careful drawings and observations about campsites are particularly useful as he gives details of housing in a different geographical location in Dhofar, for example in the desert, the drawing of a camp of ar-Rawashid (69) and a map of the layout of the interior of a tent (70). For the *nejd* area, there is a map of an al-Mahrah camp (77) and a Bayt Kathir camp (78). He also explains the different types of dwellings used by Dhofaris in the mountains, including a sun shade, open-sided tent and the typical round house with a low stone wall with woven branches as a roof (94), as well as monsoon/winter camps (121, 122), post-monsoon camps (129) and patterns of transhumance (124). He mentions some transitional buildings: small houses made with "corrugated iron" and "plywood" (Plate 32).

Cordes and Scholz's *Bedouins, Wealth, and Change: A Study of Rural Development in the United Arab Emirates and the Sultanate of Oman* (1980) also has a lot of detailed information about lifeways in Dhofar in the period after the war, for example:

> the mountain dwellers collectively designated jebalis, camp at the lower and middle elevations where they build dome-shaped huts as shelter from cool and rainy weather ... Winter pasture areas are found in the level tracts at high elevations in the mountains. Camps are built by clumps of trees

Further, some groups camp "in the deeply cut, sometimes very narrow, *wadis* and use recesses in the rocks, umbrella shaped trees, and bushes or windscreens as shelters."

They also explain which type of pastoralists live in which type of geographic regions, for example, "sand bedouins move from the Rub al-Khali, the winter pasture area, to ... the summer pasture areas, every year at the beginning of the hot season (March/beginning of April)." *Nejd* bedouins move to "with only their camels, to the watershed in the Dhofar Mountains, or to the plain of Salalah" in summer.

In this period directly after the war, Cordes and Scholz explain that the changes in lifestyle for the bedouins in the northern *nejd* and desert areas were less than for the mountain dwellers, specifically

> Little has changed in the migratory habits and settlement customs of the bedouins in Dhofar. Their movements continue to be between the area near the mountains and the country's interior. Motorized vehicles ... serve as transport from one seasonal location to another. The government has attempted to set up permanent settlements with medical stations, government and administrative offices, police station, military post, wells, and government-run markets. Up to now, however, there has been no marked settlement of bedouins in these locations.

In contrast,

> More extensive changes have taken place among the jebalis (mountain nomads) ... Many young jebalis belong to the Firqah, the sultan's native militia, and the relatively high monthly pay (80 Omani rials minimum in 1978) enables them to buy almost any of the products offered for sale in Salalah. They therefore obtain their groceries, largely provided free of charge by the government anyway, in town and, as a consequence, monsoon agriculture has been almost completely abandoned in the mountains.

For this discussion, the most important aspect is that while Cordes and Scholz note a "decrease in animal husbandry ... and the frequency and a reduction in the distance of nomadic movements" with "a transition to permanent housing and settlement" and "an increase in non-pastoral activities," pastoralism did not end. In fact, "there has been a steady increase in the number of cattle, and in some cases of camels and goats" because access to water became easier when wells were drilled throughout the mountains. Before the war, herd size was always limited by the scarcity of water during the winter and early spring. With nearby wells, owners could have more animals and use less time to take care of them.

Although pastoralism is less practiced now, there are still some adherents.[17] Ball, MacMillan, Tzanopoulos et al.'s "Contemporary Pastoralism in the Dhofar Mountains of Oman" (2020) states

> The Dhofar Mountains in Oman are one of few places in the Arabian Peninsula where an extensive form of camel pastoralism persists...a

> nd livestock populations have increased substantially since the 1970s. Over the 30-year period from 1982 to 2012, the cattle, camel, and goat populations in Dhofar increased by at least 257%, 170% and 96% respectively.[18]

Further, "Pastoralists' reasons for keeping livestock, in order of importance, were: (1) inherited from parents; (2) financial security; and (3) products for the household."

One informant took me to see a series of several small caves that he and his family lived in for part of the year during the 1970s and then to three "camps" which his father still uses. He used the term "camp" to refer to an area of land that is seen by other livestock owners and herders as under the control of a man, without any formal claims of ownership. Each camp was used in different seasons/weather.

One was in a *wadi* (dry river bed) and thus partially shaded; one was on the side of a slope and surrounded by trees. The last was on top of a hillock in the midst of an open, rolling country. Each was improved by the man's labor. The *wadi* location had a make-shift corral and a small enclosure for the male camel. The owner slept in a large tent supported by a metal frame. The camels were let loose during the day and came back at night when called (also because they were hungry and nursing mothers wanted to see the calves which were kept at camp).

The hilltop location had a long, hand-built stone wall, topped with pieces of wood as a windbreak. The camels were bedded down on the leeward side and the owner slept next to a fire pit near the wall. There was a small structure, perhaps 12 × 12 feet, made of metal bars, with a door in which fodder and supplies were kept. From this location, one could see several other nearby camps. The owner also had a cement block house with a large barn next to it. My informant had herded camels as a child and still helped his father move the camels as needed.

The most common type of transhumance still practiced is that in the *khareef* (June–September) camels are kept in camps on the flat plain at the foot of the mountains north of Salalah. To keep the camels from wandering into populated areas, between Salalah and the *jarbaeb*, as the area is known, the Dhofari municipality built a road which has a shoulder-high divide and is steeply graded so camels can't cross it; camels, either on their own or with the prompting of herders, use the roundabout to get to the other side of this divide. During the monsoon months, the owners live in tents near the temporary corrals where the camels stay. The whole area is covered with tents and camel herds, with friends and relatives of the camel owners often coming to spend a few hours at night.

Some camel owners bring their camels to the far, north, side of the mountains. The reason for moving the animals is that camel feet are flat and do not have traction on the damp earth, so if the camels stayed in the mountains in the rainy season, there would be many injuries.

Thus pastoralism is predicated on people using different types of dwellings. In the past this meant sleeping in caves, under rough shelters comprising fabric or mats strung in trees, next to windbreaks, in the shadow of a *wadi* wall, in a round stone house topped with wooden branches etc. Now, people who practice transhumance have at least one permanent house which they inhabit for at least part of the year, but some still use rough dwellings.

The round stone houses are no longer used for humans but are still occasionally being built as animal shelters. The other types of temporary housing are still used by herders, as well as picnickers and campers. Coastlines near small towns often have several small shelters made of cement blocks held together with roughly done masonry or plywood supports with old fishnet roofs covered with palm leaves. Caves that were once residences are still used on weekend trips, and, in the mountains, one can find "camel camps" consisting of several mats on the ground with the herders' supplies tied up in a tree.

Scarcity of external influences

An important aspect of housing in Dhofar is that the architecture has not been greatly influenced by other countries because of fewer expats and the infrastructure did not start to develop until the mid- to late 1970s. For various reasons including more space, weather patterns and water supplies that have supported a history of farming in parts of Oman and fewer natural resources to sell, Oman has significantly more locals and fewer expats than the other Arabian Peninsula countries except for Yemen. When I first visited Oman in 1998, I was struck that the taxi drivers were all Omanis, unlike the Emirates where I lived at that time (see Gardner 2015 and De Bel-Air 2015).

In explaining Dhofar's later development, there are two factors to consider: the historical situation and the Dhofar War (1965–75). First, Oman, unlike most of the Arabian Peninsula, has not been conquered, occupied and controlled by outside forces except for limited areas at limited times. There have been centuries of cross-cultural exchange (pilgrimages to Mecca, interchange with Oman's former colonies of Zanzibar and Gwadar, trade with India, employment in other Gulf Cooperation Council (GCC) countries, modern travel for medical treatment, education and/or tourism etc.), but direct rule from foreign powers has concentrated on a few coastal areas and ended in the late 1740s.

Specifically, the Dhofari coast was, in the far distant past, under the control of empires from the areas of present-day southern Yemen but had centuries of autonomy before being brought under the control of the Al Bu Sa'id rulers of Muscat when Sa'id bin Sultan annexed the province in 1829. From the time of annexation until the 1960s, coastal Dhofar went through alternating periods of relative calm and aggression. The mountainous areas of Dhofar are one of those rare areas where the power of outside authority was negligible until the 1960s. The cost of this autonomy was that there were no schools, clinics, permanent shops or roads beyond those built to cross the region or by employees of oil companies.

For an overview of the Dhofar War, please see Chapter 2 of *Community and Autonomy in Southern Oman* (Risse 2019).[19] For the purpose of this discussion, the important part is that as the war was between the government, represented by Sultan Said, and then his son Sultan Qaboos, against the Dhofar Liberation Front, but the small regional conflict was drawn into many larger webs of influence.

The rebels had support from the (newly formed) People's Republic of Southern Yemen (1967, changed to People's Democratic Republic of Yemen in 1970) and

> The Russians provided arms and technical assistance, the Chinese built a road to the Hadramaut and supplied medical aid, the Cubans assisted with agriculture and the training of the air force, and the East Germans organized the internal security system.
>
> (Kelly 1976 221)[20]

As is widely documented, when Sultan Qaboos assumed power by coup d'état in 1970, he used a carrot and stick approach to end the war. The government accepted aid and brought in soldiers from Jordan and Iran and paid for British military help but simultaneously made it clear that they were not targeting civilians and were ready to start development as soon as areas were cleared of rebel fighters, e.g.

> Once an area was considered secure, a CAT [Civil Aid Teams] would move in and establish a centre. A well would be dug, a school and clinic would be established, a market would be set up and a mosque would be built.
>
> (Newsinger 1998 56)

During and immediately after the war three small compounds, still in use, were built for British soldiers in Salalah, but this is the extent of the war's influence on houses. These few compounds of six or eight houses did not impact how Dhofaris conceived of or built their own houses.

Further, unlike some countries in which expat housing for oil companies influenced local styles, the oil fields in Dhofar are away from settled areas and the worker's housing is out of sight, not visited and not copied. The military base in Thumrait similarly has expat housing which is not part of the local architectural vocabulary.

And as only GCC citizens can buy land in Dhofar, expats live in Dhofari-designed houses or various types of apartment buildings designed for expats (see Chapter 4), without affecting house construction. In the one small, expat-designed compound I lived in for a few years, I had Italian, French, Indian, Iraqi, American and English neighbors. In the two Omani neighborhoods I have lived in for a total of 12 years, I am the only non-Omani who lives in the whole area.

This is an important difference as much of the writing about architecture on the Arabian Peninsula deals with, often complains about, the external influences. For example, Haggag's "The Impact of Globalization on Urban Spaces in Arab Cities" (2004) states

> By 1920, large parts of the Arab world were in western hands. Western-type apartment houses and public building started lining the street fronts of new districts. French and Italian squires and open spaces were also established in many Arab cities. Western architects and planners were commissioned to do important architectural and urban projects.
> (38)

In discussing the connection between architecture and colonization, Akcan argues

> The necessity to create controlled reorganizations in the colonies brought city planning and architecture to the fore as the main institutional setting and the crucial tool of representation in the making of colonial societies ... the colonial architects' most common concern was their confrontation with the local building traditions and the urban tissue of the colonized city ... [with] large-scale demolition of existing urban fabric, conservation according to Western values of preservation, and buildings designed as replicas of architectural styles in the mother country or imitations of local styles as a means to gain the sympathy of the colonized.
> (2014 126)

Molotch and Ponzini's article "The New Arab Urban: Test Beds, Work-arounds, and the Limits of Enacted Cities" (2019) explains, "Famously and noticeably on the land in the early period, oil companies created gated zones reserved for Western technocrats and managers" (11). These types of gated zones or communities never developed in Dhofar.

Maneval (2019) reviews texts by Saudis in which, for example, the writer expresses

> his alienation from his hometown by the spread of new building styles. The author appears to be especially disquieted by the fact that some of the new buildings reference Western architectural styles, or that Western architects were commissioned to build houses in so-called Islamic styles and even to build mosques.
> (109)

Maneval notes, "During the 1980s and 1990s ... they [Saudi authors] became concerned not only about loss of cultural identity in general but that contemporary architecture and urban design contravened the rulings of Islam in particular" (109). Adopting Western-style houses meant losing local lifeways including "appreciation and maintenance of one's neighborhood community, strong family ties, the protection of privacy and an egalitarian concept of society" (112).

I first started to think about how the loss of architectural identity is not a factor within Dhofar while looking at photos of houses. Houses made in the 1970s and 80s were often handmade and constrained by local construction knowledge and materials; they usually had a simple floor plan with few decorations beyond a crenelated roof.

Once expat labor became the norm for building, there were very few expat-designed houses and these were not used as models so Dhfoaris gathered architectural elements from various sources, such as observing other Dhofari-designed houses, traveling and looking at photos, and created amalgamations that suited the owners' tastes. Thus, most houses in Salalah have several different architectural styles: a portico with Grecian columns with clay, Spanish-style, roof tiles, for example.

This fusion of forms from different time periods and architectural vocabularies seemed strange to me at first, but I realized that it wasn't bad style or a lack of style but a happy effervesce.[21] Except for the small compounds, no two houses look alike; there are no "Little boxes on the hillside,/ Little boxes made of ticky tacky, Little boxes on the hillside, Little boxes all the same.[22] Dhofari homeowners are, in general, only constrained by budget and keep the color of the house in the field of white/beige/toast/caramel.

Development and housing changes in Dhofar after the 1970s

Development outside of Salalah

The development of infrastructure before the 1970s was impeded by Sultan Said's aversion to modernizing and then the war. Once the conflict ended and oil wealth began to be diffused through the society, the CAT centers became a model of how growth was managed throughout the mountains. Each center had provisional, then permanent (cement block) government facilities. As roads improved and people could easily move from Salalah to mountain areas, people opened stores at the centers and started to settle nearby, often building houses by hand, thus creating a series of small towns (see Janzen 1986 185–92, 193, that has two drawings of plans).

A similar process happened in the *nejd* and coastal villages listed here in reference to Salalah: Dalkut (136 km w), Rakhyut (121 km w), Taqa (30 km e), Mirbat (70 km e), Sudh (135 km e), Hadbin/Hadbeen (156 km e), Hasik (193 km e) and Shuwaymiyah (320 km e). However, these towns, albeit small, were already the centers of their respective area because of natural features such as inlets, bays, headlands and protected beaches which made fishing easier. After the early 1970s, roads were graded and paved, then mosques, schools and clinics were constructed and people built permanent dwellings.

The third group of towns was the series of urban areas along the road between Salalah and Muscat. When looking at a map, almost all of the towns (and population) of Dhofar are in the south-western section of the region. But there is a main road heading north through the mountains and then east through the desert which leads to the other regions of Oman. Along this route, the first main town is Thumrayt/Thumrait (77 kilometers north of Salalah), now home to a large military base. Then Dawkah (199 km), Qatbit (272 km) and Muqshin (350 km), the northernmost town in the Dhofar region.

Cordes and Scholz (1980) explain the beginning of this process:

> On the periphery of Salalah in Taqah and Mirbat between 6,000 and 7,000 plots (60 x 60 ft) have been distributed to Dhofaris in the past few years. Not only Hadar [city dwellers] but also many bedouins and jebalis (mountain nomads) have acquired land in Salalah in this way. At first, the inhabitants of each sector came from the same tribe, but recently the government has been trying, for political reasons, to encourage quarters with mixed tribal populations.[23]

In terms of the area to the north of Salalah

> There is a military airport near Thamarit and a military base in Mudhay, and bedouin families from different tribes, notably the Bayt Kathir, have settled in both locations. They have built their own houses, some permanently occupied, some used only seasonally or periodically.

Lastly, there are a few other towns in the desert areas: Mazyunah (176 km) to the far west, almost on the border with Yemen; the oil town of Marmul (178 km) in the desert east of Thumrait and Shalim (300 km, south-east of Marmul and north of Shuwaymiyah).

Development in Salalah

In Salalah, all land that was not built on/claimed was declared government property. As areas beyond the small commercial and residential area of coastal Salalah were planned before being built, forethought was used in that simple one-lane-each-direction roads had wide buffers so that the roads could be widened later.[24] Several maps of two Salalah neighborhoods are included in the "Salalah al-Wusta & Gharbiya: Dhofar Governorate: Documentation and Heritage Management Plan" (2016).[25]

Orientation is easy as the streets are on a fairly regular grid plan, tilted slightly in the south-west corner of Salalah. The mountains are north, and the sea is south. Most roads are of one lane in each direction;

there are very few one-way streets. Main roads are divided; if the road you want is on the other side, one might have to overshoot the road, do a U-turn and double back. In towns there are four-way stops, sometimes enhanced with speed bumps to slow traffic and traffic lights at major intersections; round/abouts are often used on the edges and outside of towns. The new airport is just to the north of town, but only accessible from the Bypass Road.

As van Nes and Yamu state, "Economic centrality is thus not a static, but a dynamic process" because "land values and rent processes tend to be influenced by the various integration values of the street net" (2018 11). When I moved to Salalah in 2005, the two main shopping areas were Haffa Souq and a long rectangle with 23rd July Street to the north, Al Matar Street to the east, As Salam to the south and Al Nadha Street to the west. 23rd July Street, also known as Bank Street, has several banks and money changers in addition to housewares, electronics, restaurants and a few more traditional stores such as fodder. Just to the north of 23rd July are the fresh food souqs: fruit, vegetables, meat and fish. At the intersection of 23rd July and Al Matar was the original Lulus, a large chain hypermarket. Behind Lulus is a small car repair/car wash area known as section 5. The old airport was at the northern end of Al Matar Street; one used to exit the airport and be downtown within two minutes.

Al Matar Street, running south from the old airport, has Haffa House, for a long time the biggest hotel in town, Al Nasr Sports club and many small shops; it ends almost at the beach to the south. As Salam Street (running east/west roughly parallel to 23rd July but further south) has small shops: furnishings, restaurants, jewelry, travel agents and many fabric, accessory and clothing stores on the western end. The corner of As Salam and Al Nadha Street has the gold souq. The short stretch north on Al Nadha Street up to 23rd July has the 24-hour pharmacy, a fire station, money exchange shops, the now-closed English language bookstore and the now-moved police station. The corner of Al Nadha and 23rd has the recently built Grand Mosque. The northern end of Al Nadha is the Royal Oman Air Force Base; it goes south almost to the beach.

In the past ten years, the formally empty space between Rubot Street and 23rd July has filled in with five or more story buildings with stores on the ground floor and apartments or a hotel on the upper stories. There is parking in front or to the sides; there are no buildings with elevated parking on the first few floors with apartments above as is common in Dubai.

Housing changes

In their article "The Architecture of Salalah and the Dhofar Littoral" Costa and Kite (1985) discuss the two architectural lineages in Dhofar: the vernacular buildings in the mountains and the more formal, usually limestone-built, buildings on the coastal plain (131).

The vernacular tradition is also discussed in Costa's "Notes on Settlement Patterns in Traditional Oman" (1983) which explains

> The Jibbali dwelling (*duqf*) is a hit with low circular walls (sometimes measuring 10m in diameter) of dry-stone construction topped by a domed roof supported by wooden posts. The roof is formed by irregular tree branches covered by a layer of cow dung and soil mixture. Each family house is formed by a cluster of interrelated huts, including sores and byres. Settlements are normally small and count an average of 15-20 houses.
>
> (250)

Sale's "The Ecology of the Mountain Region of Dhofar" (1980) includes photos of the wood being prepared (40), a house being built (46) and finished houses (47) and a description of typical dwellings and lifeways in the mountains (43–49).

Discussing the coastal plain, Costa and Kite show the plans of several "formal" limestone houses which are built around *shamsiya* (smaller than a courtyard, more like a light well)[26]. These houses are slightly similar to Yemeni houses with the ground floor used for storage and housing animals, with the living rooms above although Yemeni houses were usually much higher with five or six levels.

Yapicioglu and Cazacova (2018) explain that traditional Omani architecture in towns "can also be visualized from the narrow streets and low height buildings across many well-preserved villages; built using humble mud or stone structures" (101). Further, the "majority of the houses were made of stone, rocks, lime … Most importantly, the reference on decoration was a representation of the local craftsmanship in wood-carving" (104).

In an overview of various UK-based architecture firms working in Oman during the late 1970s/early 1980s, Smith focuses on Muscat but notes that the "traditional Salalah townhouse was limestone built" (1983 13).

Al Hinai, Batty and Probert note that in Salalah, "settlements occur in groups parallel with the coast. Houses in these groups also face south, i.e. towards the coast" (1993 253). They further detail the difference between houses close to the beach which were made of palm fronds and "often had mud-plastered walls on the north to protect from the dry, cold [often sand-bearing] northerly winter winds," while further inland, "houses were often built from limestone, two or three storeys high, with their long southerly facades facing the sea" (253).

These two types of houses (the limestone block in coastal towns and rock and timber structures in the mountains) were replaced slowly with the advent of cement block housing, expat builders and air conditioners. The transition period was gradual, with some Dhofaris still living in houses that were handbuilt by relatives.

In the 1980s, the Omani government started to impose rules covering the appearance of houses through the municipal inspectors who gave approval of house plans and permission for the building to commence. In terms of the facades for example,

> "Building Regulations for Muscat" allowed for creative designs within the frame of the local, Arabic and some Islamic architecture...Those regulations have been re-revised, evaluated and modified in 1992 and 2011. In all editions, the content of the following article was not changed: "The architectural design of facades/elevations of residential and residential/commercial buildings shall be according to the local, Arabic, or Islamic style ... [and] restricting height of buildings to a maximum of three stories for residential buildings."
>
> (Hegazy 2015 191)

In terms of the interiors, in Dhofar the first cement block houses were often in one of two styles: wheel-spoke and line. In "wheel-spoke" houses one walks directly (or after a short, narrow hallway) into a large open area, with the rooms of the house encircling the open area like spokes on a wheel, i.e. bedrooms, bathrooms and the kitchen. There might be one door on the far wall which opens to the outside. Sometimes a *majlis* is added on later with a narrow passage way from the main room to the *majlis* with a door that can be closed/locked. The center room was furnished with bolster pillows and mats. This is a single-story, smaller iteration of a courtyard house with the center room acting as the courtyard.

Another type of house had all the rooms in a line off a center, long, wide hallway that was lined with cushions might be used as a *majlis* (sitting room) or a play area for children. In this type of house, the first room on the right or left might be a *majlis*, the kitchen or a bedroom, with other bedroom doors lining the rectangular central space. Sometimes there is also a separate small concrete structure with a bathroom (sink, toilet and shower), washing machine and/or a second kitchen with a refrigerator, deep freezer and/or gas stove.[27]

In the mountains, these types of houses always have a *dekka*, an outside seating area, sometimes covered and furnished and sometimes with simply clean swept mats to sit on.

Now almost all houses are built with two main doors, a *majlis* (men's/visitor's sitting room), *salle* (women's/close friends' and family's sitting room), kitchen and bedrooms. Family residences are called "villas"; they are usually detached, but some, usually on double-lots, can share a side or back wall. They usually have extended family (sometimes three or four generations and more than 30 people) and are owned by the senior man, the senior woman and/or the older children. Some villas are so large that they are referred to jokingly as palaces, usually sitting on three or more plots of land.

In "Islamic Architecture Features and Modern Housing: A Case Study of the North Awqad District in Salalah, Oman" (2014) Al Kathiri and Cazacova note

> The modern housing of Dhofar region has been changed only in size, construction materials and building techniques' application. The dwellings are now larger, built of modern materials (mainly concrete and concrete blocks), but the layout and the exterior features did not change significantly. The cultural request for privacy remains the first consideration as well as the facades of the residence with decorative features and an attractive portico entrance.
>
> (11–12)

However, there is one noticeable change within the last decade. The authors state that

> Local regulations stating that the architectural design of façade/elevations of residential and residential/commercial buildings should be according to the local Arab Islamic style contribute to the local building traditions preservation. Consequently ... each modern residential building is a blend of features such as columns and arches, carved wooden doors and window screens with chiseled geometric or floral patterns. Yet the arch is the most common architectural attribute in local housing design and no dwelling is found without an arch.
>
> (1–2)

While this was certainly true for many decades, in the past ten years, many houses are now being built with only square windows and door frames.

In conclusion, I would like to make three general points about housing: apartments, sharing houses and older houses. First, Dhofaris rarely live in apartment units in large, multi-story buildings. If it is not feasible to be in a detached villa, there are several options. A Dhofari family might live in a rented house if there is no space in the husband's father's house or if there are temperament issues in living with in-laws. Or they might rent an apartment that is a floor or part of a house. Boys in college or men who have a house in the mountains but who are often in Salalah for work might rent a room, sometimes a *majlis* of a relative's house.

Nagy writes that

> both Qataris and others commonly assume that the new styles of housing in Qatar will encourage nuclear family households, neolocal residence patterns and the demise of extended family values. However, this does not seem to be the general pattern of change in Qatar ... I consistently found that Qataris are able and willing to expend effort

> and resources in order to establish residences within proximity to their extended family. It is incorrect to assume that villas only house nuclear family. Many of them are occupied by extended families, including three generations of kin, more than one husband and wife pair and their offspring.
>
> (2004 56)

This also holds true for Dhofaris. The change from transhumance to settled living that took place during and after the 1970s did not result in the breakdown of tightly knit family connections. Dhofaris usually live in houses with not only different generations but a changing rooster of family members as I will discuss in detail in Chapter 5.

The last factor is the age of the houses. Houses that were built from the 1970s to the early 2000s are often small, i.e. not built out to the size of the plot, and have only one story. They usually have a distinctive look: square windows placed symmetrically on either side of one main door, painted in wide stripes of two tones of beige with a noticeable overhang over windows and doors. The general appearance is plain with few decorations, heaver lines and a roof wall that looks more defensive and less decorative than more modern houses, e.g. a parapet with thick crenelations. Sometimes the concrete is starting to crumble, and the outside is not in good repair. This type of house is often rented to expats, while the family who owns it has moved to a new house.

Government-built housing

Resettlement/replacement houses

During the Dhofar War, the Omani government designated land near the coast to help mountain dwellers get out of conflict areas in the mountains. The result was *sha'biyat*, compounds of identical houses where relocated Dhofaris could live. Each family's section was called a *linat*; as explained to me, this term comes from the English word "line" as the rooms were in a line along one wall with the kitchen always in the far corner. The walls of the compound and rooms were made of whitewashed concrete blocks. Sanitary facilities were provided in large, communal bathrooms. The purpose was to bring people from the mountains into Salalah for safety and, as was explained to me by informants, to prove the government's good intentions.

Cordes and Scholz (1980) state

> During the Dhofar conflict and before the large-scale land distribution, two low-cost housing areas were built by the government, one in east Salalah and one in Taqah. Refugees from the Dhofar Mountains (jebalis) were provided with free houses. There were 54 houses in Salalah and nine houses of five units each in Taqah.

In 1977, the Salalah compound housed "about 3,000 jebalis." It was torn down that year and most of the families living there had "acquired land on the periphery of Salalah under the land distribution programme."[28]

In the post-war period, the government again provided free housing when the government wanted people to settle into permanent dwellings, to move settled people from their current location which was prone to flooding and/or as recompense because the government wanted the land for new roads or developments. There is a small government complex in Sa'adh (north-eastern section of Salalah), a larger scheme in Muqsal (35 kilometers west of Salalah), and a development of about 200 houses in Hasik (190 kilometers east of Salalah). In each settlement, each house was built with the same plan, which might be altered by the owner, and given to Dhofaris without cost.[29]

Housing provided with jobs

In an effort to make the country more united, the Omani government requires that citizens in certain kinds of jobs such as teachers and police must work away from their native area for several years. During this time, men and women are provided with free housing in a government-built complex. Depending on the person's job level, utilities are either subsidized or free and a cleaning service is provided. The second option, which is frequently used now, is to give each person a housing allowance for renting a house or apartment.

Sometimes this also happens when a person is posted more than an hour's drive from their home so that they will stay in the government-provided apartment during the week and return home on weekends and holidays. Some apartments are set up within work compounds; others have open access so the apartment can be shared, e.g. given to friends who are visiting.

House histories

To explain in more concrete terms the changes in housing as explained above, I asked two Dhofari informants to share their "house history" with me: which houses they have lived in, who they have lived with and which houses they visited often. I am very grateful for their time, their trust and their faith in this research as eliciting this information meant a lot of personal questions and talking about topics not usually discussed with non-family members such as details of their parent's marriage(s) and how the worth of a house is divided after the owner dies.

Example 1: male

X is a *hakli* man in his early 40s. He was born in his mother's father's house which had five rooms and a kitchen. His maternal grandfather had built the house himself in one of the coastal towns. X lived there for two or three years staying in a room with his parents and siblings. This house is still standing and is now rented to expat workers.

When he was still a toddler, his father built his own house and X moved with his parents and siblings to the new house. For 37 years, he lived in his father's house which had seven rooms, a kitchen, two bathrooms and a central open space used as a *majlis/salle*, e.g. a "wheel-spoke" design. Until he was about 10 years old, he shared a room with his parents and other siblings; then, he moved into a separate room with his brothers. His father's other wife and her children also lived in the house. Later, a daughter from his father's previous wife, who had passed away, lived with them. As the daughter had children but was no longer married, she came to live with her father and half-siblings.

Many relatives from the mountains came to visit this house when they were in the coastal town for shopping or taking care of government formalities such as registering marriages.

When X married, he spent most of his time in his wife's house as she is a cousin (father's brother's daughter) and she has most of the responsibility for taking care of a sick relative. This house was in the mountains, about 20 km away, but the uncle and his family moved to the same coastal town as X's family six years ago.

In 2020, X and his brothers finished building a new house for all the children of his mother, near the houses of his half-siblings from another wife of his father. X has his own suite (two rooms and a bathroom) but still spends most of his time at his wife's house. Even though it is likely he will spend at least the next 10–20 years in his wife's father's house, he was an equal partner in paying for the house his siblings built and his suite is his inviolate. There is no discussion about when the couple will move into X's house as that would only happen if the person his wife is taking care of dies, something that would never be talked about.

Another important aspect of X's housing history is that he has a government job and has spent over six years working too far away from his home town to commute, three years in one city and three years in a second city. In both places he was given furnished accommodation as part of his benefits. At the first place he had to pay a nominal fee (about 15 OR) per month for water and electricity in a studio apartment. In the second place, there were no fees.

Other houses he stayed in growing up include his brothers' houses, his sisters' houses and both maternal and paternal uncles' houses.

I asked X what happened to his maternal grandfather's and his father's house after their deaths and the two very different answers show how families can approach the idea of house ownership within the framework of Islam which mandates that each close relative be given a certain share of a deceased person's goods.[30]

When X's maternal grandfather died, all of his children met and decided that one of the children (A) would have the responsibility for renting the house. A would oversee the house, paying for any necessary upkeep from the rent money and then dividing the rest as per shares. Thus the task of dividing the house/the worth of the house is forestalled.

When X's father (B) died, all the children from the father's wives met and discussed what to do. All the children were in their 20s or older and had a house to live in; there was no one in hardship. The children decided that one child would buy the house at a less-than-market value so that there would be no issues arising about costs, debts or ownership. When that child had the money in hand to distribute according to Islamic guidelines, each brother/step-brother in turn renounced his share so that the money was split among the sisters/step-sisters.[31]

Example 2: female

Y is a *hakli* woman in her 40s. She was born in the first hospital in Salalah and spent her first year in the Salalah *sha'biyat*, as explained above this was a housing complex made by the government to help Dhofaris relocate from the war-torn mountains to the coastal plain. Usually, and as with the case of Y, her father was from the mountains. Y's father's parents had died so her father and his much younger brother lived with her mother's family in a *linat*, a small, walled compound with a series of rooms along one wall.

In 1975, the government gave away free plots of land, and Y's father obtained one. He moved his family, Y's maternal grandmother and Y's paternal uncle to a plot of land located in the south-central part of Salalah. This residence was a walled compound with two rooms, a *salle* and a kitchen with a toilet room in the farthest corner. In the middle of the plot, there was space for gathering, children playing and a garden; unlike the *linat*, the rooms were arranged along three sides.

In 1979 Y's father "broke the house," meaning torn down the rooms. Y and her family moved to a house which was rented from a father's cousin, while Y's father and uncle built a house with two *salle*, three rooms, two bathrooms and a kitchen. This house took up about half the space of the plot, so there was still room to play and a garden.

While they lived in this house, Y's paternal uncle got married and had children. Eventually there was not enough room for both families so the uncle and his family moved out to a nearby rented house in 1983. Later he built his own house near Y's family in Sa'dah, the north-east area of Salalah. Y's maternal grandmother left in 1994 to live in the house of her oldest grandson, near her two other daughters and other relatives.

During this time many relatives from one of the coastal towns and/or the mountains came to stay for visits or because they needed to be in Salalah for shopping or government formalities. As in X's house, having many relatives stopping over was viewed as "so nice" and "it's good to have the people come" with no negative feeling of disruption or money lost in feeding and taking care of frequent guests.

In 2001, Y's mother and siblings moved to a rented house in the Sa'dah, the north-east section of Salalah. That house had a *majlis*, two *salle*, five rooms, a kitchen and four bathrooms. They rented for ten years, much longer than they planned or hoped for because they first had to decide whether to buy or build a house, and then it took a long time to build the house as they did not want to take bank loans.

In 2011 Y moved to "her house" with her mom and siblings. She lives there now with unmarried sisters, unmarried brother and married brothers with their families: 18 people plus a live-in maid. Her married sisters visit often; other frequent visitors are Y's aunts (her mother's sisters) and their daughters, as well as her father's brother's daughters who are cousins and sisters-in-law as one is married to Y's brother. This house has a *majlis* with a bathroom, two *salle* one of which has a bathroom, a kitchen, storeroom, room for the maid, a ground-floor bedroom and six suites (small apartments with two rooms and a bathroom, some have a mini-kitchen).

When she was a child, she visited her father's aunt in a traditional, round mountain house made of stone courses topped by wooden branches. This great-aunt's son eventually built her a small cement block house near her house with two rooms, a bathroom and a kitchen.

Her maternal grandmother, who lived with Y's family for many years, lives in the house of her oldest grandson, next to the house of her divorced husband and near her other daughters (Y's aunts). Y visited her grandmother often, sometimes incurring the anger of her grandfather who wanted Y and Y's family to stay with him in his house.

Y and her family also visited her paternal uncle's house, the younger brother of her father. However, after he took a second wife, there was less space in the house with more children so, although Y still has a close relationship with these cousins, she and her sisters rarely spent the night in that house.

She also visits her married sisters' houses and sometimes spends the night if the sister and brother-in-law have their own house. Y would not spend the night if the house was owned by her sister's father-in-law.

Her married sisters come to visit Y's house often and, if she does not have several small children, the sister would spend the night. With several children, the logistics become more difficult and the sister would visit for several hours, then go home to sleep.

Example 3: camping

Z is a *hakli* man in his early 40s. He was born in a small settlement at the foothills of the mountains and remembers ("I can see it in my eyes") moving to one of the coastal towns with his family when he was a toddler.

As camping is such an integral part of the lives of many Dhofari men, I interviewed him about living outside his house. As many other informants explained to me, as a child he slept in different places in and close to his home. "His" room was shared with his mother and younger siblings, but he also slept in the *majlis* area. He could also stay at cousins' houses.

He started camping when he was about 12 or 13 years old with older half-siblings and cousins. This time was an apprenticeship (my term, not his) in learning how to pick a place to fish and sleep, to cook over a fire and to arrange the camping area. Within a year or two, he started camping with friends and by 14 he could "drive a car and boat."

He and his friends went camping frequently, sometimes every weekend, along the coast near his town, by walking or catching rides to different beaches. He learned the names of each area, the types of fish etc.

There were "funny times" in which the food they cooked didn't taste good, or there wasn't enough food. He can remember occasional long walks into town when there were no passing cars, and sometimes it was very cold, but he can't remember any emergencies during these years. He knows of a few boys who were hurt while camping, such as twisting their ankles, but no major disasters.

By the time he was 16 or 17, Z would be away from home for a week or longer, sometimes as long as a month in the *khareef* (monsoon) season. He and his friends had access to cars so sometimes they would come into town to sell their fish, drive to Salalah to see a movie in the cinema, come back to the beach to sleep, wake up the next morning and fish.

He would stop by his house sometimes to check-in. How much contact the boys had with their families varied; some boys checked in frequently or sent word with other fishermen. In general, families knew which boys were fishing/camping together and that they would be along the coast.

For the abalone season, Z would rent an apartment or create a campsite with older half-brothers and cousins and dive with them, occasionally bringing friends in the same boat. He got a job soon after high school but for many years continued to camp and fish frequently with friends. He sees fishing as "good work because you are with good people, there is fresh air and quiet, you are outside the house."[32]

The most frequent type of camping was simply laying on a mat while covered with a blanket. He also stayed in rough shelters (plywood posts supporting roofs of old fishnets, plywood sheets, palm fronds and/or old blankets) or under rock overhangs.

He stated that most Dhofari men go camping in places that are similar to where they live, i.e. "in the mountains, the men go to some different mountain."

Discussion: housing trajectories, married daughter in parent's house, impact of divorce/second wives and maids

I would like to pull out a few issues from the information presented above. First, although I did not know their housing history before I started that set of interviews, both X and Y are good examples of the changes in housing in the past half-century. X lived in two houses that were hand-built by the owner and then moved to a large, modern house built by expat labor. Y spent a lot of time as a child in a traditional, round, stone-walled mountain house while visiting her great-aunt. Her first house memories are of a Dhofari-style courtyard house with rooms in a line along one side of an enclosed space and then a walled space with rooms along different sides. Later, she and her family moved to an expat-built rented house and, finally, to a house they had built to their specifications. Both followed the common trajectory of people moving out of the mountains as both of their fathers moved from rural areas into towns.

Secondly, as part of the discussion about a daughter staying in her parent's house with her husband, X and I had a long discussion about when this happens and why as I had heard from female informants that this rarely occurred. According to X, in the past, a young married woman would stay in her father's house for several years until she learned to take care of her children and run a house by herself. Normally her father would make a room for the married couple, but if he did not have enough money, the groom would pay for an additional room to be built. Women might stay in their parent's house for three to ten years until she was "ready to do everything."

Another issue was that in the past travel was more difficult so if a husband and wife went to visit her family, he would stay with her. But now that it is easier to move about, X explained that a good man will take his wife to her family's house and "let her take her rest and visit the people," meaning that if the husband stayed, she would have to pay attention to him instead of focusing on her mom, sisters and neighbors.

Now a man can simply drive back to his home, a relative's home or go camping and pick his wife up after a few days. According to X, if there is a room available and the couple lives far away or the woman will visit for an extended time, then the husband might stay, but a man should take care not to monopolize her time so she can socialize with her relatives.[33]

I had heard that a husband would not stay in his wife's father's house as he would have to walk through the private part of this house; for example, his wife's room might be near the room of an unmarried sister. X agreed in principle but gave two counter-examples from his family. In one case the wife was the only daughter and would visit her mother often. She had her own room on the ground floor so that the husband was never on the upper floors where his wife's brothers' wives lived.

In a second example, an unmarried man who didn't have a car lived in his maternal uncle's house which was close to his workplace. He stayed in a male cousin's room during the week for about six years. He carefully kept the same schedule every day so that the female cousins could "have their freedom." After work, he would stay in the room until the sunset call to prayer so the women could clean, cook, socialize and watch TV in the *salle* or *majlis* without having to be "formal," i.e. worried about their appearance. They wore *dhobes* and covered their hair at all times, but the man did not want to surprise one of them unaware, so he organized his life so that the women would know when he would be in the public areas.[34]

In Y's life, married sisters come home (i.e. the house where their mother lives) after the birth of a child and come often for visits. They sleep overnight if they have one or two kids, but never with their husbands.

A third theme I want to highlight is the impact of second marriages and divorce on housing (see also Chapter 5). X and Y both have step-mothers and step-siblings. X grew up with this step-mother and step-siblings in the same house, as well as an older step-sister with her children. In time, the children sorted themselves out into nearby but different houses. X refers to his step-siblings as "my older brother and sisters."

Y's father became physically distanced from Y's mother and her siblings in that he did not live with them after they left the plot of land that was given by the government and later divorced Y's mother. He remarried and had additional children.

Thus X and Y are examples of how having multiple wives affects living situations. X's mother lived with a co-wife for decades, and Y's mother was divorced; both mothers eventually lived in a house with their children. X and Y get along well with their step-siblings and also consider it a matter of respect to both their fathers and themselves to keep a close relationship, e.g. to pay visits, attend weddings and give condolences, but their living preference was with full siblings.

The last topic is live-in help. X remembers his family first had a live-in maid in 2005. She washed clothes and took care of "inside the house," meaning the bedrooms, bathrooms and *salle*. From that time until the pandemic, there was always a maid in the house, supervised by his mother. When government regulations changed making it harder to get a visa for a maid and the pandemic made it more difficult for expats to enter Oman, X's family hired a man to come every day to help cook and clean the kitchen. The women in the family took over the work of doing the laundry as it would not be appropriate for a man to do this.

Y remembers that her family first had a maid in 1988 as her mom began classes in a government program to teach middle-aged Dhofaris who did not have a chance to go to school when they were younger. This maid worked for the family for eight years and is still in touch with Y's mom, Y's sisters and Y. Since that maid left, there has always been a maid in the house, including women from India, Indonesia, Nigeria and Ethiopia. Most have stayed at least two years or longer. The maid has always had her own room.

Several informants told me that there were very few maids until the 1990s, and after that, most large families had one. Because he is a man, X had very little communication with the maids in his house; he knew their names and greeted them, but he did not give them work. Male informants told me that men will do the paperwork, e.g. bring a maid to renew her visa, but otherwise not interact with the maid.

Whereas Y and her sisters had a close relationship with the women who worked for them and stories about the different maids come up in conversation. In particular, when one maid arrived from the hiring agency, Y and her family were amazed to find that she was very young, so Y's family tried to take care of her by giving her less work and lots of phone cards so she could call her family.

Notes

1 As of April 2022, the total population of the Dhofar governorate was 435,683 (221,870 Omani and 213, 813 expat); for the year 2021, the population of the *wilayat* (region) of Salalah was 333,688 (153,488 Omani and 180,240 expat). All the other regions of Dhofar have fewer expats than Omanis. For comparison, in April 2017, there were 461,439 total (209,019 Omani and 252,420 expat). In 2012 there were 346,046 (175,416 Omani and 183, 178 expat), and in 2002 there were 237,523 (158,910 Omani and 78,613 expat). This information is from the Omani government's data portal ("Population" 2022).

2 In more detail:

> The Jebel Qara massif ... gently slopes towards the south with elevations ranging from between ~400-500 m a.s.l. [meters above sea level] near the southern escarpment, and up to ~1000 m a.s.l. at its northern watershed. Most of the top of the Jebel is heavily affected by surface erosion and soil loss; as a consequence, exposed outcrops of limestone and dolomitic limestone are common.
>
> (Zerboni, Perego, Mariani, et al. 2020 189)

3 I am very grateful to Vincent Charpentier from the Institut National de Recherches Archéologiques Préventives for reviewing this section. Any mistakes that remain are mine.

Background information to help understand the articles' titles: in the system of dating geological data across continents the Pleistocene is the time period from c. 2.588 million years ago until c. 11.7 thousand years ago; the Holocene is c. 11.7 thousand years ago until today.

The Paleolithic is the time period from when archaic human species started to use stone tools to the end of the Pleistocene. The Paleolithic is followed by the Neolithic period which started c. 6500 BC and lasted until 3200 BC in Dhofar (earlier and later in other parts of the world).

The next period is the Bronze Age, which in parts of the Arabian Peninsula archeology is divided into three sub-periods. The Hafit Period (apx 3200–2700 BC) is named after Jebel Hafit in Abu Dhabi where several hundred stone cairns were discovered. The Umm an Nar Period (apx 2700–2000 BC) is named after a small island located near Abu Dhabi and is typified by circular tombs. The Wadi Suq Period (apx 2000 and 1300 BC) is named after Wadi Suq west of the town of Sohar in Oman and signifies long, narrow graves. I am adding this information as background as these Bronze Age dates are used to discuss sites in northern Oman; correspondence to Dhofar sites has not been verified.

4 In more detail:

> Evidence of human occupation (lithic industry and charcoal) in the cavities of Jebel Qara is mostly concentrated in the Unit C, apart from the occasional find of charcoal in Unit B, and it is systematically associated with high concentration of mollusc shells ... Inside the cave deposits molluscs

> are associated with organic layers, charcoal, and in some case to small fragments of burnt bones and to lithic artefacts ... In thin section, the evidence of human activity is clearer as shells of land snail are often broken and redistribute in flat layers with planar distribution of clasts and associated to finely subdivided organic matter and charcoal lenses; these are indicative for occupational trampling.
>
> (Zerboni, Perego, Mariani et al. 2020 11)

Further, Zerboni, Perego, Mariani et al. state that they

> interpreted the shells layers inside the studied rock shelters as intentional accumulations related to human activities ... The lithic assemblages associated to these sites, including laminar debitage, sometimes Fasad points, represent the remains of hunter gathers populations ... the identification of accumulations of land snails at Jebel Qara represents an unprecedented evidence of foraging strategy adopted by the Early Holocene human groups in southern Arabia. The frequentation of the area was made possible thanks to a main climatic shift towards wet conditions, in contrast with the aridity that dominated in the area at the transition between the Late Pleistocene and the Early Holocene. New and wetter environmental conditions promoted the ecological settings suitable to the development of the molluscs fauna of the Jebel Qara, representing another type of food resources for these populations.
>
> (2020 11)

5 See also Hilbert, Rose and Roberts' "Late Paleolithic Core Reduction Strategies in Dhofar, Oman" (2012) and Hilbert, Usik, Galletti, Parton et al. (2015).

6 Although it concentrates on northern Oman, Potts's "Trends and Patterns in the Archaeology and Pre-Modern History of the Gulf Region" (2016) is a helpful geographic/historical overview.

7 For an overview, see Zarins' *The Land of Incense: Archaeological Work in the Governorate of Dhofar, Sultanate of Oman, 1990-1995* (2001) and Newton and Zarins' *The Archaeological Heritage of Oman. Dhofar Through the Ages. An Ecological, Archaeological and Historical Landscape* (2017).

8 When I first visited Dhofar in 1999, the archeological site of Samhuram was known as "the Queen of Sheba's palace" which was a brilliant and poetic untruth. That usage has now faded as less lyrical, more realistic and academic descriptions prevail.

9 In more detail:

> A large amount of imported pottery items reached the site from many different lands: northern Oman, Yemen, Arabian Peninsula, the Gulf area, Iran, Egypt, Eastern Africa, the Indian subcontinent, China and South-East Asia. The recent studies of C. Visconti seem to point to the existence of at least two main phases of imports towards Al Balid coming from East Asia: one dated to the 14th-15th century and a second one dated to the 18th century ... the recent study of the coins by A. Annucci proves the relationship between the site of Al Balid and Kilwa, confirming the strong and well known commercial connections between the south of the Arabian Peninsula and the Sultanate of Kilwa until the arrival of the Portuguese in the 16th century.
>
> (Pavan, Fusaro, Visconti et al. 2020 196)

10 For more details, see Smith and Porter (1988).

11 *Nejd* means the arid, sandy and rocky area to the north of the mountains (Jebel Quman, Jebel Qara and Jebel Samhan), i.e. the area between the high mountains and the pure, sand desert of the *Rub al Khali* (the Empty Quarter).

12 "Vernacular" means local and/or informal; in terms of architecture, it means buildings that are created from what is possible given limitations such was which building materials are nearby/attainable, climate, geology and intangibles such as religious and regional beliefs about how to create living quarters.

13 There are a few mentions of Dhofar in the intervening years. One early traveler is Ibn al-Mujāwir, who wrote in approximately 1226–30 that Dhofar had at one time been connected to Baghdad by a trade route which was cut off in 616/1219 (2008 261). "Ibn Battuta visited Dhofar in 1325 and again in 1347" (Morris 1987 55; see 51–60 for an overview of early visitors), but there is no description of the inhabitants beyond "its people closely resemble the people of Northwest Africa in their customs" (Ibn Battuta 1929).

There is a short shipwreck narrative of two Spanish Jesuit priests on their way from India to Ethiopia who were kidnapped by pirates on February 14, 1590. Antonio de Montserrat and Pedro Páez landed at "Dofâr" where they were held for several days until they were told that the "captain of the city" was going to send them "to the place where his King was staying so that the latter could condemn us to whatever death he chose" (Beckingham and Sarjeant 1950 195). They were taken to Hainan and then to the Turkish leader in San'a, proof that at that time the coast of Dhofar was under the rule of Turks based in Yemen (201, 203; see also Beckingham 1949).

In Ovington's *A Voyage to Surat in the Year 1689* (1929) there is a very brief description of Dhofar, confusingly in a chapter about locations in the Red Sea. He mentions the production of frankincense, coconuts and butter (268).

Another shipwreck narrative is by Daniel Saunders, who was castaway when his ship, *Commerce* out of Boston, sank on July 10, 1792, near Mirbat. His brief re-telling of his adventures has no information on Dhofar.

14 He calls the region "Dhufar" and discusses the villages of Auqad, Salala, Hafa and Al Husn as separate entities. Today Auqad, Hafa (now Haffa) and Al Husn are sections within the city of Salalah.

15 This is not the same place that the Bents stayed in. That "castle" was torn down in an insurrection and the fort built later.

16 For more details, see Tabook (1997 26) and Chapter 2 of *Foodways in Southern Oman* (Risse 2021).

17 One difference that is not discussed in these texts is that in rural areas until the 1970s/1980s, many women worked with animals, especially herds of goats. This still happens, but much less frequently (see Tabook 1997).

18 In more detail:

> Following the Dhofar Rebellion (1962–1975) the region rapidly developed under the leadership of Oman's ruler Sultan Qaboos bin Said and with revenue from an expanding oil industry. Many pastoralists were offered government-paid employment, predominantly in the Firqat, an irregular military force. With regularly paid employment, families were quick to start acquiring higher-status livestock, namely camels. The government improved road infrastructure, installed a water supply network, constructed high-capacity livestock watering troughs, built dams at springs, and established a system of manufacturing and distributing subsidised feedstuffs. Families settled in villages close to the new amenities. Expatriate workers from South Asia were hired to carry out the everyday work of livestock husbandry. The Oman government imposed a new land tenure system that ensured that everyone had access to common-pool grazing resources, which replaced the tribal land tenure institutions. The use of four-wheel drive vehicles became widespread to transport feedstuff, water, and livestock in the state owned rangelands.
>
> (Ball, MacMillan, Tzanopoulos et al. 2020)

19 See Takriti's *Monsoon Revolution: Republicans, Sultans and Empires in Oman 1965-1976* (2013) if you would like an unabashedly anti-government interpretation.

20 Takriti's *Monsoon Revolution* (2013) stresses how the revolutionaries in Dhofar were "reflecting incorporation into the anti-colonial cultural system" of countries such as Algeria, China, Cuba, Egypt, Iraq, Palestine, Vietnam, Yemen and Zanzibar (236, 237). He believes the Chinese, East German, Russian and Yemen's aid and influence during the Dhofar War were positive but

> By 1975, the combined impact of Iranian, Jordanian, and Anglo-Sultanic forces – backed by generous funding from Saudi Arabia and Abu Dhabi – overwhelmed the revolutionaries. Thus the indigenous inhabitants were defeated on their own land by a foreign force seeking to determine who governed them.
>
> (306)

One of my concerns with the book is that it is never explained how China, Cuba, East Germany, Russia and others were not foreign forces seeking to determine who governed Dhofar.

21 My website, https://mariellerisse.com/, has dozens of photos as examples.

22 Words from the song "Little Boxes" by Malvina Reynolds. This song is about the monotony of house styles in San Francisco and is often used as a shorthand to refer to unimaginative, boring urban planning.

23 In more detail:

> All construction on these sites must be of natural stone and/or cement blocks. In an effort to check land speculation there is a law that a piece of property can be sold only when at least one stone building has been constructed on it ... Many families that still engage in animal husbandry in the desert or the jebel use their urban dwellings only irregularly. In part they serve as shelters during the work week for those members of the family who have found work in town.
>
> (Cordes and Scholz 1980)

24 When I moved to Dhofar in 2005, driving was a joy as almost every major road had same-level, gravel shoulders that were one or two lanes wide. One could pull off easily and safely at any moment. Over the years, the roads have been built out to divided, two-lanes-each-direction.

25 I am not engaging with issues of who planned which areas within Dhofar as urban planning is beyond the scope of this book, and given that several entities were involved, I do not want to get involved in a discussion of who was responsible for what.

26 See also Al Hinai, Batty and Probert 1993 253.

27 My website, https://mariellerisse.com/, has dozens of photos and house plans as examples.

28 A drawing can be found at: https://archive.unu.edu/unupress/unupbooks/80143e/80143E0h.gif.

29 Sometimes the plan to have people move into government housing has not worked as the citizens refuse to inhabit the buildings for a variety of reasons.

30 The rules of inheritance are beyond the scope of this book. As an overview, first, all of the person's debts must be paid off. In Dhofar, this necessitates a close male relative standing up after Friday prayers and asking any person who is owed money by the deceased to come and see him. Sometimes people come and state that there is a debt, but that debt is forgiven, to forestall any questions if the family finds a written reminder. Second any person has the right to give

only up to 1/3 of their wealth as they choose to a non-family member, charity etc. The balance is then distributed according to statutes explained in the Holy Qu'ran which covers topics such as a child dying before parents, multiple wives, half-siblings etc.

Thus a close family member (husband, wife, son, daughter, father, mother, grandfather, grandmother, full brother, full sister and half-siblings) can never be disinherited but also may never be given more than the share set out in religious guidelines (see also Carter 1982 104–5).

31 This is clearly a good behavior on the part of X, his brothers and half-brothers, but their decision would never be discussed positively by X. Discussing, much less praising, one's generous conduct is not often part of *hakli* culture. During the interview, X stated what happened and then immediately changed the subject.

32 I will come back to the point of men's opinion that outside of this house is "quiet" in more detail in Chapter 8.

33 This is a moot point if there is not a separate room that the married couple could use; often, a woman will sleep in her mom or a sister's room.

34 As is usual in Dhofar, the uncle would not accept payment for hosting his nephew, i.e. there was no expectation of a monthly reimbursement. However, the nephew, for his own self-esteem not predicated on anything expected, done or said by his uncle's family, made the kind of gesture typical in Dhofar. Several times he gave a huge fish haul of 70 kilos or more to his uncle so that the uncle had plenty of fish to give to other relatives and neighbors.

References

For photos and a full bibliography, please see: *Come From Away*, https://mariellerisse.com

Adam, Khalid and Liudmila Cazacova, 2012. "The Round Dhofari House Popularity Uniting the Past and the Present." *Proceedings of the 6th International Seminar on Vernacular Settlements*. Famagusta, North Cyprus: Eastern Mediterranean University. 365–74.

Akcan, Esra. 2014. "Postcolonial Theories in Architecture," in *A Critical History of Contemporary Architecture (1960–2010)*. Elie Haddad and David Rifkind, eds. London: Ashgate. 119–40.

Al Hinai, H., W. J. Batty and S. D. Probert. 1993. "Vernacular Architecture of Oman: Features that Enhance Thermal Comfort Achieved within Buildings." *Applied Energy* 44.3: 233–244. https://doi.org/10.1016/0306-2619(93)90019-L

Al Kathiri, Muna Salim and Liudmila Cazacova. 2014. "Islamic Architecture Features and Modern Housing: A Case Study of the North Awqad District in Salalah, Oman." *The International Journal of the Constructed Environment* 4: 1–18.

Al Mohannadi, Asmaa Saleh, Raffaelo Furlan and Mark David Major. 2019. "Socio-Cultural Factors Shaping the Spatial Form of Traditional and Contemporary Housing in Qatar: A Comparative Analysis based on Space Syntax." Proceedings of the 12th Space Syntax Symposium.

Alkhalidi, Abdulsamad. 2013. "Sustainable Application of Interior Spaces in Traditional Houses of the United Arab Emirates." *Procedia: Social and Behavioral Sciences* 102: 288–299.

Atlas of Archaeological Survey in the Governorate of Dhofar Sultanate of Oman. 2013. Muscat: Office of the Advisor to His Majesty the Sultan for Cultural Affairs.

Avanzini, Alessandra, ed. 2008. *A Port in Arabia between Rome and the Indian Ocean (3rd C.BC. - 5th C.AD) Khor Rori Report 2*. Rome: L'Erma di Bretschneider.

———. 2007."Sumhuram: A Hadrami Port on the Indian Ocean," in *The Indian Ocean in the Ancient Period: Definite Places, Translocal Exchange BAR International Series 1593*. Eivind Heldaas Seland, ed. Oxford: Archaeopress. 23–31.

———. 2002. "Incense Routes and Pre-Islamic South Arabian Kingdoms." *Journal of Oman Studies* 12: 17–24.

Ball, Lawrence, Douglas MacMillan, Joseph Tzanopoulos, Andrew Spalton, Hadi Al Hikmani and Mark Moritz. 2020. "Contemporary Pastoralism in the Dhofar Mountains of Oman." *Human Ecology*. https://doi.org/10.1007/s10745-020-00153-5

Beckingham, C. F. 1949. "Some Early Travels in Arabia." *Journal of the Royal Asiatic Society of Great Britain* 81: 156–76.

Beckingham. C. F. and R. B. Sarjeant. 1950. "A Journey of Two Jesuits from Dhufār to San'ā in 1590." *The Geographical Journal* 115.4/6: 194–207.

Bent, J.T. 1895. "Exploration of the Frankincense Country, Southern Arabia." *The Geographical Journal* 6.2: 109–33.

Bent, James and Mabel Bent. 1900. *Southern Arabia*. London: Elibron, 2005.

Carter, Henry. 1852. "Memoir of the Geology of the South-East Coast of Arabia", *Journal of the Bombay Branch of the Royal Asiatic Society*: 21–96.

———. 1851. "A Geographical Description of Certain Parts of the Southeast Coast of Arabia." *Journal of the Bombay Branch of the Royal Asiatic Society*: 224–317.

———. 1847. "Notes on the Mahra Tribe of Southern Arabia, with a Vocabulary of their Language, to which is appended additional Observations on the Gara Tribe." *Journal of the Bombay Branch of the Royal Asiatic Society* 2: 339–364.

———. 1846. "The Ruins of El Balad," *Journal of the Royal Geographical Society of London* 16: 187–199.

———. 1845. "Notes on the Gara Tribe." *Journal of the Bombay Branch of the Royal Asiatic Society* 2: 195–201 and an illustration.

Carter, J. R. L. 1982. *Tribes in Oman*. London: Peninsular Publishing.

Cazacova, Liudmila., M. Hidalgo, M. Farhan, F. Al-Masikhi, F. Al-Hafidh, H. Qatan, J. Hubais, L. Ghafoor, M. Al-Marhoon, M. Darwish, M. Al-Amri, S. Al-Baraami, S. Al-Shanfari and S. Al-Rawas, 2014. "Recognition of Mirbat Town's Old Area as Historical Environment." Proceedings of REHAB 2014 [International Conference on Preservation, Maintenance and Rehabilitation of Historical Buildings and Structures]. Tomar, Portugal. 581–91. https://doi.org/10.14575/gl/rehab2014

Charpentier, Vincent, Jean-Francois Berger, Rémy Crassard, Fredico Borgi and Philippe Béarez. 2016. "Les Premiers Chasseurs-collecteurs Maritimes d'Arabie (IXe-IVe millénaires avant notre ère) [Early Maritime Hunter-Gatherers in Arabia (9th–4th Millennium before the Current Era)]," in *Archéologie des Chasseurs-collecteurs Maritimes*. Catherine Dupont and Gregor Marchand, eds. Paris: Société Préhistorique Française. 345–66.

Clapp, Nicholas. 1999. *The Road to Ubar: Finding the Atlantis of the Sands*. Boston: Houghton Mifflin.

Cordes, Rainer and Fred Scholz. 1980. "Changes in the Nomad Region of Oman" and "Settlement Projects in Inner Oman, and Other Measures to Develop the

Rural/Nomad Region," in *Bedouins, Wealth, and Change: A Study of Rural Development in the United Arab Emirates and the Sultanate of Oman*. Tokyo: United Nations University. https://archive.unu.edu/unupress/unupbooks/80143e/80143E00.htm

Costa, Paulo. 1983. "Notes on Settlement Patterns in Traditional Oman." *Journal of Oman Studies* 6.2: 247–68.

Costa, Paulo and Stephen Kite. 1985. "The Architecture of Salalah and the Dhofar Littoral." *Journal of Oman Studies* 7: 131–58.

Craufurd, C. 1919. 'The Dhofar District.' *The Geographical Journal* 53.2: 97–105.

Cremaschi, Mauro, Andrea Zerboni, Vincent Charpentier, Remy Crassard, Ilaria Isola, Eleonora Regattieri and Giovanni Zanchetta. 2015. "Early-Middle Holocene Environmental Changes and pre-Neolithic Human Occupations as Recorded in the Cavities of Jebel Qara (Dhofar, southern Sultanate of Oman)." *Quaternary International* 382: 264–76.

Cruttenden, Charles. 1838. "Journal of an Excursion from Morbat to Dyreez, the Principal Town of Dhofar." *Transactions of the Bombay Geographical Society* 1: 184–188.

De Bel-Air, Françoise. 2015. "Demography, Migration, and the Labour Market in Oman." Gulf Research Center - Gulf Labor Markets and Migration - EN - 9/2015. https://cadmus.eui.eu/bitstream/handle/1814/37398/GLMM_ExpNote_09_2015.pdf;jsessionid=D57068437CF3E9B040792393699299B9?sequence=1

Degli Esposti, Michele and Alexia Pavan. 2020. "Water and Power in South Arabia: The Excavation of 'Monumental Building 1' (MB1) at Sumhuram (Sultanate of Oman)." *Arabian Archeology and Epigraphy*: 1–29. https://doi.org/10.1111/aae.12159

Galletti, Christopher, Billie Turner and Soe W. Myint. 2016. "Land Changes and their Drivers in the Cloud Forest and Coastal Zone of Dhofar, Oman, between 1988 and 2013." *Regional Environmental Change* 16.7: 2141–53.

Gardner, Andrew. 2015. "*Migration, Labor and Business in the Worlding Cities of the Arabian Peninsula*." Institute of Developing Economies - Discussion Paper no. 513. 1–11.

Haggag, Mahmoud. 2004. "The Impact of Globalization on Urban Spaces in Arab Cities." 35–46. https://www.irbnet.de/daten/iconda/CIB5930.pdf

Haines, Stafford. 1845. "Memoir of the South and East Coasts of Arabia, Part II." *Journal of the Royal Geographical Society of London* 15: 104–60.

———. 1839. "Memoir to Accompany a Chart of the South Coast of Arabia from the Entrance of the Red Sea to Misenat, in 50, 43, 25 E. Part I." *Journal of the Royal Geographical Society of London* 9: 125–56.

Hegazy, Soheir. 2015. "Cultural Sustainability between Traditional and Contemporary Omani Residences: A Comparative Case Study." *European Journal of Sustainable Development* 42: 185–94.

Hilbert, Yamandu. 2013. "Khamseen Rock Shelter and the Late Palaeolithic-Neolithic Transition in Dhofar." *Arabian Archeology and Epigraphy* 24: 51–8.

Hilbert, Yamandu, Ash Parton, Mike Morley, Lauren Linnenlucke, Zenobia Jacobs, Laine Clark-Balzan, Richard Roberts, Chris Galletti, Jean-Luc Schwenninger and Jeff Rose. 2015a. "Terminal Pleistocene and Early Holocene Archaeology and Stratigraphy of the Southern Nejd, Oman." *Quaternary International* 282: 250–263. https://www.sciencedirect.com/science/article/abs/pii/S1040618215001603

Hilbert, Yamandú, Vitaly Usik, Christopher Galletti, Ash Parton, Laine Clark-Balzan, Jean-Luc Schwenninger, Mike Morley, Zenobia Jacobs, Lauren Linnenlucke, Richard Roberts and Jeffrey Rose. 2015b. "Archaeological Evidence for Indigenous Human Occupation of Southern Arabia at the Pleistocene/Holocene Transition: The Case of al-Hatab in Dhofar, Southern Oman." *Paléorient* 41.2: 31–49.

Hilbert, Yamandu, Jeff Rose and Richard Roberts. 2012. "Late Paleolithic Core Reduction Strategies in Dhofar, Oman." *Proceedings of the Seminar for Arabian Studies* 42: 1–18.

Hulton, Jessop. 2003/1844. *South Arabia: The 'Palinurus' Journals*. W. A. Hulton, ed. London, Oleander. (original journal self-published by older brother)

Hulton, Jessop and James Smith. 1839. "Account of some Inscriptions found on the Southern Coast of Arabia," *Journal of the Royal Asiatic Society* 5: 91–101.

———. 1835. "Report on some Inscriptions found at Hammam, on the Southern Coast of Arabia," *Journal of the Asiatic Society of Bengal* 4: 533–7.

Ibn al-Mujawir. 2008. *A Traveller in Thirteenth-century Arabia. 1204/1291. Hakluyt Society – third series; no. 19*. G. Rex Smith, trans. London: The Hakluty Society.

Ibn Battuta. 1929. *Travels in Asia and Africa 1325–1354*, H.A, R. Gibb, trans. London: Routledge.

Janzen, Jorg. 1986 *Nomads in the Sultanate of Oman: Tradition and Development in Dhofar*. London: Westview Press.

Kelly, J.B. 1976. "Hadramaut, Oman, Dhufar: The Experience Of Revolution." *Middle East Studies Association Bulletin*, 12.2: 213–30.

Lees, G. M. 1928. "The Physical Geography of South-Eastern Arabia." *Geographical Journal* 71.5: 441–70.

Maneval, Stefan. 2019. *New Islamic Urbanism: The Architecture of Public and Private Space in Jeddah, Saudi Arabia*. London: University College London Press.

Molotch, Harvey and Davide Ponzini. 2019. "The New Arab Urban: Test Beds, Work-arounds, and the Limits of Enacted Cities." *AlMuntaqa* 2.1: 9–23. https://www.jstor.org/stable/10.31430/almuntaqa.2.1.0009

Morris, Jan. 1957/2008. *Sultan in Oman*. London: Eland.

Morris, Miranda. 1987. "Dhofar: What Made it Different," in *Oman: Economic, Social and Strategic Development*. B.R. Pridham, ed. London: Croom Helm. 51–78.

Nagy, Sharon. 2004. "Keeping Families Together: Housing Policy, Social Strategies and Family in Qatar." *The MIT Electronic Journal of Middle East Studies* 4: 42–58.

Newsinger, John. 1998. "Jebel Akhdar and Dhofar: Footnote to Empire." *Race and Class* 39.3: 41–59.

Newton, Lynne and Juris Zarins. 2017. *The Archaeological Heritage of Oman. Dhofar Through the Ages. An Ecological, Archaeological and Historical Landscape*. Muscat: Ministry of Heritage and Culture Sultanate of Oman.

Ovington, John. 1929. *A Voyage to Surat in the Year 1689*. H. G. Rawlinson, ed. London: Oxford University Press.

Pavan, Alexia and Chiara Visconti. 2020. "Trade and Contacts between Southern Arabia and East Asia: The Evidence from al-Balīd (southern Oman)." *Proceedings of the Seminar for Arabian Studies* 50: 243–57.

Pavan, Alexia and Michele Degli Esposti. 2016. *The Urban Shrine in Quarter A at Sumhuram: Stratigraphy, Architecture, Material Culture*. Quaderni di Arabia Antica 4, Roma: L'Erma di Bretschneider.

Pavan, Alexia, Agnese Fusaro, Chiara Visconti, Alessandro Ghidoni and Arturo Annucci. 2020. "New Researches at The Port of Al Balid and Its Castle (Husn): Interim Report (2016–2018)." *The Journal of Oman Studies* 21: 172–99.

"Population." 2022. Data Portal: National Centre for Statistics and Information. https://data.gov.om/OMPOP2016/population. June 2.

Potts, Daniel. 2016. "Trends and Patterns in the Archaeology and Pre-Modern History of the Gulf Region," in *The Emergence of the Gulf States: Studies in Modern History*. J.E. Peterson (ed.). London: Bloomsbury. 19–42.

Ragette, Friedrich. 2003. *Traditional Domestic Architecture of the Arab Region.* Felbach: Edition Axel Menges.

Reynolds, Malvina. 1962. "Little Boxes." Schroder Music Company.

Risse, Marielle. 2021. *Foodways in Southern Oman.* London: Routledge.

———. 2019. *Community and Autonomy in Southern Oman.* New York: Palgrave Macmillan.

"Salalah al-Wusta & Gharbiya: Dhofar Governorate: Documentation and Heritage Management Plan." 2016. University of Liverpool and the Ministry of Heritage and Culture. https://issuu.com/archiam/docs/20170908_hmp_salalah

Sale, J. 1980. "The Ecology of the Mountain Region of Dhofar." *The Journal of Oman Studies: Special Report 2: The Oman Flora and Fauna Survey 1975.* Muscat: Diwan of H. M. for Protocol. 25–54.

Saunders, J. P. 1846. "A Short Memoir of the Proceedings of the Honorable Company's Surveying Brig "Palinurus," during Her Late Examination of the Coast between Ras Morbat and Ras Seger, and between Ras Fartak and the Ruins of Mesinah," *Journal of the Royal Geographical Society of London* 16: 169–186.

Smith, G. Rex and Venetia Porter. 1988. "The Rasulids in Dhofar in the VIIth-VIIIth/XIII-XIVth Centuries." *The Journal of the Royal Asiatic Society of Great Britain and Ireland* 1: 26–44.

Smith, John Alexander. 1983. "Desert Developments." *Building Design* 11: 18–21.

St Albans, Suzanne. 1980. *Where Time Stood Still: Portrait of Oman.* London: Quartet Books.

Tabook, Salim Bakhit. 1997. *Tribal Practices and Folklore of Dhofar, Sultanate of Oman.* Unpublished PhD thesis, Faculty of Arts, Exeter University.

Takriti, Abdul Razzaq. 2013. *Monsoon Revolution: Republicans, Sultans and Empires in Oman 1965–1976.* Oxford: Oxford University Press.

Thesiger, Wilfred. 1991/1959. *Arabian Sands.* New York: Penguin.

Thomas, Bertram. 1932, reprint. *Arabia Felix: Across the Empty Quarter of Arabia.* London: Jonathan Cape.

van Nes, Akkelies and Claudia Yamu. 2018. "Space Syntax: A Method to Measure Urban Space Related to Social, Economic and Cognitive Factors," in *The Virtual And the Real in Planning and Urban Design: Perspectives, Practices and Applications.* C. Yamu, A. Poplin, O. Devisch and G. de Roo, eds. New York: Routledge.

Yapicioglu, Balkiz and Liudmila Cazacova. 2018. ""Omani Burqa" vs. Decorated Facade of Modern Omani House: The Case of Salalah, Dhofar Region, Oman." *The Academic Research Community Publication.* 101–111. ISSN online: 2537–0162

———. 2016a. "The Building as a Statement of an Artefact: The Mijmara." *International Journal of Ecology & Development* 31.3: 99–116.

———. 2016b. "Culture Embedded in City's Architecture; Incense Burning Custom and Its Effects on Modern Buildings' Features of Salalah, Oman." Proceedings of the 5th International Conference on Sustainable Tourism and Cultural Heritage. Istanbul, Turkey.

Zarins, Juris. 2009. "The Latest on the Archaeology of Southern Oman." *Journal of the American Oriental Society* 129.4: 665–74.

———. 2007. "Aspects of Recent Archaeological Work at al-Balid (Zafar), Sultanate of Oman." *Proceedings of the Seminar of Arabian Studies* 37: 309–24.

———. 2001. *The Land of Incense: Archaeological Work in the Governorate of Dhofar, Sultanate of Oman, 1990–1995*. Muscat, Oman: Sultan Qaboos University Publications.

Zerboni, Andrea, Alessandro Perego, Guido Mariani, Filippo Brandolini, Mohammed Al Kindi, Eleonora Regattieri, Giovanni Zanchetta, Federico Borgi, Vincent Charpentier and Mauro Cremaschi. 2020. "Geomorphology of the Jebel Qara and Coastal Plain of Salalah (Dhofar, southern Sultanate of Oman)." *Journal of Maps* 16.2: 187–98.

3 Creating modern houses

Researching landownership and occupancy[1]

Discussing who owns which piece of land is a good example of the kind of navigation I do to understand issues pertaining to houseways in Dhofar. For more than a decade, I heard informants speak about houses and plots of land in the mountains with the vocabulary of ownership, e.g. "my father's house." When I asked questions, the answers came in terms of possession, "I will build a house on my land next year."

I know that technically the government owns all the land in the mountains and this would come into play when informants talked about camel camps, farms and water rights. Some men practicing transhumance would bed their camels in certain areas which they referred to as "theirs" or "their families," but there were no deeds attesting to this claim. Their use was by right of long custom and their improvements, such as long windbreaks made of stones and/or wooden sticks.

Similarly, I was told that enclosed small fields in the mountains officially belonged to the government but were discussed as "X's farm" and ownership (without paperwork) was handed down to children. If a person took a piece of land, surrounded it with a wall and planted trees, that land was seen as "theirs," even though such plots were sometimes bulldozed by the government if they were in an area slated for development, such as a road being expanded (see Carter 1982 105 and following). Who "owns" which water source can still be a sensitive topic; even though the answer is "the government," some tribes assert their rights of control, leading to stand-offs and heated discussions.

But even with this background, I was surprised when I heard one expat researcher say that it was not allowed to own land in the mountains; thus, no one owned their house. Of course, I took this back to the research guys. One replied, "No, that is not true." Another said, "Yes, it's true," but then qualified his answer by explaining that the government might own the land, but they would never take a person's house.

This is the kind of moment that I try to catch and elucidate; as the American cliché goes: there's the right way, the wrong way and the army

DOI: 10.4324/9781003270317-3

way. For many of the issues I will discuss there is an official rule that is publicly stated or an understanding that is agreed to, then there is what people actually do which, while not necessarily illegal, might not be exactly in keeping with the spirit of the law. For example, one informant told me that a man (X) had bought a piece of land from his brother (Y). Y's land had been given by the government so he was not allowed by law to sell it for ten years, but Y needed the money so he sold it to his brother "without paper" and X built a house. My informant was worried that if anything happened to Y, the land would be given to Y's children; X might have to move and lose the money he had paid.

In the same way, if three brothers (A, B and C) build a house together then C moves out, A and B will attempt to give C his monetary share of the house. Perhaps C's name is not on the deed so there is no legal proof of ownership, but everyone in the family would know of C's rights and issues of who inherits what would be handled within the family.

Thus there are a lot of possible permutations as house/land ownership and house/land occupancy are not necessarily the same. For example, it's rare but an older woman might live alone in her father's house when all the others in the family have moved away. The house might legally belong to a brother or a nephew, but the house is discussed as being "hers," with the understanding that she has the right to live in it until she passes away. On the other hand, as explained above, when herding camels, a man might set up a camp and stay for several weeks on land his family has traditionally used but does not legally belong to him.

I would like to highlight that both men and women can buy, sell and inherit lands and houses, but a married couple usually lives in a house (partially) owned by the husband and/or husband's father. The land a woman owns can be sold or she can, with her own money or family's help, build a house, which can then be rented or sold.

Some examples I know of pertaining to house ownership/residency are

- one man owning the land/house where his wife, married sons and unmarried sons and daughters live
- one man owning the land/house where his wife and children, divorced mother, married brothers and unmarried brothers and sisters live
- brothers and sisters pooling money to buy land and build a house for their mother to live in with them, with the deed in the name of several siblings who acknowledge the ownership rights of all siblings although those rights are not legally represented
- one woman owning a house which is rented out, her husband and son do the up-keep and vet the renters
- one woman owning a piece of land which she sold to help pay for her child's education
- one man building a house for only his immediate family

- one man who lives with his wife and children in his father's house but as he travels frequently for work, his wife and children often stay at her parent's house
- one man building a house for a previous wife and their children while staying in a rental house, then building a house for his current wife and their children

Buying and selling lands

There are three important aspects of owning land in Dhofar. First, land and house ownership is linked; the person (or people) who owns the land owns the house. Second, it is almost impossible to alienate someone from their land/house as there are no yearly taxes once the house is built. If the government takes the house by right of eminent domain, a new land with a house or money to pay for a house will be given. I have never seen or heard of a homeless Omani as there is an extensive social support network within families and government gives monthly salaries to jobseekers, disabled people, widows and orphans, etc.[2] Further, there are no old-age homes or retirement villages; the elderly are cared for in their homes by relatives or expats.

Third, any piece of land that is not specifically owned by a person, "having paper" as it is commonly called, is under the control of the government. If a person has staked out a plot with even ad-hoc, temporary markers such as outlining the space in cement blocks, then there is no interference, but a plot of land that is not marked might be used in ways that do not fundamentally change the space.

For example, municipal workers come to neighborhoods several times a year to trim back plants in public spaces and open ground. They will cut back even clearly cultivated gardens which are not enclosed by a house wall and will trim off branches which fall on the outside of house walls. They might use an open plot to dump rocks, soil or equipment such as cables or culverts for nearby road construction or to erect small tents for workers to eat and rest in. Thus, if there is evidence of owner involvement, the area is treated as if there was a complete house. If there is not, then it is treated as open land on which the government might place materials and temporary shelters and neighbors might park and/or grow plants.

Land is acquired by inheriting, buying or being given a plot by the government after putting in an application and paying a nominal fee. In the past men could be given government land when unmarried and women could only apply if married or divorced, but women can now apply even if never married.

Land given by the government can be used to build a primary or secondary house (for rent) or sold. This means that a person with no work or little funds can accrue money to help build a family house or swap lots to own land close to family members.

In almost all cases in Dhofar, people are given land in the mountains only in areas where they were born, which usually means areas that were traditionally controlled by their tribe. Otherwise, people are randomly given plots of land in the area between the sea and the mountains, spreading east and west from Salalah.[3]

Any Omani can buy land in town areas although people will usually try to buy land in proximity to relatives. In neighborhoods with predominantly one family or tribe, the right of first refusal is given to family members. As one informant told me, "choose the neighbor before the house."

Houses in towns are on lots of 600 square meters. People with double or treble lots will sometimes build two, three or four houses together for co-wives or one large house with a garden. With the exception of some Gulf Cooperation Council countries, foreigners are not allowed to buy land/houses in Oman outside of a few developments which grant residence visas to buyers, such as The Wave/Al Mouj in Muscat.[4] There is a small such development in Dhofar that has been plagued with various problems.

Houses are rarely built on spec; almost all homes are designed by the people who live in them according to their taste although, to help pay for the building costs, the house might be rented out for a few years before the owner moves in. If the family decides to move out, the house will either be given to a relative or sold, normally using the family grapevine. Men who want to buy a house will make this clear to his family and the men he has tea with at night; this information will be circulated until someone within this network is found with a house for sale.

In a few cases, a large and wealthy family will build a complex, i.e. a group of houses, for themselves. A smaller complex might have four houses and a separate *majlis* (guest/male sitting room) for a man with four wives or a father with several sons. There are a very few larger complexes with over 20 large houses for one extended family.

Financing the build and deciding to build

The cost of building a house varies widely depending on size and location and rests on four main outlays: land, building materials, builders and fittings. For example, a plot in an unpopular area might cost only 5,000 Omani Riyal (OR[5]); other plots might cost over 50,000 OR. In Salalah, the materials, labor and fittings are usually a minimum of 60,000 OR for a simple, one-story house, 200,000 OR for a three-story house with extras such as a tiled exterior and elevator. Outside of the city, prices drop, for example 40,000 OR for a simple, one-story house.

If a person does not have money on hand, one can borrow from family, friends or a bank. An anonymous reviewer of an article I wrote stated that Omanis (in their experience) did not take bank loans because it is seen as "shame" and that their Omani informants were "afraid" to talk about issues related to paying for building.

My *hakli* informants and friends talk freely about costs and how they are paying for the house. Everyone knows it is expensive to build so people share stories, tell costs, explain what steps they took etc. I only know one man who bought an already-built house; more than ten informants have gone through the process of building their own house.

Some Dhofaris will not take a loan to make a house and will build piece-meal, paying for each stage as they have money.[6] Not having all the money in hand at the start of construction is usual, but if the money runs out early, it can cause problems. For example, if the foundation hole is dug but not re-filled by the monsoon season, it will fill with water and then plants. The best stopping point is to have the roof finished as then the walls and floors are largely protected from sun and rain. Sometimes a family will build a one-story house, live in it for a few years, then add a few rooms upstairs (for example, for a son who will marry) or build out the entire second story.

Once the house is finished, the owner(s) often can't compute the total cost as there were dozens of cash outlays over several months, often with relatives helping. What is always known is the amounts to be paid back if loans were taken from friends and relatives and/or a female relative sold gold jewelry. Owners might pay back these loans for years.

The decision to build does not rest solely with the men of a *hakli* family. Mothers, wives, sisters and daughters are part of the decision, and although they are not expected to pay, they may give financial help if they are working or have their own money, such as an inheritance. Men may not say publicly that they are making decisions based on their wives' and daughters' wishes, but it is expected that the women's opinions will be consulted. I have heard complaints from Dhofari women that, for example, the kitchen is not well designed, but among my *hakli* informants and the *hakli* houses I know/have been in, the women always had a say in how the house was set up, and several men I know simply handed over the room location and decoration to the women.

Blueprints and permissions

The term "vernacular domestic architecture" refers to buildings made with materials found locally and the knowledge of local usage needs and weather patterns, without professional architects. But in Dhofar, architects are viewed as similar to tailors, carpenters and iron-mongers: skilled people who create what the purchaser specifies. Architects might provide checks on unrealistic or illegal suggestions to keep the house within the limitations of government regulations and design constraints (three-story buildings made of cement blocks), but the buyer will rarely purchase a ready-made plan. Dhofaris will come in with a plan from a relative's house, a hand-drawn sketch or photos on their phone or simply talk through what they would like. The first-draft plans are often carried around, shown to people who will live in the house, friend or relatives, and then revised.

Ideas can come from all the houses one has visited, social media, and/or simply driving around and looking at houses as, except for government housing or small compounds, all houses are different.[7] For example, a row of houses might include a modernist one with square windows and sleek lines, one with a Greek-style portico, a Spanish revival style with red tiles gracing a mansard roof and elaborate iron work, a high-arched portal topped with a dome, and a house with arched windows and a castellated roofline. Architectural styles are regularly mixed within the façade of one house.

The blueprints (called "maps") can range from about 200 OR to over 1,000 OR, with an approximate cost of 1 OR for 1 square meter. For example, 120 OR for a one-story house outside of the city; 400 OR for a two-story building on two plots of land with a large entrance hallway, *majlis* (guest/male sitting room), *salle* (female guest and family sitting room), kitchen and two suites on the first floor with four suites on the second; and 600 OR for a three-story house with a large entrance hallway, *majlis*, *salle*, kitchen and a suite on the first floor with seven additional suites on the upper two floors.

Alkhalidi complains that "architects build and leave their buildings with no study of how these buildings work while occupied, in order to repeat positive attitudes and avoid mistakes" (2013 298). However, beyond making sure that the building code is obeyed, architects in Dhofar are following, not leading.

The blueprints must be registered with the government, but if drawn up by an Omani-based firm there are no difficulties as it is expected local architectural firms know and follow official rules. Government inspectors come to verify the site and outline of the house (the chalk lines explained below) and when the municipal water and electricity is hooked up. Informants told me that it is easy to schedule the inspectors and they are perceived as helpful in making sure everything is done correctly.

Siting

There are three important factors to consider when siting a house: weather conditions, view and privacy. In the past, the placement of a house was extremely important, Alkhalidi argues that

> The ancestors in the Middle East area erected sophisticated buildings. Their main concerns were the thermal, social and functional performance of their designs. Generally speaking, these buildings are integrated to their physical environment and their designs and construction were based much more on the performances rather than decorations.
> (2013 298)

In terms of Dhofar, Smith notes

> Inland from the groves, the traditional Salalah townhouse was limestone built and featured an extensive open yard to the front which faced

> the sea. In this way the onshore breezes passed undisturbed towards and through large openings in the upper levels of the south wall, thus ensuring ventilation within.
>
> (1983 19)

With the advent of air conditioners (ACs), houses are no longer placed in view of climate considerations. Houses in town are somewhat constrained by the orientation of the lot, i.e. the entrance must be on the side facing the road, but prevailing winds are no longer taken into account. To my great unhappiness, one house I lived in had a front door which faced due north and every winter sandstorm brought small dunes of sand into the hallway and *salle*. A house facing south might have huge picture windows with only a small awning over the door, exposing the house to direct sun all day, yet a north-facing house might have the door placed at the back of a recess.

In the mountains, houses are usually placed at the end of driveways not directly on streets, so house owners/builders can pick the orientation for the house. Since there are fewer passers-by, privacy is not part of the calculation. Houses are placed to capture/guard against winds and for the *dekka* (outside seating area next to the house) to have a good view of the surrounding area, including the driveway.

In towns, the weather and a scenic view are much less important than creating and preserving privacy. Someone building a house will take the height and location of a neighbor's windows into consideration so that the windows do not line up. Sometimes this results in houses with no windows on a wall which faces/is close to a neighbor's house.

An interesting point is that the prime location for a house in Salalah is on or close to a main road. While a house should be built/decorated so that it is impossible to see into, it should have easy access to a main street. This is in contrast to most descriptions of houses in Arabian Peninsula cities. For example, Kotnik writes

> As an effect of this pattern of development, residential districts are shielded from the main streams of public life. Access from public areas to residential quarters is broken down into a series of hierarchical units through the use of dead-end alleyways and progressive sequences of gates and thresholds, in spatial analogy to the patrilineal division of Yemenite tribes into sections, local communities, and families with increasing levels of closeness of their members.
>
> (2005 479)

The siting effects land/house prices so that in Salalah a small, one-story house on a slip road a few hundred meters from a major round/about near my house was on sale for 95,000 OR; the same size house on a back street would be 50,000 or 60,000 OR.

Construction

It is impossible to speak of an "average" time to build a house as there are too many variables – getting a building permit, finding/hiring a building crew, hiring the digger and bulldozer, buying and having the supplies delivered, etc. If the owner has cash in hand, an experienced crew and no distractions, a one-story house can take less than three months, but the time can vary widely.

Near where I live a two-story "palace" with a separate *majlis* went up in a few months with the crew starting at 6 am seven days a week.[8] The three-story house next to it took over two years; almost a year until the roof was poured, another eight months to get the exterior tiles fixed and holes drilled for water pipes and several months to get windows framed, interior painting and tiling, electricity and furniture moved in.

Once the plan has been approved and the necessary government permissions are secured, a notice must be put up on the lot with information about the owner, including a contact number.

Then the owner must arrange for the building crew by making a contract with an Omani business which will hire and supervise the workers or directly with a group of workers. This contract will specify all the details of the house and the number of men who will work, but not how much time the building will take as many factors are out of the control of the workers. For example, the workers will create the wooden frames and set up the metal support poles for the roof, but the owner must arrange for the cement truck and crane to carry the liquid cement up to the roof. If the owner does not do this quickly, the workers will be paid but have no work to do.

There is usually one crew of five to eight expat men who do most of the work of creating the foundation, walls, wooden frames, ceilings, staircases, surrounding wall, etc.[9] The team usually works six days a week from around 7 am to 4 or 5 pm, with a short morning and afternoon break and a long break for lunch to eat and nap.

Specialist workers are hired for specific tasks; for example, a driver with a backhoe is brought in to dig the foundation and a master-plaster is hired for gypsum work on the ceilings.

Even if a manager is hired with the crew, it is expected that the owner will come to inspect the building site at least once a day. Although the owner is not doing physical labor, having a house built is time consuming and exhausting as the owner is expected to take care of the government formalities, arrange for the heavy construction equipment to be rented and make sure the supplies arrive in time and that the blueprints are followed. If several brothers are building a house together, one is put in charge and he may, for example, be given the best room as compensation. Relatives will also come to see the site frequently. Towards the end of the process, people who will live in the house may come and ask for changes.

Once the crew is hired, the next step is to arrange for electricity for drills and water to make concrete. Usually someone building a house will ask a neighbor to run a long extension cord. For water, either a spigot from the municipal water supply is installed, a water tank is brought in during the building period or a neighbor agrees to give water.[10]

There is the same sequence for all houses.[11] The outline of the house is surveyed and painted on the ground with white chalk; this is the stage where a government inspector makes sure the plot and shape of the house correspond to the official permissions. The foundation is dug, cement block squares about six blocks high are built and painted with waterproof paint and then a rebar frame is placed inside. Then the squares are filled with liquid concrete. Next earth is repacked around and above the squares.

Then the outline of the house and load-bearing walls is again traced on the ground. Wooden frames are built to hold poured concrete to create the foundation walls, and then low cement block walls are built following the outline of the interior walls. This frame (now about 1 meter or more off the ground) is filled with dirt which is packed by rollers and then liquid cement is poured on top so that a few inches of the load-bearing interior walls and upright rebar frames show above the smooth cement floor.

Thus there is a dirt-filled, cement-encased, raised foundation which is resting on sunken reinforced cement squares. The walls are then built up. The rebar supports are framed in wooden supports[12] into which liquid cement is poured. Wooden frames are also used to create arches and staircases. Many metal poles are brought in to support the wooden frames to hold the poured cement for the roof/second floor. On the top floor, a small square room is built for the internal staircase to reach the roof; the ceiling of this small room might be made from liquid cement, or it might be an elaborate, glass-paneled cupola. The roof is then finished with a low wall around the edges.

Before windows and doors are fitted, holes are drilled for water pipes which usually run down the outside of the building, sometimes covered with decorative screens. The outside is then painted or tiled, then the inside is plastered, additional (non-load-bearing) walls might be put in and floors are tiled. Lastly wiring for electricity, telephones and Wi-Fi is put in, and the water pipes are connected to the water tank on the roof. At this stage, a government inspector checks the house before allowing the building to be connected to the municipal water and electric supply.

There are usually pauses (days, weeks, months or years) between various stages as the owner might be too busy to supervise or there might be a problem with the crew, finding equipment like concrete mixers or paying for supplies. One often sees houses in various stages of construction such as just the foundation hole dug, the cement foundation finished, walls and ceiling finished or the house complete but no paint/windows because of lack of money.[13] As explained above, the best stopping point is to have the roof poured so once this happens the owner might stop work for several months to collect money for paint, tiles, windows, doors and furnishings.

Exterior design

Almost all houses are painted in the spectrum of beige/ivory/toast. Some are tiled in the same range of colors as "[a]ccording to the Dhofar Municipality Building regulation (1996) the buildings should be of sandy color matching the surrounding environment" (Yapicioglu and Cazacova 2018 105). A few are painted in brighter colors such as strawberry pink and tropical green.

The first cement block houses built in the 1970s and 1980s had simple designs, usually they were one-story buildings with a window on either side of the main door. They were utilitarian, devoid of ornamentation, with plain walls, small windows and metal gates with a postern. Decorations were the roof castellations and, perhaps, wide stripes (a lighter and darker shade of beige) painted on the exterior.

Most houses now have "Arabic" details; as Al Kathiri and Cazacova explain

> Local regulations stating that the architectural design of façade/elevations of residential and residential/commercial buildings should be according to the local Arab Islamic style contribute to the local building traditions preservation. Consequently, traditional elements are widely used in contemporary design and each modern residential building is a blend of features such as columns and arches, carved wooden doors and window screens with chiseled geometric or floral patterns.
>
> (2014 1–2)

Almost all houses have window air conditioners which are partially concealed by an ornamental box, which is also said to be a government requirement. Newer/more expensive houses have "split" ACs, where the compressor is on the roof. Usually the ground floor windows have bars.

In "'Omani Burqa' vs. Decorated Facade of Modern Omani House" (2018) Yapicioglu and Cazacova argue that "the facade design of a modern Omani house and its walls are like the modern 'burqa' and the 'eye'" in that both "attempt to hide what is considered private in a closed society" (101, 102). The abstract states

> Visiting Oman, one firstly encounters wide roads and exaggerated decorations of house facades—situated behind high walls .... Another encounter one might have is the traditional "Omani burqa." It is worn by some Omani women, originally designed for protection from dust and sand, which mimics the features of a falcon. Lately, the "Omani burqa" has developed into a true fashion-item and is used as a "face mask" with different colors and shapes. Fashionable burqas are often

> decorated with shimmering crystals or diamonds which differs from the traditional design. What is visible behind the "burqa", the "eye", and the "burqa" itself, become quite embellished, subsiding the importance of the other parts of the face.
>
> (101)

Thus the decorated façade, with "eaves, pediment, moldings, pilasters, arches, columns, balconies, quoins, colour, etc." acts as a *burqa* which forces the viewer to concentrate the eyes (usually decorated with kohl, eye shadow and/or mascara), simultaneously attracting and resisting the gaze of outsiders (107).

On roofs, parapets (low walls surrounding the edge) with battlements/crenellations which together form castellations are a frequently used design motif; the battlements can be around the entire roof or only placed only at the corners with small (sometimes curved) merlons and wider embrasures. As Yapicioglu and Cazacova explain in "The Building as a Statement of an Artefact" (2016), the castellations repeat design elements of the locally made and used style of clay incense burner. The article argues that the "incense burner, *mijmara*, manifests itself visually in architecture practice through visual clues" (99) by linking, for example, *mijmara* central facade motifs and perimeter designs to roof-line patterns (106).[14]

As explained in Chapter 5, houses are usually only given exterior extra/temporary exterior decorations for weddings and/or National Day.

For houses in the mountain, the constant drizzle in the monsoon season often turns the exterior of houses black with mold. Some are repainted often, while others gradually turn into a permanent dark color.

Lastly, the exterior decoration is usually only paint and/or tile work, with some newer houses adding in historic features such as projections painted to look like load-bearing wooden logs. A few recently built houses include many types of media such as painted cement blocks, wooden screens, intricate tile works and columns. These embellishments are geometric, rarely shaped to represent objects such as flowers and never depict animals or humans. As Alkhalidi explains, "In Islam, any decoration or painting representing any creature with a spirit is prohibited. This instruction is the reason for the usage of plants, calligraphy, and basic geometrical shapes as tools used to decorate the different spaces" (2013 290).

Interior design[15]

If possible, furnishings are bought from outside Salalah where there is a better choice and often cheaper prices. Some owners travel to China to buy everything; people who have done this pass on details about how to arrange the trip and the name of companies and hotels.[16] It is more usual for the entire family or a husband and wife to go to Muscat or Dubai to order furniture and plumbing fixtures which are shipped to Dhofar. Furniture can also be made to order in the *saniya*, an industrial area with many small ironmongers, carpentry and car repair shops. Salalah's *saniya* is in the northwest corner of the city.

Houses are decorated when they are new or when the family moves in, usually with new furniture with the old furniture either thrown away or given to poorer relatives. Refurbishment, new furniture and/or painting, usually takes place before the two *Eids* and/or before a wedding. Decorating decisions are made by the men and women together, usually with older family members having a more decisive say.

Women often help with the design and decoration of their own bedrooms, the kitchen, the *salle*, the *majlis* and the exterior whether or not they made a financial contribution to the house. Some Dhofari women are frustrated that they don't have a say in designing and decorating, but this is often a function of age and tribe. In the *hakli* families I know mothers, sisters, daughters and/or wives were always consulted or had design control over at least part of the houses they lived in. However, unmarried women in their teens or early 20s might not be consulted, except for the color choices in their rooms, because of age and the expectation that they will not stay in the house for long given that almost all women move to their husband's house when married.

When a man is going to get married, he is either given a new room or his room is completely redone: repainted, new furniture, new lighting and often a new dropped or decorated ceiling. As men often marry their cousins, sisters of the groom and sisters of the bride can sometimes talk to choose colors and designs the bride likes, but sometimes the groom will just decorate as he sees fit or gives the task to a sister without ever asking the bride. This room, out of respect for whoever decorated it, should not be changed for several years, so a woman might not have power over her living space until she is in her late 20s or 30s, but from then on, the decorating is made in consultation with her husband/family or left up to her.

The most important rooms are the *majlis* and *salle*; usually the *majlis* is more showy with a larger TV, elaborate curtains, wall hangings, gypsum decorations on the ceiling, etc. Care is taken that the two rooms do not have the same color scheme, but the spaces are not color-coded for gender in Western terms, i.e. the *majlis* might be light purple, while the *salle* is dark blue.

The main design element in kitchens and bathrooms is the choice of tile for floors and ceilings which is often gray, cream or brown.

Getting design ideas for the exterior of houses is simple, one only has to drive around and see what other people have done. But there are not many chances to get design ideas about interior spaces beyond a few, large furnishing stores that have opened in the past few years. Dhofaris will visit relatives' houses and might stay in hotels or vacation rentals, but there are limited opportunities to see a wide variety of interior styles. Social media often has photos of bedrooms made up for weddings, and people renting houses might post photos of interiors, but there is, for example, no Omani equivalent of Zillow or Redfin with photos of the inside of millions of homes.[17]

On the other hand, there are many carpenters, iron-mongers and tailors so that Dhofaris are not limited to furniture and curtains they find in stores. As with designing the house, people can take a photo or hand-drawn sketch to a workshop and have beds, wardrobes, sofas, chairs, etc. made to their specifications.

Once the house is enclosed (fitted with windows and doors) and tiled, furniture can be dropped off and left for weeks until the final work of putting in ACs, lighting and sanitary fixtures, running water and electricity.

Moving in

The getting-ready-to-move process is usually slow, taking weeks if not months given that most of the furnishings are coming from out of town and some people will buy only when they have cash on hand. For one family I know, the *majlis* and *salle* furniture was in place and covered in plastic for a month before the family moved in.

Part of the slowness is because there is a cultural understanding that "new house" means "new everything"; some Dhofaris only take their clothes when moving into a new house. Even if the furnishings such as beds, rugs, sofas and tables are in very good condition, everything is usually left behind.[18] The former house, fully furnished, is often given to a family member or rented out.

Given this framework, shifting houses can be done swiftly as there are usually only clothes and a few personal items to transfer, but then it can take weeks to adjust to new stoves, furniture etc.

If the family was not able to buy all new furnishing before the move-in date, they might live for weeks or months with a nicely decorated *majlis* and *salle* but have only very simple items in the other rooms and make do, for example sleeping on the floor on portable mattresses, until they can accumulate all the necessary items. This might happen when a family needs to leave a rented house or there is an occasion which they want to celebrate in their new house, such as a wedding or *Eid*.

Some people will have a party to celebrate the new house although this is not necessary.[19] If there is a party, it will take place on a weekend evening soon after moving in and all neighbors and close family members are invited.[20] The family will slaughter an animal or animals (goat, cow or camel) depending on their finances, serving some of the meat and giving some away to relatives or poor people.

One Dhofari informant explained that when a family member moved into a new house, there was no house party because there was a wedding within a week. That family had rushed to get into the house and prepare for the wedding, so there was no need to have a "new house" party.

Redecorating/repairing

For the two *Eids*, when Dhofaris usually visit and are visited by all close family members, there is usually some sprucing up of the *majlis* and *salle*, such as a new rug or new coffee table. Major redecorating is usually only done for weddings although sometimes family members will redecorate for each other as a gift; more than one female Dhofari friend has refurbished her mother's room, without any input from the mother.

I will talk about this point more in Chapter 5 in the section on "reading a house," but the outside of a house is not an effective indicator of the wealth or intentions of the inhabitants. Redecorating is very much a feast or famine. For example, a house that looks run-down, e.g. in need of a new paint job, fresh gravel around the exterior wall and a new gate, might be owned by people who are waiting for a particular event. I have seen Dhofaris live in truly dismal surroundings while saving money to move or completely refurnish a room.

Once the redecoration is complete, the room will stay pretty much the same until the next complete overhaul. As explained above, this is particularly the case with new brides who live in rooms designed by their husband and/or his sisters. For even small changes, she should not just consult but go shopping with her husband for items such as a nightstand. After a few years of marriage, the room becomes fully "hers" and she can make changes as she likes.

In terms of repairing, I keep a log of which workers come to my house and here is a summary of problems that cropped up within one typical month as I was writing this book. The electricity went off in half the apartment for eight hours, and in trying to fix the problem, the electrician started a small fire when the whole building was without power for another four hours. Twice in the next few days, the power was turned off without warning for an hour to make more repairs. My modem (supplied by the telephone company) died, one curtain pull stopped working, one AC leaked water, the light bulb fixture over the front door had to be replaced and the water pipes were full of algae. The metal gate was stuck closed twice and, as the windows are not well fitted, a sandstorm deposited a layer of sand on everything.

The house is well made, and my landlord is meticulous about up-keep, but there is always something that needs fixing: a florescent tube is burnt out or needs a new starter, the door lock isn't working, the Wi-Fi wires need to be replaced, cracks in the wall need to be filled, the bathroom floor needs new grouting etc. During seven years in this house, I have replaced all the sink faucets at least twice, the shower heads three times, four ACs and two extractor fans. There have been two water pipe leaks which required breaking wall tiles and significant damage under windows from rain storms.

As many Dhofari men supervise the building of their house, they can diagnose, and sometimes fix, problems themselves. Sometimes landlords have a repair person on call, but getting help usually means driving to a nearby hardware store and asking one of the men sitting outside with a bag of tools to get into the car, driving him to the house, watching him fix the problem and then driving him back to the store.[21]

This means that it is easy and inexpensive to find a plumber at 10 pm on a weeknight or one can decide to paint a room at 9 am and have painters at work by 11 am. The bad news is that a repair person might not be qualified, such as the one who replaced my leaking water tank, only for me to discover two days later that it was a pipe, not the tank, that was leaking.

Repairmen have a sense of self-respect amounting to an *amour-propre* which means they will not do other actions except their job. I respect this, but it causes a lot of headaches. A man who has come to fix the AC will fix it but leave handprints all over the wall, the empty boxes for the spare parts on the floor, drops of dirty water all over the rugs and slam the ladder into the wall causing chunks of plaster to fall out. Usually any major repair will necessitate calling another repair person: having my gate fixed meant repainting the garden wall.[22]

The research guys do not complain about scorpion bites or older relatives who ask for attention and/or money at inconvenient times, but they have a lot of say about repair people. Yet, the examples in this section are from my life as the research guys did not want to talk on the record about issues with repairmen as part of their cultural understanding of not focusing on negative people or situations. Repair people are perceived as not honest and thus not it's worth their time or self-respect to speak about them, especially as I would be writing down their words.

Notes

1 For an older discussion of land rights and usage in Oman, see Carter (1982 104 and following).

2 There might be homeless refugees in some towns, but never publicly such as sleeping on sidewalks. There have been clusters of refugees living in the mountains who have walked into Oman from Yemen, sometimes after crossing the Red Sea, but there are fewer now because the border is more carefully guarded.

3 A reviewer mentioned a Dhofari could receive a plot allocation through the "Governor's Office" in an attempt to exercise "some form of influence on the decision." I asked my informants about this and was told that this was only an option for a very poor person who was asking for assistance.

4 In 2020, the law was changed so that expatriates who have lived in Oman for at least two years and meet stringent requirements may buy apartments and offices in parts of Muscat Governorate.

5 One Omani Riyal [OR] is approximately 2.6 dollars, 1.8 pounds or 2.2 Euros. Each riyal has 100 *baisa*.

6 Charging interest is forbidden in Islam, but there are banks which charge a straight fee without interest, but some prefer not to be in debt and some men are not able to get loans.

7 I will talk about photos of houses in Chapter 8.

8 Elaborately decorated houses on two or more plots of land are often referred to as "palaces." This one has a small footprint, with a *hosh* (courtyard) in front

of the house, a separate *majlis*, a large portico, a stained glass cupola and extra parking space outside the wall. Given the shouting among themselves, drilling, pounding etc., it was impossible to sleep once they started working and a few times I opened a window and yelled at them to be quiet. Waking up at 6 am every weekend morning for months made me furious, but the research guys thought I was being ridiculous. Everyone has stories about not being able to sleep because of house construction; this is seen as something not worth complaining about. I have not reached that level of *sangfroid*; I have never met this neighbor and I sincerely hope I never do.

9 Usually, only one crew will build a house, but sometimes an owner will run out of money, pay off the workers, end the contract and hire a new group when he has money again. One informant told me about one friend who built his house slowly, having to start and stop so he ended up using four different crews.

10 Sometimes in the corner of a lot (i.e. not within the footprint of the house), a small room is built of cement blocks which are not mortared together, only placed on top of each other. This is fitted with a door made of scrap wood which can be locked to secure tools inside. However, rebar, cement blocks, sacks of cement mix, etc. are left in piles out in the open. I have never heard of such items being stolen. If the building is stalled, the piles of rebar, for example, can be overgrown with plants.

11 There are photos of each stage on my website in two essays titled "House construction, parts 1 and 2."

12 The wooden frames for the rebar columns, arches and the roof are used over and over again. Usually a large heap of pieces is brought to the construction site, and workers sort through the pieces to find the right size. The used wood is then taken away when no longer needed.

13 One expat who had just arrived asked me why there were so many "burnt houses," referring to the many gray cement block shells of houses. One house near where I live has been in this condition for nine years.

14 See Smith (1991) "reminiscent of the upper silhouettes of the [Muscat] harbour forts" (191) and "The 'qarn' or crenellation on the top of a fortified wall or parapet has appeared on many civic scale buildings in recent years, thereby hoping to establish, arguably to re-establish, a national style of architecture peculiar to Oman" (footnote 13, 205).

15 I also discuss decorating in Chapter 6.

16 Before Covid.

17 Also some countries have hundreds of movies and TV shows filmed in various places so that it's easy to see how other people live. For example I love *Mystery Road* because it's fascinating to see how houses are arranged in remote areas of Australia. There are no such equivalents in Oman.

18 I don't think this is an issue of, as Belk terms it, the "contagion" or "sympathetic magic" of items (2012 22). I discuss this in my texts *Community and Autonomy in Southern Oman* (2019) and "Generosity, Gift-giving and Gift-avoiding in Southern Oman" (2015) and it bears repeating in terms of house decorations. For the *hakli* people I know, the stuff in your house is the stuff in your house – it's not you or an extension of you.

19 For a specific example, see the Methodology section in Chapter 1. Some Dhofaris remember in the distant past that the blood of a slaughtered animal was put on the threshold, but not in recent memory.

20 The men who built the house are not invited and will never be associated with it again.

21 This is one of the main reasons expats live in complexes. The manager of a group of villas will hire one or two men to run interference on all repairs. Because repairmen are often Pakistani and would refuse to go with a single woman or

be in the house with one, I often had to ask one of the research guys to help me until I found a fix-it guy who could run interference for me. One of the guys in particular (X) was of great help. Just after I moved into one house, I called him in a panic: two sinks were leaking and there was no hot water in the shower. He showed up with a plumber about 15 minutes later.

A few weeks later, he brought an electrician to fix the lights in the *majlis*. When I went to check on how the repairs were going, I couldn't find them until I heard shouting so I looked out the window and saw X and the electrician balanced on top of my garden wall fixing the lanterns. I hadn't mentioned that none of the outdoor lights worked, but he had noticed and decided to fix them. Ten minutes later, they were up on the roof with X perched on the "battlements" (thick, four-foot high wall that goes around the edge of the roof) fixing the lanterns up there. When he finished and came in, he never mentioned what he had been doing.

22 When I walk outside to discover that the painter has poured out a can of paint thinner underneath my car, it's hard to figure out if then was done because of pure malice, incompetence, boredom or confusion. Is this hatred or expedience? The frustration of living in a foreign culture or dislike of a Christian woman? The result of exhaustion from not getting enough sleep or anger at having to do two coats of paint?

References

For photos and a full bibliography, please see: *Come From Away*, https://mariellerisse.com

Al Kathiri, Muna Salim and Liudmila Cazacova. 2014. "Islamic Architecture Features and Modern Housing: A Case Study of the North Awqad District in Salalah, Oman." *The International Journal of the Constructed Environment* 4: 1–18.

Alkhalidi, Abdulsamad. 2013. "Sustainable Application of Interior Spaces in Traditional Houses of the United Arab Emirates." *Procedia – Social and Behavioral Sciences* 102: 288–99.

Belk, Russell. 2012. "People and Things," in *Handbook of Developments in Consumer Behavior*. Victoria Wells and Gordon Foxall, eds. Cheltenham: Elgar. 15–46.

Carter, J. R. L. 1982. *Tribes in Oman*. London: Peninsular Publishing.

Kotnik, Toni. 2005. "The Mirrored Public Architecture and Gender Relationship in Yemen." *Space and Culture* 8.4: 472–83.

Risse, Marielle. 2019. *Community and Autonomy in Southern Oman*. Cham, Switzerland: Palgrave Macmillan.

———. 2015. "Generosity, Gift-giving and Gift-avoiding in Southern Oman." *Proceedings of the Seminar for Arabian Studies* 45: 289–96.

Smith, John Alexander. 1991."The Islamic Garden in Oman: Sanctuary and Paradise." *Garden History* 19: 187–208.

———. 1983. "Desert Developments." *Building Design* 11: 18–21.

Yapicioglu, Balkiz and Liudmila Cazacova. 2018. ""Omani Burqa" vs. Decorated Facade of Modern Omani House: The Case of Salalah, Dhofar Region, Oman." *The Academic Research Community Publication*: 101–111. ISSN online: 2537–0162.

———. 2016. "The Building as a Statement of an Artefact: The Mijmara." *International Journal of Ecology & Development* 31.3: 99–116.

4 The physical house

Basic elements of a house-space

Hosh

In the heavily built-up areas of Salalah, the front door opens directly onto a small landing, and then there are a few steps down to the sidewalk, but most houses have a 2-meter high cement block wall with two openings.[1] One is a sliding gate for a car to enter the *hosh*, the area between the wall and the house which is usually paved with bricks/Interlock. The second is a door (*bab*) which is usually left partially ajar or completely open. The door and the sliding door are often made of metal, with geometric designs and painted the same color as the wall.

In the *hosh*, there is usually an open space for kids to play and an area to park cars. Along the side of the house or at the back of the house, sometimes there are clotheslines (or they are on the roof) and occasionally plants such as mint, thyme or basil; trees such as henna, lime, coconut or papaya; or decorative plants such as hibiscus, oleander or bougainvillea. If the house is built on a double plot, there might be a large paved area with trees at the back as a private garden.

Some people, wanting to increase the footprint, build the house to within a few feet of the border wall on all sides and push the border wall to within a few feet of the street, leaving a *hosh* barely a meter wide and there is no place for parking.

Set into the outside of the *hosh* wall, there is sometimes a tank of water with a spigot and a slanted overhang to keep it shaded. This is free drinking water and house owners keep the tank full as a charity. Given the high temperatures and absence of drinking fountains, these tanks are used frequently. When I saw a house in my neighborhood with a broken wall, I asked one of the research guys about it. He told me that the head of the household had recently died and that the family were constructing a tank in his honor.[2]

Doors

Only older houses are built at (or below) ground level; all concrete block houses are above ground level at least 1 meter[3] so one walks up a short set

DOI: 10.4324/9781003270317-4

of stairs to a landing (2 meters by 2 meters or larger) usually with a decorative lamp hanging from the ceiling and perhaps a few plants or clay vases. Sometimes the only objects on the landing are a mat in front of each door and a collection of shoes as most Dhofaris wear sandals which are kicked off and left outside the house. It is sometimes possible to know who is visiting by examining the shoes in front of the two entry doors.

The doors are often recessed to shade from the sun and to allow more privacy at the threshold. Doors are sometimes left ajar, but because they are usually set back from the front plane of the house, it is impossible to see inside unless you are standing directly in front of the door.[4]

Main doors of houses that are set back from the street are often embellished with decorative elements such as carved wood trim and/or an arched transom window and thin vertical windows with opaque glass on either side. Given that the two doors are usually made of wood and shrink/expand because of weather changes (hot humid springs, cool humid summers, cool dry winters), there is often at least an inch gap between the bottom of the door and the floor. This is sometimes stopped with rags during rain or wind storms.

When looking at the two doors on the landing, it is easy to distinguish between which one leads to the *majlis* (male/guest sitting room) and to the main hallway/*salle* (female guest/family sitting room). The main hallway door is often more decorated, directly facing the street and larger. It is wider than average to allow large furniture to be moved in and out. This usually means either one wide door or double doors in which the right-side door is used daily, while the left is locked in place and only opened when more space is needed. There is never a post between the two doors as this would defeat the purpose of having a large open space. Screen doors are seldom, if ever, used.

The *majlis* door usually has similar decorations, but it is standard sized (apx 115 cm wide, 210 cm high) and set at an angle to the street and the main door. In larger houses the doors might be on different landings; the larger, more elaborate door is always the main hallway door.

Talking about front doors is, to me, a chicken-and-egg issue. Did behaviors help form door shapes or did door shapes help form behaviors? Impossible to tell. Having wider doors at the main entrance makes sense as a Dhofari woman does not often go visiting by herself, she will bring children, sisters, her mother and/or aunts along and when they arrive, they are greeted by the children who live in the house so that perhaps ten people are standing in/near the doorway or just inside in the foyer.

Whereas it is more usual for a man to visit a house by himself, and even if a group of men approach the *majlis* door together there are, as one Dhofari friend says, "protocols" of how men should enter a building. Anyone who visits Dhofar will get used to the logjam/shuffle that occurs when several men walk up to a doorway. Younger men will step to the side or backward to show respect; older men will move aside to avoid acting as if they want to go ahead, sometimes gently pulling on the shoulder of another man's *dishdash* to allow him the honor of going first. Sometimes the negotiations will take 15 seconds until one man is persuaded to enter, then there might be further parleys until it is decided who will go second. Dhofari men go through doorways one at a time after careful demonstrations of respect and goodwill.

The same sequence does not usually occur with women. If four women approach a doorway at the same time, there will not be a delay in entering. Perhaps a young woman might let an older woman go first, but for example, children might race ahead or tug their mother's *abayah* to pull her forward or a younger woman might enter and then turn around to help an older woman over the threshold.

When leaving, the same dichotomy exists. Women leave together by the main door, unconcerned about who goes through the door first and, in any case, the door is usually wide enough to allow two or more to walk through at the same time. The doorway cluster can be the group of women who came together or if a single woman came to visit, then the hostess, children and perhaps other women in the house will be near the door to say "goodbye."

From the *majlis*, unrelated men leave singly, trying to time "goodbyes" so that one is not approaching the door at the same moment as another man which would necessitate at least a symbolic "after you – oh no, you first – please, I insist – I couldn't, please go ahead" sort of exchange. Men who are related or friends can leave in groups as the order of precedence (or lack thereof) is established and will not require gestures of politeness.

To explain this phenomenon another way, there is a general cultural understanding in Dhofar that the person standing on the right-hand side of a doorway should enter first. But whereas men will actively try to maneuver themselves towards the left and another man towards the right, women will not attempt to change their position or the position of another woman as they approach a door.

I don't know all the reasons for this behavior. I think it is partly due to women not wanting to draw attention to themselves in public and wanting to get to an inside space as quickly as possible. Women are also often carrying or leading children and a crying baby or sleeping toddler who needs to be settled is of more importance than who walks in the door first. Also, as women's faces are usually covered while men's aren't, a man stepping aside to let another man go first is publicly showing his good behavior.

From watching men's behaviors in a cafe and on picnics, the same dichotomy exists in the *majlis* and *salle*: men actively try to give other men the "best seat" (most central, closest to air conditioner [AC], most comfortable), while women sit where there is space closest to women they know. If there are no seats open on a sofa in the *salle*, younger women and/or women who live in the house will stand up to make place, but if the guest waves them down, there is not a protracted back and forth. Some older women prefer to sit on cushions on the floor and if a woman has settled herself, no one will try to force her to another place.

Floors

One of the most dangerous events in a Dhofari house is spilling water on the floor. Dhofari floors are usually white tile: cold, unforgivingly hard and perilously slick when freshly polished or wet. Floor tiles are usually large, for example 20″ square, and it's impossible to get traction on them.

The tiles are usually made of ceramic or porcelain, and sometimes glass in bathrooms; marble and stone tiles are rare. The floors of the *majlis* and *salle* are often at least partially covered with rugs, which are swept clean at least once a day.

In bathrooms and kitchens the tiles can be of other colors, often cream, beige, brown or gray, and are usually smaller, sometimes with a domed/rounded shape which is safer as they are not as slippery.

Floors of the kitchen and bathroom are often slightly raised to accommodate floor drains and have a 1- or 2-inch barrier at the threshold to prevent water that is sluiced for cleaning from escaping. Some home owners will ask workers to slightly (almost imperceptibly) tilt the cement base of stairs and floors near doors to keep water out of rooms.

For example, my roof wall had drilled holes for the water to escape and the roof door had a ledge in front of it but the huge amount of water from hurricane Mekunu (2018) meant that water came into the landing at the top of the stairs. However, the stairs were slightly canted so that the rain ran down the left side of the stairs, and at the first landing the water spilled over the edge into the stairwell instead of continuing down the stairs. For several hours, there was a waterfall in the stairwell, but no roof water entered my apartment or the apartment downstairs as the water seeped out in the gap under the front door.

As shoes are taken off at the door to prevent dirt from entering the house, floors are usually very clean, although during sand storms sand usually piles up near doorways and under windows. Shower shoes/slip-ons are worn in the bathroom.

Walls and ceilings

Walls are usually cement blocks, but some (non-load-bearing) are plasterboard. Cement block walls are plastered and then painted or tiled. Given the vagaries of handset block courses, walls often bulge or recess slightly in places; plus the plastering is not always even, leaving slight dimpling that can be noticeable in low light.

I am not sure of the reasons why there are no closets, perhaps for ease of building and given the high humidity, people want to ensure good airflow. Rooms are built with straight walls, and the interest/decoration is provided by archways and plastered decoration on ceilings. Walls often develop alarming cracks which is explained, for example by my Dhofari landlord, as "it always happens, building on sand."[5]

The colors of walls for the main hallway and *salle* coordinate and can be any shade from a calm shade of beige to violently bright tangerine, blue or green. The *majlis* is always in a different color, as is each of the bedrooms. For example, when one of the research guys was building a new house with his brothers, the brother in charge of construction picked one base color that was used for every inside wall. Then the mother picked the colors of the *majlis* and *salle*, and each brother and his wife picked the color for their own rooms.

Ceilings are high (usually at least 3 meters) and usually have plaster decorations, referred to as gypsums, such as cornices, ceiling roses and square or rectangular frames. Suspended (dropped) ceilings are common, as are hidden/recessed lights.

AC, fans and smoke detectors

There is almost always moving air because of the heat and dampness; in the *khareef* (monsoon) season, it's normal to have 90% humidity. There are window ACs which are fairly cheap, but loud, and "split" ACs which have the motor on the roof so they are quieter but more expensive.[6] It is rare to have central air conditioning in a house as it creates much more work during the construction phase and thus is much more expensive. It is also rare to have an AC in a kitchen or bathroom.

Most rooms have fans. Kitchens and bathrooms always have extractor fans to remove odors; the *majlis*, *salle* and bedrooms have ceiling fans for air circulation. Some are attached to light fixtures; a common set-up is to have fluorescent tube lighting placed near the four corners of the rooms, a fan in the middle of the ceiling and a few lights on the wall or recessed into a ceiling.

Switches and sockets are usually gathered at shoulder height next to the door of a room.[7] There can be, for example, nine identical switches to control the ceiling lights, wall lights and fans. As most ceiling lights are florescent which take a few seconds to turn on and the fan has a separate circular switch for speed adjustment, you can spend over a minute pushing switches trying to figure out how to turn things on and off.

Bathroom switches are outside next to the door and will be for the ceiling light, vanity light and extractor fan, as well as hallway lights. Kitchens and bathrooms will also have a switch to turn on the water heater; other rooms will have the AC power switch.

Whenever an AC repairman comes to fix an AC, he will leave the AC set at the "normal" temperature of 16°C (60°F)[8], far too cold for me. Yet, when I visit Dhofari friends, 16°C makes sense as women are always dressed in a *dhobe* and *lossi* (headscarf) in the home so their bodies and heads are covered. Also there are sometimes spaces, such as hallways or a kitchen, which don't have an AC so the cool air created is needed for other rooms and with over 30 people living in one house, the *salle* and *majlis* can get very crowded and hot.

ACs are turned off if no one will be sitting in the room, but some people use them in bedrooms even in the winter as white noise.

I have never seen a smoke detector in a Dhofari house as frankincense and/or *oud* (wood perfumed with oil) is burnt on small pieces of charcoal every morning so that the thick scented smoke fills the house.[9] This cleans and purifies the air and is also done after meals or when guests are visiting. Perhaps some people have a smoke detector in the kitchen.

Dhofaris also "smoke," as it is called in Dhofari-English, at work as well. The provisionary quarters for the university where I teach was a group of villas and staff burned frankincense every morning; it was normal to see billows of smoke floating down the hallways. When we all moved to the campus, they continued to do so, setting off fire alarms constantly. It was an interesting stand-off: safety vs a comforting tradition.[10]

Windows

Over the last 20 years or so, the predominant style for living and bedroom windows is two- or three-panel, lift-out, sliding windows placed about 1 meter from the floor with the window either single pane or divided. Usually the window itself is rectangular (for example with a height of 110 cm and a width of 120 cm) with an inset plastered/painted arched niche or an arched fanlight above (for example with a height of 45 cm).[11]

In the last few years, there is a greater mix of styles. While some houses continue to have arched windows, square windows, large picture windows and/or an entire wall (one or more stories high) of windows are more common. In particular, rental houses often have floor-to-ceiling windows with sliding glass or French doors. Bay and bow windows are rare.

Most windows are reflective – either because the glass itself has been treated while being made or because a thin reflective film was put on. This is done to cut cooling costs as it means less direct sunlight enters a room; it also means windows are difficult or impossible to see through during a sunny day. Regardless, most windows are completely covered with drapes/curtains.

Kitchen windows are usually smaller (for example, 1 m × 80 cm) and set above the sink. Bathroom windows are smaller still (for example 65 cm × 50 cm). Both have opaque glass, and sometimes there is a small fan incorporated into the window space or the arched fan light. Both rooms might have two-panel, lift-out sliding windows or hopper (the top of the window inclines inward); awning (the bottom of the window inclines outward) is less common.

Sometimes windows are incorporated into the front door frame: either as transom/fan lights above the doors and/or as thin windows on either side of the door. These windows are opaque, perhaps made of translucent glass blocks or colored with real stained glass or a plastic, press-on designs, that looks like stained glass.

Window frames are metal, usually 3–5 m wide and, as can be expected when fitting arched windows in metal frames into cement block buildings, there are often thin gaps which let in wind, sand and rain. As windows are often completely covered with curtains/drapes, wind and sand are not that much of a problem, although drifts of sand appear on the floor during sandstorms. For rainstorms, some Dhofaris take the preventative option and nail plastic sheeting over windows; some simply move furniture and rugs away from the window and mop up the water.

Rooms in houses

I think of Dhofari houses as the antithesis of expensive Victorian-era houses in the United Kingdom with all those little rooms with separate purposes: the morning room, the seamstress' room, the billiard room, the music room, the library etc. In Dhofari houses, there are usually only four types of rooms: sitting room, bedroom, kitchen and bathroom, and the first three types are furnished with the same pattern of furniture next to the walls and empty space in the middle.

Or, as an opposite example, some North American homes have a "great room" with combined kitchen, dining and sitting areas. In Dhofar, kitchens are isolated and dining tables are usually incorporated into sitting rooms, not in separate rooms.

Another way to think about types of rooms is to consider that many middle- and upper-class North American homes have rooms for work, relaxation and/or exercise such as a home office, craft room, gym, yoga studio etc. which might be the former bedroom of a child who has moved out. There is a standard trope of a child going to college and his/her room "disappears" as it has been entirely repurposed.

Whereas in Dhofar, while the people who stay in a room might change, the purpose seldom does. For example, three brothers might share a bedroom on the ground floor. In time, an additional story is added and two boys move to an upstairs bedroom, while the original room is redone for the oldest boy and his bride. After this couple have a few children, they move to a suite on the first floor and the room is refurbished for a grandparent who cannot manage to walk upstairs.

Majlis

The *majlis* is usually explained as the "male" or "male visitor's sitting room" in contrast to the *salle* which is usually explained as the women's sitting room.[12] For example, the "Majlees is a reception hall of a residence for male visitors only, which is used on different festive occasions. Usually is easily accessible from the street and has a segregated entrance and bathroom" (Yapicioglu and Cazacova 2018 104). Al Thahab, Mushatat and Abdelmonem state that

> The separation of public/private spaces summarizes the impact of the cultural and behavioral value systems on the sequence and hierarchy of spaces that largely defines the organic pattern of the traditional fabric at large ... The traditional house obtains its priority over public realms as it accommodates the social and cultural aspects of life. It demonstrates, moreover, the thresholds of social interaction between male and female members of the same family in the everyday social practices ... This is reflected in the architecture of the house through dividing it into two distinct parts: male section "Diwan-khana", and female part "Haram". (2014 238)

But this strict division does not obtain in Dhofar among the *hakli* tribes. A woman, for example, might sit in the *majlis* and speak with her uncles or male cousins who have come to visit. Older men who are close neighbors can sit with women in the *salle* if there are no men in the house to entertain them.

Further, the *majlis* can have a variety of uses. Children might use it as a temporary classroom with a tutor in the early evening. Women might use it to entertain female guests or for wedding parties, during which women usually take over the whole house while men are entertained outside. A husband might use the *majlis* in his wife's parent's house as a place to talk to his wife when she is temporarily living at her parent's house if she is caring for a sick member of her family or if there is an argument between the couple.

When I visit female Dhofari friends at home, where we sit depends on several factors. If their husbands and/or brothers are not at home, we sit in the *majlis*. When I visited one male Dhofari friend, we sat in the *majlis*, but I went to the *salle* to eat lunch with the women.

The *majlis* is usually decorated with sofas or cushions on a low wooden frame surrounding the sides of the room, a few coffee tables, a TV and sometimes decorations such as photos of the Sultan Qaboos or Sultan Haitham. There is an AC and a short hallway which leads to two doors, one leads to a sink area which has another door leading into a small toilet/shower room. The second door leads to the main part of the house and is almost always closed, if not locked. The walls are always painted to coordinate with the curtains and sofas; often, there is a rug in the (empty) center of the room; the color scheme might be shades of beige, pastels or dark shades of brown, blue or green. Red is usually not used.

In a very small house, sometimes the *majlis* is completely repurposed by becoming a bedroom. Then the *salle* functions as *majlis*. In one house which was arranged like this, when I was sitting with women and a man entered to meet with the husband, the women and I went to sit in the couple's bedroom.

There can also be a *majlis* in the house as well as another *majlis* in a separate building. This is not common in Dhofar and is usually a marker of a religiously conservative and/or wealthy family. The outside *majlis* is usually located close to the wall (sometimes with a doorway cut into the wall) so that visitors do not go anywhere near the house. This *majlis* often has a large sitting room and bathroom with sometimes a small kitchen (with its own entrance) and/or a bedroom. When I was with some of the men in the research group visiting a man we knew, we sat in the separate *majlis* and lunch was brought to us, carried by our friend.

Foyer/main hallway

The main door usually opens into a large, wide hallway. As Al Thahab, Mushatat and Abdelmonem explain, "The space of the entrance has been articulated in a way that prevents any kind of direct visual intrusion from the outside towards the main social core of the house associated with the courtyard or the family room" (2014 242). This hallway, which runs from the front to the back of most houses, is widest by the front door.

Several members of my family work in the fields of design and planning, so I grew up listening to a lot of talk about architectural details and effective organization between and within buildings. A favorite mantra was: form follows function, meaning the purpose of the space determines the shape of the space. This is a good way to start to think of entrances to houses.

When I first visited Dhofari houses, I was surprised by the large space near the front door that leads to the main hall. The foyers were empty and, to me, unnecessary. Kids did not use the area to play, no one sat there and there was no furniture except perhaps a tall, rectangular side table pushed against the wall with a mirror above it or nearby; it was just a large empty space that had to be air conditioned.

After more visits, I started to see the purpose and began to be very grateful for the entrance as a helpful liminal space between being public (outside where everyone could see me) and private (in the *salle* in view of women and children).[13]

To aggregate several dozen experiences, when I arrive at a house, I wear a *dhobe* (loose, Dhofari housedress) which is covered by a "head *abayah*" (a large, black polyester square that is pulled over the head and drapes to cover the body down to the knees). It is often worn for short distances, such as from the car to inside a house or between neighbors' houses; some older women wear it while shopping.

If the front door is open, I call out to show that I am there, step into the foyer, take off my head *abayah* and put it in my purse, check that my *lossi* (headscarf) is covering my hair and then walk into the *salle*, the women's and family's sitting room.

If the door is locked, I ring the bell, and when it is answered, there is usually one woman with a group of children behind her who have come to see who it is. The woman will welcome me but not ask me questions. She will stay back a few feet and not give any pressure such as saying "everyone's waiting for you!" as I check that I am ready to go into the *salle*. When I start to move, she will walk to the opening of the *salle* with me then sit in her place. Once in the *salle*, all eyes will turn to me and there are sometimes questions and explanations as to who I am as I walk in a circle, greeting each woman and shaking her hand, then I find a place to sit and get ready to talk.

The large, empty foyer gives me the chance to move from the outside presentation (shapeless black figure) to inside (still shapeless but brightly colored). I can check my hair and lipstick, smooth down my *dhobe* and get ready to be part of the conversation. Even if there is a wedding party with over 50 women in the house, the foyer is empty and women who are further down the hallway will not come to say "hello," until I have moved away from the door area.

The area makes me think of texts from the 1800s and 1900s in which there are depictions of women going into a small dressing room to take off their wraps and change into dancing shoes such as in Katherine Mansfield's "Her First Ball." It's public, women in the hallway can see me and sometimes children stand nearby, but also private in that I am not expected to make small talk or answer questions.

When I leave the house, the space again is useful as, after I say my goodbyes, I step out of the *salle* and into the foyer, I have a moment to get my head *abayah* back on, check my phone and get out my car keys. Perhaps my friend will come stand with me, to walk to the portico with me to wave goodbye, but the talk is easy: "say hello to your mother for me" and "I hope you have a nice weekend" sort of phrases.

At the end of a wedding party, there might be several women standing near the door waiting for a car to drive them home, but there is plenty of space even with children running about. And there are no expectations of doing formal greetings; when I walk into the foyer, I don't have to say "hello" to each woman. We see each other and shift to give room for whoever is leaving to get to the door, but we don't have to interact.

Thus, it's a space that is used only for a few moments of time several times during the day but is necessary given common Dhofar behaviors. A large foyer is not needed because there are usually more than five small children living in one house, but because children love to run together to the door when someone knocks (or are sent to see who it is) and often stand near the door to look at a person arriving or leaving.

As children like to move in groups, they might all gather in the entrance way when school-age children are leaving. Mini-vans/buses come into or next to the *hosh* as children don't usually walk to and wait at a bus stop since it is often very hot. With a large foyer, there is space for the mom, the children who are going to school and young children to all wait inside where it is cool. Or the space can be used by a group of sisters waiting for a car to take them shopping or visiting relatives so they don't have to stand outside the house in view of the neighborhood.

In some large, recently built houses, there is no hallway but a circular, open area with a *salle* through a wide open archway, the door to the *majlis*, the door to the kitchen and the steps leading to upper floors. This space is sometimes big enough for chairs/a sofa and is used as a play area for children, a pass-through/staging area and an intermediate/indeterminate location. For example, a strange man would come to the *majlis* through the outside door, but a new bride's brother who wants to visit might not want to ask her to come to the *majlis* (where there are other men) and might not be comfortable in the *salle* (where there are women he doesn't know and is not related to) but could stand with her in this open space to chat.

Salle

The *salle* is always at the front of the house, close to the front door but usually not visible to people standing at the door. The room has three sides, often with windows to the front and side of the house, the side to the front hallway completely open, with a blank back wall. Like the *majlis*, it is usually decorated with sofas or cushions on a low wooden frame surrounding the sides of the room, a few coffee tables, a TV and decorative elements such as vases. The color scheme is always different than the *majlis* and not always in keeping with stereotypical Western ideas of male/female colors, for example the *majlis* might be decorated in pale peach, with a dark brown *salle*. The bathroom area might be attached to the *salle* or further down the main hallway of the house.

Although the norm in Dhofar is for a house to have one *majlis* and one *salle*, some larger houses have a series of rooms, i.e. a formal *salle* at the front of the house and then a (usually less formal) *salle* further inside, sometimes also a few sofas are placed upstairs in an open area at the head of the stairs (out of sight of the front door) for only family members.

Many Omani families in Dhofar eat while sitting on the floor of the *salle* or *majlis*. When the food is ready and the person in charge of the meal has decided it is time to eat, instructions are given to lay the "table" (light plastic drop cloth that comes in a roll) and people will clear the area. Those who are eating gather in a circle around platters of food which are usually placed on the floor, with women bringing small children next to them to hand feed. Usually four to six people share one round platter, depending on its size. If there are guests, the men will eat in the *majlis*; sometimes guests are put in the *majlis* alone, so they can "feel free" to eat as much as they want. Although a separate dining room is rare, sometimes a dining table is set in the *salle*, *majlis* or, if there is space, in the hall.

A *salle* can be a place for siblings to watch horror movies at 1 am, somber when the house is in mourning and women come to pay condolence visits, joyful for a graduation celebration, intimate when sisters come to visit and share all the family news, loud when the children are playing and welcoming for neighbors and guests. Whereas, for example, an American family might gather in the kitchen for a meal, on the porch to chat with neighbors, in the den or basement to relax, in the living room for formal visits and in bedrooms for children to play with friends, the *salle* is the center of a Dhofari house.

Kitchen/dining room

The kitchen is located to the side or back of the house; in newer houses, it has its own entrance used by expat workers who don't live in the house, people bringing in supplies such as bags of groceries and/or jugs of water for water dispensers and family members if there is parking near that entrance.

Like bathrooms, kitchens have tiled walls and floors, with a floor drain. There are fluorescent tube lights, a ceiling fan and an extractor fan, but usually not AC. If there is a window (most often over the sink), it has opaque glass.

Often there are long, high counters along one or two walls, with shelving underneath and cupboards above.[14] The below-counter cupboards, as well as the stove, fridge and washing machine, are set slightly above floor level on platforms so that the floor can be cleaned by mopping/sluicing.[15] Usually the gas canisters for the stoves are located outside the house, next to the kitchen door, with a small hole drilled in the cement wall to bring the gas pipe to the stove/oven.

As it is common to have 20 or more people (from different generations) in one house, kitchens are big enough to make large meals. Like most rooms, everything is placed around the sides of the room. Sometimes there is a table, but often you can find an empty area in the middle of the room that is five feet square or larger. This is so a lot of women can work together for parties and also because some cooking is done on the floor. For example, large pots of meat are sometimes cooked on gas rings set on the floor because it is easier to stir from a standing position than trying to reach into a pot set on the stovetop. Some kinds of bread are cooked using small gas burners set on the floor.

Kitchens are utilitarian; pretty trays might be leaned against the backsplash or there might be a vase to hold wooden spoons etc., but kitchens are seldom decorated or set up as welcoming/comforting spaces in which to sit and relax.

As soon as you walk in, it's easy to visually orient yourself; often, the cupboards have glass fronts so you can see inside them. Most families will have items for hosting in sight and easy to reach: several sets of teacups and saucers, tea and coffee pots, carafes, glass bowls or plates. There are usually several trays as almost all food, drinks and eating utensils, plates, cups etc. are moved on trays, not carried by hand.

Clean-up is done while cooking or as soon as the meal is finished. Dirty dishes and food are never left sitting on the counter for long. All dishes are cleaned and put away, the countertop wiped down and the floor swept; the garbage bin is usually covered and if mostly full might be put outside on the steps up to the kitchen. Thus, most of the time, the kitchen is empty and very clean. Dhofaris only go into the kitchen to supervise or cook before meals or to prepare dishes ahead of time for Ramadan/*Eids* and to clean up afterward.

Larger and newer houses may have small suites for each married son. This will usually consist of a bedroom with an attached bathroom and a sitting room which might have a galley kitchen with a small sink and microwave so they can make tea and simple meals for themselves. Thus there will be one large kitchen for the house, with perhaps a few smaller kitchens for couples.

Bedrooms

If the house has one floor, bedrooms are at the back of the house, usually behind the kitchen. In a two- or three-story house there are usually one or two bedrooms on the ground floor for an older or senior relative with the rest of the bedrooms on the upper floors.

There is usually a bed with matching nightstands and large wardrobes, as well as a sofa or padded chairs and coffee table. Sometimes there is a desk and chair if the inhabitant is school age. I have never seen a built-in closet. Everything is stored on or in shelving units or cupboards.

In addition to the overhead, usually fluorescent, lights, bedrooms often have wall lights, usually with a low-watt or colored bulb so, if the room is shared, one person can move around and/or parents can look in on children without waking anyone. There is always a fan and AC.

As many Dhofari houses have over 30 people living in them, room ownership changes over time. Children sleep in their parent's room/bed for the first few years and then into their own room or a shared room, with same-sex siblings or cousins of a similar age. Sometimes a child will move into their own room when they are in their late teens if there is enough space. Usually when a man gets married, with the help of the entire family he will make a room for himself and his bride, either completely redecorating his room, moving him to a new room or building a new room, for example on the roof.

Thus it is very common for the upper stories to have a series of suites, meaning a door on the main corridor which leads to a small space with three or four doors: two rooms and a bathroom, perhaps a storage room. This configuration can be easily changed as needed. For example it could be used as a bedroom and a sitting room for a newly married couple or single older relative; a bedroom and a study/playroom for several children; two bedrooms with a variety of configurations such as younger children in one room, one older child in the other; the married couple in one room, children in the other etc. If the second room is used as a sitting room, there is often a small kitchen area.

If a man has more than one wife in the same house, each suite will be considered as belonging to the wife and the husband will move between the suites. If his second wife is in another house, he will move between houses. In Islam, a man should spend equal time with each wife; in practice, this does not always happen. In old age or in times of sickness, he might sleep alone in what was a room for guests.

Especially in a house where a man lives with co-wives, a mother's bedroom is the focal point for her children. Her personal sitting room is an important private space as the *salle* near the front door would be used by female neighbors, relatives of the husband and of all the wives. If she is widowed or divorced, daughters or grand-children might sleep in her bed.

Sometimes a Dhofari woman will stay in her parent's house and her husband will move in with her. This doesn't happen often; usually, it occurs when the husband works close to his wife's family house if she is the only daughter or her mother has no sons living with her. He will pay for the room to be redone and may or may not contribute to the household expenses.

Whether a married woman will have a bedroom in her family's house will depend on several factors. One is the size of the house. Sometimes a bedroom is set aside for married daughters and their children. Another is the husband's degree of closeness to the wife's family, i.e. if he is a cousin or in the same tribe it is more usual for him to be able to stay in the house. Other considerations are how conservative the family is and where her bedroom is located. For example, if her bedroom is next to the bedroom of unmarried sisters, it can be seen as impolite for him to stay.[16] For one family I know, the sons-in-law might visit but never spend the night. In another family, sons-in-law sleep in the *majlis* and in a third family, the married daughter has her own bedroom where her husband stays with her for short visits.[17]

Bathrooms

For some houses built in the mountains in the 1980s and before, the bathroom can be a small, separate building. In this case it is a low ceilinged, tiled space with a toilet, sink, shower and washing machine.

Since the 1980s, they are a room within the house, usually rectangular and built with the narrow end on an outside wall or light well to allow for the window and extractor fan.[18] They usually have tiled walls and floors with an open design (e.g. no interior walls such as a low partition to screen the toilet), a pedestal sink or sink on a counter with empty space beneath and a shelving unit next to the wall. The sink is always closest to the door.

The shower area usually does not have a curtain and is marked off with a slightly lowered floor with a drain. Some have tiled steps along one side. Bathtubs are rare; if there is one, it usually has a seat. The steps and seat are for the ritual washing before prayers during which the face, hands and feet must be cleaned.

The entrance, with or without a door, to a guest bathroom that is attached to or near the *majlis* and *salle* often opens to a space with one or more sinks, then there is an inner door which leads to a small room with a toilet, shower and sink so that guests might wash their hands while the toilet/shower room is in use. Their rooms are usually nicely appointed with fancy faucets and attractive tiles.

Bathrooms in the family/private area of the house are usually more plainly decorated and are built open plan for one person to use at a time unless it is a parent helping a small child. Some North American bathrooms are set up with the toilet half-hidden behind a low wall and shower curtains so that two people might use the room at the same time, but I have not heard of that in Dhofar.

For unmarried inhabitants, if there is not a bathroom attached to the bedroom, there is one nearby.

Some bathrooms don't have electricity outlets as men either shave with a razor or go to a barber for a shave. Women often arrange their hair and put on make-up at a vanity table in their bedroom. There is no sense of a bathroom being a space one should linger in; even if the room has been recently cleaned with bleach, it is perceived as a tainted place. One goes in to remove impurities from one's body, then quickly leave.

"Store"

Sometimes there is a small, usually windowless room called the "store." Its door can be inside the kitchen or near the kitchen and it is usually locked to keep children from taking things. It is often lined with shelves and holds sacks of rice, flats of drinks and other large commodities; it can also have a deep freeze or second refrigerator.

Another type of store can be found on one of the upper levels. This would also be locked to stop children from playing in it and could hold extra furniture and bedding such as blankets, portable foam mattresses, camping equipment etc. Within the small suite for a married couple, there might be a store in which the children's clothes and desks for homework are kept so that the children's rooms would just have beds and perhaps a TV and seating.

Servant's room

There is sometimes a small bedroom with a tiny adjacent bathroom for live-in female help either directly off or next to the kitchen. In houses built for expats, the maid's room often has its own entrance as there can be a cultural understanding that both the maid and the family should have their own privacy. For Dhofari-built houses, the maid's room is always integrated within the house. It would be unthinkable for a male worker to live in the house. Sometimes a detached *majlis* will have a small bedroom for a male servant.

Roofs

All houses have flat roofs in Salalah; outside of town there are some older houses with pitched roofs, but that is rare. There is always an internal staircase leading up to the roof which creates certain "rules" about house architecture and space use.

First, because the floors, ceilings, roof and steps are from poured cement and there needs to be space for the support poles, staircases are never built straight and narrow between two walls, thus it is easy to get large pieces of furniture to the upper stories. Even the back set of stairs (in large houses) is wide with an open area at the bottom. Further, because there is always open space on at least one side of the main staircase, there are always banisters (handrails supported by balusters).

Second, there is always empty space under the stairs which can be used for storage or decorated with a piece of furniture. Third, there is always a landing at the top of the stairs which is usually used as a storage space. This landing space can look like, from the outside, a small, four-sided "hat" or cupola. Often the cupola has clear- or stained-glass windows on several or all sides which, depending on the house design, brings light into the main hallway below.

The roof of the upper landing is accessed by a ladder and often holds satellite dishes and a round, white plastic water tank. Water comes from the municipal supply or a well and comes into the house using gravity, although some houses have a small pump to increase the force of water up into the tank.

When cement block houses started to be built, rooflines often looked like battlements with the edge wall as a parapet with crenelations[19], sometimes fashioned to look like the distinctive local style of incense burners (*majmar*; see Yapicioglu and Cazacova 2018). Now there are many choices including closely spaced decorated balusters, glass inserts, metal railings etc.

Roofs are not seen as part of the living space although there might be a metal or poured cement roofed area for women and children to sit outside, instead of sitting on the front steps. If there is not enough room in the *hosh*, there might be a clothesline (as clothes dryers are rare) and miscellaneous objects which wouldn't be damaged by being outside, such as leftover tiles. Sometimes there is a laundry room, an extra room for the maid and/or a small room for storage, either free-standing or sharing a wall with the small room at the top of the stairs.

A roof can be finished, meaning that the home owner does not mean to build another story, or unfinished, meaning that, although the roof might be tiled and/or have decorations such as crenelations, the owner plans to build an additional story. If more stories are planned, the roof will have short, rectangular poured cement pillars which cover reinforcing bars, aka rebar. When an upper story is added, the tiles, decorations and tops of the short pillars are broken.

By law, all roofs have some sort of wall around the edge for safety. The most common type is plastered cement blocks up to waist height. Sometimes there is no discernible difference between the wall of the highest floor and the roof wall, e.g. there is a smooth facade from the ground to the top of the roof wall, which often has a cornice with a dentil pattern. Sometimes there is a clear division in that the roof wall protrudes slightly and is painted/decorated. Some newer houses have a flat roof that is smaller than the footprint, a wall at the edge and then a slope of three to five courses of clay tile which meet the wall of the upper story. Most roofs have a series of lights, often looking like small lanterns, placed at intervals along the roof wall.

Often owners will drill holes at the bottom of the wall to allow rain to run off after the infrequent, but heavy rainstorms. Sometimes there are several drain pipes which are angled away from the house's foundation. One neighbor did not drill holes in his roof wall, and after hurricane Mekunu (2018) hit, his roof looked like a swimming pool for over a week.[20]

Apartments

Types of apartments

I would like to informally divide apartment buildings into two types: "public" meaning available to be rented to any person (usually expat or non-Dhofari Omani) and "family," meaning built to be given or rented to only people who the owner knows (usually family or tribe members) or someone vouched for by a close friend or relative.

This difference is sometimes, but not always, by location, as some sections of land in Salalah are occupied by inter-related families within one tribe while others, especially newly built areas, have a mix.

In general, "public" buildings have several floors and an on-site manager who has a small office and/or lives in a small apartment near the front door and is responsible for upkeep, fixing problems and keeping an eye on the building. The building will have stairwells or elevators which are used by all the residents. The person who owns a "public" apartment building will advertise widely, for example hanging a "for rent" sign, taking photos and putting them on social media and/or registering the apartment with rental companies.

"Family apartment" buildings are usually smaller, either two or three floors. For example, a two-story building with four flats in which two flats (ground floor and first floor) are accessed through one gate and the other two flats (ground floor and first floor) are accessed through a second gate, with a cement block wall dividing the *hosh* into two spaces. Thus only one family would use the stairs to the upper level. The apartments can also be connected to a house (see below).

When the apartments are ready, the owner will not advertise in any way but fill the apartments by word of mouth among friends and relatives. There would never be an on-site manager for a family-only building as no one would want someone watching who comes and goes and when.

Apartments attached to houses

For the past 50 years or so, a "house" meant a cement block-built living space for a father, mother, unmarried sons and daughters, married sons and their families, older relatives and temporary guests, for example a married daughter whose husband is out of town for work. Sometimes the house would be built to two or three floors, or one floor was built, then upper floors added when more space was needed.

From the 1990s until recently, sometimes the *majlis* was rented out in *khareef*, the monsoon season from the end of June until the end of August. The owner would give the space to family living in other parts of Oman or rent it by letting friends and relatives know the space was available.

Sometimes there was the opposite use of space, in which a house was rented out, but the *majlis* was kept for the owner. For example, if the owner worked in Salalah but lived in the mountains, the owner would be able to use the *majlis* as a place to nap/relax and occasionally sleep in and rarely see/interact with renters who lived in the house.

Another division I have seen (only once) was for the owner to put a new interior wall and a wall in the *hosh* (courtyard) and then broke an exterior wall to make a door, thus lengthwise dividing a one-story house into two apartments: one with the *majlis* and *salle* (women's sitting room) at the front of the house and the other with the kitchen and two bedrooms at the rear. The renters of the back half of the house had a narrow driveway to reach the kitchen door.

A newer (within the last ten years) trend is that some home owners find it easier to take (no-interest) loans from the bank or family/friends and build a large (three-story) house with a few small, separate apartments which are entered through a second door. The flats are then rented out to help repay the loan and/or given to older relatives, married sons or relatives in need, for example a young nephew who is attending college in Salalah.

To do this, the land must have street access on two sides, usually a main road to the front and an alley to one side. The house is designed with a front gate opening to the main road and a smaller gate on the side (which would normally lead to the kitchen) leading to a door which opens to a small landing with one or two small apartments. If it is not possible to have access on two sides, the apartment doors are along one side of the house and there might be a wall dividing the *hosh*.

Thus the family lives in the main house, sharing a wall (but not entrance) with several small apartments so that the family has privacy.

Example of an apartment

The owner's (X) family lives in a three-story house which is accessible through a gate facing the main road. The apartment is on the south side, facing an unpaved alley, and is entered through a side gate which leads to a small paved area and steps up to the entry door. On the ground floor landing, there are two doors (with metal numbers attached so food delivery workers know which doorbell to ring) and then steps up to the upper floors. On the ground floor, one apartment belongs to my informant (Y, who is a member of X's extended family) and the other is for a relative of X who only uses it during the *khareef* (summer monsoon) months. On the first floor are two apartments: one is used by X as a retreat; the other is for X's brother. The top floor has one apartment rented by a relative of X, who is also related to Y. Thus everyone is connected.

When you open Y's door, there is an L-shaped sectional sofa along the left wall and straight ahead with a coffee table in front of it. At the end of the sofa is an archway leading into a hallway off of which are the family/private areas. To the right of the archway is a door leading to the *salle* and to the far right is the public bathroom.

As explained above, houses have two front doors, one leading to the *majlis* and the other that leads into the main hallway and *salle*. Some apartments are set up like this, but in an apartment with one door, the *majlis* area is directly in front of the door, with the *salle* further inside the apartment, off of a hallway that can be blocked with a curtain.

In this apartment, guests are placed on the longer part of the sofa (under the AC, facing the front door) so that if women were in the *salle*, they could get up and move to the kitchen and bedrooms without being seen. Or women can simply stay in the *salle* and close the door.

Standing under the arch, looking down the hallway, the kitchen door is to the left, and then there is a hallway door so that the two bedrooms (each with its own bathroom) can be completely shut off from the front of the apartment. Thus a man can entertain male friends in the *majlis* area, with access to a bathroom and the kitchen without disturbing other inhabitants. And women, children and other men can also access the kitchen without disturbing guests.

Notes

1 Even if the neighbor has built a wall, usually home owners build their own rather than use the extra 20 centimeters of yard space. The walls are so close together that it would be impossible to take one down without damaging/destroying the other.

2 This water-giving is *sudaka*, a voluntary charity given to people who are in need, including poorer members of one's extended family and neighbors. *Sudaka* produces *hasanat*, an undetermined/undeterminable religious benefit that accrues to the giver.

3 Some houses built in the 1980s and 1990s are slightly smaller than then-built-up, poured foundation so that there is a concrete shelf, about 30 centimeters wide, around the house, and then the drop-off of the foundation wall. I have not seen this in newer houses in which the house wall is seamlessly connected to the concrete base.

4 One should never crowd the door. Every visitor, even if well known, should step back off the welcome mat. I once answered the doorbell to find a Dhofari

neighbor who had stepped back down several steps from the landing. He then gripped the stair rail with his left hand and leaned forward, offering a bag of dates with his right hand. I stepped out of the doorway and took the dates, greeting and thanking him.

5 Not loose sand but very compacted sand and gravel. I can't even call it "top soil" as the gardens I have had were impossible to dig in by hand with a trowel.

6 Al Hinai, Batty and Probert write in 1993, "The air conditioning of buildings accounts for at least 70% of the national annual electricity consumption" (236).

7 It's not always clear where the wires are located, so one has to always be careful about drilling to hang pictures.

8 According to Khan, Al-Saadi, Benkari and Al-Hashim,

> relatively low-temperature thermostat setting, alongside other factors, has increased energy consumption in Oman by fifteen times during the thirty years from 1980-2010. Around 77% of this energy goes to the building sector, with 48-55% used in the housing sector, and 80% of this share is dedicated to running air conditioning systems ... In order to bring these very high values to more reasonable and sustainable levels, there is a need to focus on reducing the use of air conditioning in houses to reduce energy consumption, especially with the prediction that energy consumption will increase in the coming years.
>
> (2022 92)

9 See Cazacova and Yapicioglu's "Fertile Crescent Defensive Cities Architectural Features Influenced by the Land of Incense Culture" (2014) and Yapicioglu and Cazacova's "Culture Embedded in City's Architecture; Incense Burning Custom and Its Effects on Modern Buildings' Features of Salalah, Oman" (2016), as well as Al Gandel and Finn (2017 49-53).

10 Even large stores use frankincense. I am not sure how they manage, but a few times I have arrived just as a large hypermarket opened to find wisps of smoke drifting through the aisles; perhaps they disable the alarms for a few moments.

11 More common: flat arch /French arch, nested, ogee, "oriental," lancet, segmental, trefoil (Gothic), Tudor. Some have a flat lintel with a relieving arch; in brick houses, this pattern is created by bricks angled on the vertical, but in Dhofari houses, the arch pattern is created by plaster or tile work, unrelated to structural support. Occasionally used: onion, Venetian. Less common: art nouveau (non-symmetrical), draped, horseshoe (Syrian), inflexed, keyhole, parabolic. In general, window and door arches do not curve inward, nor are the sides narrower than the maximum span (width of the arch), i.e. the arch usually connects to the sides seamlessly, without a large differential of size.

12 *Salle* is pronounced "sall-la," not as the French, "sall."

13 There is a difference between houses in towns and in the countryside, as rural houses usually have a *dekka* (seating area in the front or side of the house) which means you are on display as soon as you leave the car.

14 I live in a Dhofari-designed apartment which does not have overhead shelving, but there are 22 feet of counter-space: 9′2″ on the north side and 12′10″ on the south side.

15 The preferred place for a washing machine is in its own room (near the kitchen or on the roof), but not all houses have that much space so it is usually in the kitchen or a bathroom. They are usually top loading and made of plastic so they are easy to move around. Dryers aren't used.

16 In the same way, an adult male *hakli* might be invited to sleep in a guest bedroom or his male cousin's bedroom but instead sleep in the *majlis*, as he would not want to walk around the upper stories of the house, near his female cousin's bedrooms.

17 I discuss this issue in detail in Chapter 2.
18 Bathrooms are almost always "dead-end." I have seen only one example of a "pass-through" bathroom with two entrances in a house built before 2000.
19 This feature can help cool the house. In discussing a house in the northern Al Batinah region, Khan, Al-Saadi, Benkari and Al-Hashim state

> Another feature of this building is the design of the roof's parapet wall. In the house, many slit openings were used and were located just above the roof to increase the airflow near the upper surface of the roof. This is important because the roof is usually hotter than the rest of the building and the ambient air due to solar radiation. This extra flow of air can cool it back to a slightly higher temperature than the ambient temperature.
>
> (2022 97)

20 The day after the storm, I told my landlord who called the neighbor, but he did not come and fix the problem, perhaps because he would have needed to climb up a ladder carrying a pump. Opening the roof door would have meant all that water coursing into the house. As the water evaporated slowly, I could see the damp seeping into the cement blocks, eventually reaching halfway down the side of the house. I wonder how the neighbor's roof door was so watertight, but I don't know him well enough to ask if I can prowl around his house.

References

For photos and a full bibliography, please see: *Come From Away*, https://mariellerisse.com

Al Gandel, Thamna and Ibrahim Bryan Finn. 2017. *Learn About Dhofar from 530 Questions and Answers*. Muscat: Dar al Wraq.

Al Hinai, H., W.J. Batty and S.D. Probert. 1993. "Vernacular Architecture of Oman: Features that Enhance Thermal Comfort Achieved within Buildings." *Applied Energy* 44.3: 233–244. https://doi.org/10.1016/0306-2619(93)90019-L

Al Thahab, Ali, Sabah Mushatat and Mohammed Abdelmonem. 2014. "Between Tradition and Modernity: Determining Spatial Systems of Privacy in the Domestic Architecture of Contemporary Iraq." *ArchNet - International Journal of Architectural Research* 8.3: 238–50.

Cazacova, Liudmila and Balkiz Yapicioglu. 2014. "Fertile Crescent Defensive Cities Architectural Features Influenced by the Land of Incense Culture," in *Proceedings of the CAUMME II International Symposium: Architectural and Urban, Architectural and Urban Research, Education, and Practice in the Era of Post-Professionalism*. Girne, North Cyprus: Girne American University. 322–46.

Khan, Hayder, Saleh Al-Saadi, Naima Benkari and Aliya Al-Hashim. (2022). "Numerical Simulation of Ventilation Potential in Traditional Omani House: Bait Al Khandaq as an Example." *The Journal of Engineering Research* 18.2: 91–100.

Yapicioglu, Balkiz and Liudmila Cazacova. 2018. "'Omani Burqa' vs. Decorated Facade of Modern Omani House: The Case of Salalah, Dhofar Region, Oman." *The Academic Research Community Publication*. 101–11. ISSN online: 2537–0162.

———. 2016. "Culture Embedded in City's Architecture; Incense Burning Custom and Its Effects on Modern Buildings' Features of Salalah, Oman," in Proceedings of the 5th International Conference on Sustainable Tourism and Cultural Heritage. Istanbul, Turkey.

5 Cultural understandings of houses

A day in the life of a house

This is an approximation of daily space usage which, of course, varies between houses. For example, older relatives might sit in the *salle/majlis* for the entire day or a new bride might spend almost all her time in her room until she adjusts to the new household. This section explains for readers who are not Muslim and/or have not been to the Middle East how the five daily prayers impact who is in which room at which time.

A *hakli* house wakes up at *fajr*, the first prayer which takes place just at dawn. If locked overnight, doors are unlocked. In small towns, the front door, the door from the kitchen to outside the house and the door between the *majlis* and the rest of the house might be locked or not; in Salalah, these doors often are.[1]

Men might walk to a neighborhood mosque or the men of the house might pray together.[2] After this, men might sit in the *majlis* or *salle* to drink tea and then watch the news or talk to family members or might return to their rooms to talk to their wives and children. In the mountains, whoever is responsible will leave the house to check on livestock.

Either an expat worker or one of the women in the house will make tea and/or coffee and set it out in the *salle* and *majlis* with bread, fruits or snacks. If there are school-age children, they will be woken up and fed breakfast. On work days, by 6:30, 7 or 7:30 am everyone who works or is going to school is getting ready to leave.

In the mountains, the house is now awake and ready for visitors; in towns, after those who work and go to school have left, older inhabitants might stay awake in their rooms or relax in the *salle/majlis*, but some might go back to sleep for a few hours. Around 10 or 11 am in town, visits are welcome, phones are ringing, small children are playing and lunch is discussed/being prepared for. On weekends and holidays, usually everyone sleeps late and there is usually no visiting in the morning.

The mid-day, *dhuhr*, prayer is usually done at work/school. Around 1 pm, people who have been out of the house start to return as lunch is the main meal of the day and usually eaten with all the members of the

DOI: 10.4324/9781003270317-5

household. Unless invited for lunch, guests should leave. Lunch, usually rice with meat or fish, is normally eaten together in the *salle*, but if there are male visitors or if the family is more conservative, men will eat in the *majlis* and women in the *salle*. After lunch, women or expat will help clean up and everyone retires to their room.

Around 3 or 3:30 pm, houses are again open as people get in for the *'asr* prayer which falls in Dhofar between 3:30 and 4:30 pm depending on the time of year. After the prayer boys and men might go to play football or sit in the *salle* or *majlis* talking to the other people in the house, sending messages to friends or watching TV.

Girls stay closer to the house but can also play football in the courtyard or on the street near their house. Girls who are approaching puberty and/or have started to cover their hair (usually around the time they get their period, but it can be earlier or later depending on the family) stay in their room to study or text with friends/cousins, sit in the *salle* or on the front steps with the mom and female relatives or visit relatives. Women who live near roads with adjacent brick walking paths can go singly or in groups for a walk.

By the sunset prayer (*mughrab*), everyone is back in the house. Men will usually go to the mosque for this prayer and then return home to discuss plans for the night, e.g. men might drop women at a relatives' house for the evening. The last prayer is at 7–8 pm, after which dinner plans are usually made/dinner is eaten.

By ten or so, most movements (shopping/errands/eating) have stopped and most men go to hang out with their male friends; in towns, they go to cafes, along the coast they go to the beach and in the mountains they may hang out on the *dekka* (front porch) of one person's house or a scenic place.

The time the house "closes" varies from family to family, usually around midnight or 1 am in towns, earlier in the mountains where people follow "farm hours," up at *fajr* and in bed soon after the last prayer. Depending on the house, the *bab* in the wall might be closed (usually not locked). Between when the household usually sleeps and *fajr*, visits and phone calls should only be for emergencies.

Thus a *salle* /*majlis* is usually empty from late at night until dawn, then often not used again until 10 or 11 am, just for family over the lunchtime, empty again until around 3 pm and then in use frequently until late at night. A kitchen is only occupied during meal preparation and clean-up. Bedrooms are in use from late at night until dawn, or after, and again during mid-day. Times for social visits, dropping off goods and repair work are late mornings, mid-afternoons and after sunset. It is normal for me to call my Dhofari landlord at 11 pm to discuss an issue with my house, but I would never call him at 2 pm.

Who controls the house and what does "control" mean?

Control of a house, in terms of who has the power to fulfill their choices, is multi-directional. To use a term from political science, there are several veto players who can accept or reject various decisions such as when and where the house is built, how long it takes to build, how and when the rooms are decorated etc.

The Omani government has control at the start of the process as blueprints must be approved before building can start, and every building site must have a specific type of sign with the building permit number and the owner's name. Inspectors come at various stages, for example to check the chalk outline before the foundation is dug, as well as the electricity wiring and water pipes. I have never heard complaints about these examinations as owners know they are done for safety.

The building crew has some control as the speed with which the house is built depends on their work and their ability to follow the blueprints. The usual work day is 7 or 8 am until 4 or 5 pm with a few short breaks and a long (usually one hour) lunch break/nap time. There are often criticisms about the work crews, but it's hard to differentiate between valid complaints, cultural differences and unrealistic expectations.

It might be thought that the land/building owner has complete control, but *haklis*, and most Dhofaris, live within family- and community-oriented tribal structures so that the actions of one person are of interest and can be commented on/influenced by many.

A person might want to build, but the family intervenes by suggesting that the money saved go towards a sibling's wedding or university fees, medical expenses for an older relative etc. Conversely, a person may not want to build but is given money and encouragement by siblings or parents. Once the decision is made, many people will want to see and comment on the blueprints.

If a man announces he will build, friends and family will give money unasked for or loan money and offer advice in terms of who to hire as manager, which building supply company to use, where to hire the heavy equipment etc.

Women are not usually involved in the nuts and bolts of house building (such as renting cement mixers), but mothers, sisters, wives, and daughters are apprised of every step, look at the blueprints, visit the house when it is being built and may help fund it either directly by giving cash from their salary or selling jewelry or indirectly by buying furnishings with their own money. If it is a house on her land, a woman might be more involved but still leave the building details to her husband or a son.

Once finished, a house is referred to by the name of the oldest man[3], but women are not passive inhabitants. Unmarried girls in their late-teens and early twenties have the least control, but as they grow older, get married and/or work, they have the power to influence the home, for example a woman might entirely re-decorate her mother's or sister's room as a gift. She might support her husband if he decides to help build a home for a relative, pressure him to build for their nuclear family and/or hire or not hire live-in help.

The eldest man (the father or oldest brother) is nominally in control of certain aspects; for example, he might be in charge of the Wi-Fi password and locking the door between the *majlis* and the house at a certain time so that sons who are not home by that time will sleep in the *majlis* and not in their rooms. But this can be subverted by other members who unlock the door or open a window.[4]

In terms of the daily running of the house, there are several people making different types of decisions. Perhaps the senior man is incapacitated by illness or the oldest brother is living in another town or often away for work, a younger brother might then take on paying bills. Or a sister will take the responsibility for preparing for her brother's wedding or redecorating for *Eid*. A senior woman in consultation with other women and men will decide what parties to have and who to invite to the house. As children grow up, the parents and other adults will figure out who will sleep in which bedroom.

Except for rare cases, usually older people in the mountains, a man or a woman will never live in a house alone, and even in those cases, many people will be involved in the running of that house. Neighbors, children and grand-children will stop by to bring supplies, do upkeep, help prepare for storms and to check on the health of the person.

Significantly, people in a house do not have control over who comes. Among *hakli* families, any man or woman who comes to the door should be invited in and given tea/refreshments. It is normal for family and neighbors to drop by uninvited and whatever plans family members had must be put on hold to host the guest, never betraying tiredness or a desire for the guest to leave.

I think it is partially because of this lack of control over space that Dhofaris rent weekend houses. It might seem odd from an American point of view for a family to rent a house close (5–25 miles) from their house. But, for example, a group of sisters who are married might find it difficult to all stay together in one place. To return to their parents' house *en masse* might overwhelm it as large families are the norm and between five sisters there might be 30 children. Further, if sitting in the *salle*, their conversation would be interrupted by any neighbor or relative who arrived. In a rental house, there is space for everyone and no chance of being disturbed.

Movement within houses

Upper-class, English, Victorian-era homes had a set of rooms for children which would include a day nursery, night nursery, schoolroom, bathroom and the nanny's room. In present-day America, a middle-class child might play on the kitchen floor while a parent is cooking, do homework on the dining room table, play in a basement rec room, watch TV in the living room, i.e. sit in different rooms for different purposes during one day.

Whereas young Dhofari children spend most of their indoor time in their parent's bedroom and the *salle*. When they are close to puberty, they will move to their own bedroom or a room with several children who are the same gender and around the same age. Children are only in the *majlis* in the presence of adults and for a reason, for example an uncle is visiting or they are working with a tutor as a male teacher would not be allowed in either the *salle* or the child's bedroom.

Adult women spend their days between the *salle*, their room and the kitchen if they are responsible for cooking. If it is their family house, they might visit their mother's room to talk to her and/or a sister's room. Adult men who are awake are usually in the *majlis* or *salle* depending on the time of day and are only in the kitchen to drop off supplies.

However, while Dhofari children and adults are usually in a limited number of rooms during the day, they might sleep in various places. This is in contrast to, for example, American children who normally have bedtimes and are expected to sleep in their own beds. In some cultures, going to sleep is taken seriously with a whole series of bedtime rituals such as saying "good-night," being read to, good-night kisses, being tucked in etc. Dhofari children may not have set bedtimes or routines. For example, if a young boy was talking to his grandmother, mom, aunt or sister and fell asleep in her room, he would spend the night there as there would be no necessity of putting him in his room.

This continues when people get older. Sisters might sleep in each other's rooms, a boy might fall asleep in the *majlis*, a daughter might sleep in her mother's room and a married man might sleep on the floor of his children's room if he comes in late.[5] When I ask, "Where do your children sleep?" and "Where do you sleep?" informants list off a variety of rooms as going to sleep, even for grown-ups, does not carry the burden of following a series of procedures.

Informants explained to me that as kids they would fall asleep in brightly lit rooms with lots of adults talking, and this approach continued as they grew up. When they are tired, they sleep without having to make adjustments to their surroundings, for example, window curtains are closed at sundown not bedtime and there are minimal or no clothing adjustments necessary. Only one or two people in a household of 30 or more would have nighttime responsibilities such as turning on or off lights, locking a door/checking that a door was locked or making sure the kitchen is clean.

Movement between houses

Dhofari children spend a lot of their free time out of the house once they can walk. If younger than three or four, kids are usually in the *hosh* or in front/near house, and then within the neighborhood in mixed gender/mixed age groups until close to puberty. They also know the *salle* and *majlis* of many houses (grandparents, uncles/aunts and older siblings) but will usually not play/hang out in a cousin's bedroom, although they might sleep there if it is an overnight visit. Children sleeping over at relatives' houses is common, even among families which live close to each other. For example, when a female Dhofari friend got Covid, she didn't want anyone to know so she sent her young child to live with her parents. The child was there for over two weeks before anyone suspected there was a reason the child wasn't at home.

As children grow older, they experience the same house differently as the use of rooms is linked to both gender and age. For example, a *hakli* girl visiting her paternal uncle's house: as a baby, she might be taken into the *majlis* by her father who is holding her; as a five-year-old, she might spend the visit playing in the *hosh* with male and female cousins; as a 14-year-old, she might sit in the *salle* with her mom and older sisters. If she marries a cousin from this family, she will be expected to go into the *majlis* when there are visitors to bring tea and, perhaps, sit and visit.

Further, men experience houses differently according to what their relationship is with the house owners. A boy will spend time in the *salle* of relatives' houses when young and the *majlis* when older, but there are many variables. For example, a 25-year-old *hakli* man with three sisters (A, B and C) would have different visiting patterns depending on who owns/controls the house that the sister lives in. He visits sister A in her *salle* because A and her husband own their own home; he visits sister B in her *salle* because B married a cousin, thus the other women in the *salle* are his relatives. But he visits sister C in the *majlis* because C lives in her husband's father's home who are not relatives, so the *salle* is for C's mother- and sisters-in-laws.[6]

Families usually have WhatsApp groups to inform each other about who is where, but a man might come home to find his aunts visiting in the *salle* (or *majlis*), a married daughter staying for the night because her husband is out of town, younger children gone to stay with cousins and a repairman working in the kitchen under the supervision of a son.

There are still a few people, mainly older men with camel herds, who practice transhumance in Dhofar. Usually one of the places they live during the year is a concrete block house with nearby permanent camel pens/stables. The other places are "camps," i.e. metal-framed tents covered with tarps that they have used for decades and/or rock and timber windbreaks for the camels to bed down next to. Their pattern of movement is known to their families and other men who live in the same manner.

A second type of transhumance is families with camels bringing the herds down from the mountains in *khareef* to live on the *jarbaeb*, the flat plain to the north of Salalah or on the dry, northern side of the mountains. Camels need to be on dry, flat land in the monsoon season because their feet are smooth so they don't have any traction and can easily slip and fall on wet ground. As the camels must spend the monsoon season out of the mountains, the owners and herded live in tents in the *jarbaeb*, with relatives or in a house used only for the season.[7]

I see echoes of transhumance in *hakli* living arrangements in that who stays in which room is not stable, beyond the necessity of respecting age and gender issues, i.e. teenage girls and boys would never share a room. A relative coming to a *hakli* house would know who normally lives in the house, but not who is actually there. An older female relative might be visiting for several days, a nephew might be staying for a few days to conduct business in the area, one of the son's wives may have gone back to stay in her parent's house because her mother is sick, one of the men in the household might have gone camping with his friends for several nights, a young child might be visiting grandparents etc.

Thus *haklis* have many houses in which to stay – their own, their parents, their aunts and uncles, their grandparents and, for men, the *majlis* of friends' houses.[8] This is possible because, first, houses are set up to handle overnight guests. The sofas in the *majlis* are usually long and wide enough to sleep on, and all houses are equipped with extra blankets and foam mattresses. Second, there is a cultural understanding that a person is always dressed while sleeping. Babies will be in diapers and t-shirts; girls wear *dhobes* (loose cotton housedresses), leggings and shirts or full nightgowns and boys wear long shorts. Adult women wear *dhobes*, and men wear a *wazar* (cotton sarong).

Therefore, it's easy for a person to stay if they find themselves outside of their home at night. A boy visiting a cousin will tell his mother where he is and stay on a mattress in his cousin's room. A man drinking tea with friends might take a blanket from his car and sleep next to the fire. A married woman visiting her family's house might share a bed with her mother or a sister or sleep in a guest room. Sometimes people make much longer visits to relatives' houses; an older, male, *hakli* friend moved with wife and children back to his father's house for several years when his father was sick.

Movement between houses: marriages, divorces, births and deaths[9]

Marriages usually mean a wife moves to the husband's or husband's father's house; in some cases, he moves to hers. Second marriages can result in various housing shifts such as a man buying or renting a second accommodation for the second wife or he and the first wife reassigning rooms in the family house to make space for the second wife.

Usually a husband will take his first wife back to her parent's house before his second marriage and she often stays for a few weeks. If she is upset, sometimes she will simply continue to live there, whether or not they divorce.

Parents are closely involved in all the marriages of a son and can directly influence housing choices. In one example I know of, a young woman (X) was seen as taking care of an older relative of a man in her tribe (Y) in a somewhat extravagant manner, not in keeping with her normal demeanor. Then "suddenly" Y announced that he was going to take X as a second wife. His close female relatives were all angry, they felt that X had been putting on a persona to catch Y. Also Y's current wife (Z) was loved and respected within his family. Y's father, unhappy at the situation, insisted that Y must bring X to live in the family house and Y had no choice but to agree. Now, years later, Z continues to have the admiration of all of Y's family for staying married to Y so that her children can stay with their father and grandparents.

It is also possible for Dhofari men to take a second wife without telling their wives. Given that most men stay out of the house every evening and/or keep an apartment in Salalah if they live outside of town, this is not as difficult as it seems. He might pay for the housing or have the second wife stay in her parent's house. There is a prevailing understanding that it is wrong to talk about other people so that people who know about the second marriage might not tell the first wife. The people who do inform the first wife are usually blamed for involving themselves in a situation that has nothing to do with them.[10]

In the past, young brides stayed in their father's home for a few years after marriage so she would give birth in her family's house and stay until she had several children and could manage a household on her own. In the pre-war and war years, some men would have a wife, and possibly, children, in several settlements in the mountains and move between them.

Several informants were born in the middle of the shift from home-birth to hospital-birth with older siblings born at home while they were born in a hospital or they were born at home while younger siblings were born in a hospital. Now almost all births are in the hospital and, if there are no complications, the new mother leaves after a day or so and stays in her mother's house for several weeks if it is a first or second child. If it is the third child, the new mother might return to her own house (usually her husband's father's house), but that depends on space, her relationship with her parents and her in-laws etc.

In situations where a woman remarries after being divorced or widowed, the children may or may not move houses. In Islam, boys should stay with their mother until they are seven and girls until they reach puberty (sometimes understood as nine years old). Most Dhofari children will stay with their mother, i.e. return with their mother to her father's or a brother's house. Some men insist on the children staying with them, but this is rare and seen as "not good" unless the divorce is because of the wife's immoral behavior.

If a woman is widowed or divorced then remarries into another tribe, there will be various negotiations as it is felt that teenage daughters should not be living in a "strangers' house," so they might stay in their father's or grandfather's house and occasionally visit their remarried mother. The father's family and tribe will be less involved in housing decisions after a divorce, but if a woman is widowed they will, in the name of the husband, make sure the children are raised in their specific tribal customs and traditions.

As people age, housing choices can become more flexible. Older couples will often not sleep in the same room and sometimes the husband will live in the mountains and come to a town rarely. The parents of one Dhofari friend are divorced, but when the ex-husband comes to Salalah, he stays with his ex-wife and their children, sleeping in the *majlis*. Once a woman goes through menopause, this situation is accepted and, if mentioned at all, the ex-wife is praised for her positive behavior.

There are no hospice services in Dhofar. I would not say it is "usual" to die at home, but I have heard of many cases of a sick person asking to be released from the hospital to die at home. This wish is sometimes countered by family members who insist on doctors performing treatments, even if the doctor argues that further intervention is useless. This can lead to various problems as a doctor saying "this person will die" can be understood by family members as the doctor is not trying/doesn't care/has given up and the family becomes more strident in asking for interventions. From the doctor's point of view, a realistic assessment should help the patient and family prepare, but stating a negative is sometimes interpreted as a wish. Families given a fatal diagnosis may insist on taking the family member by plane to another country at great expense.

I know of cases in which the doctor picked one family member, or a family member asked directly, and this family member lied to everyone else, checked the patient out of the hospital and the patient died at home, having believed that the release from hospital was because of a positive prognosis.

According to Islam, a person should be buried before nightfall on the day they die, which means when a person dies, there are immediate changes. Women will take off jewelry, make-up and bright dresses and start to prepare to greet mourners. Female visitors will sit in the *salle*; men will come either to the *majlis* or to a large tent erected near the house. Usually animals are slaughtered to feed the guests; the work of taking care of guests should be done by those close to the deceased, but not the most affected, i.e. a wife should be comforted and not expected to serve drinks or check that guests have enough to eat (more details about a house in mourning are below).

Usually, only the death of a husband will cause a change in residence. In Islam, a widow should live in seclusion for four months and ten days; if she is young and does not have children, she might spend the mourning period in her family home then continue to live there. If she has children, she might continue to live in her father-in-law's house, return to her parent's or go to a brother's house depending on the age of her children and her relationship with her in-laws.

If she stays in her father-in-law's house, it will usually be only until one of her sons builds his own house and then she will then live with him. If she and her husband had their own house, she will stay there if she and/or a son can take responsibility for the house, i.e. can drive, bring food and make repairs.

If the person who died had their own room, it is usually left "as is" for a short period of several days to a few weeks. Friends have spoken with shock over people who have cleaned out the deceased's room the next day; even if there is pressure for space within the house, informants have told me that, out of respect, the family should not move quickly to erase all traces. On the opposite side of the issue, I have heard of a person who did not allow a family member's room to be changed for years. After the body was taken for burial, the door was locked and no one could enter.

Movement between houses: non-residents

I want to briefly discuss who might visit a house beyond the usual reasons of visiting/friendship. One main reason is the circulation of prepared food and foodstuffs. In *Foodways in Southern Oman* (Risse 2021), I explain how relatives, friends and neighbors often drop off items including cakes, fruits such as limes, fresh fish and meat, vegetables such as sweet potatoes, honey, *samn* (clarified butter, called "oil" in English) and fresh camel, cow or goat milk.

Hired workers might come to cook, clean inside the house, sweep the *hosh* and/or clean cars. Workers from nearby shops come to pick up rugs, curtains and/or bedclothes to be cleaned and then return them. If the family has bubblers (water dispensers), the company might send out someone weekly to take empty water jugs and bring full ones. By using "pins," an electronic signal of where the house is located, workers might be called to bring gas canisters or deliver food from restaurants. Sometimes expat men will bike around residential neighborhoods ringing a bell, indicating that he is selling sweets and chips from his saddlebags, rather like a North American/UK ice-cream truck with a distinctive, musical song.

It is normal within some Dhofari cultures for men to visit houses in which they don't know anyone; there are also other types of people, not known to the inhabitants, who might show up without warning. One is during Ramadan; some people will drop off prepared food (this is usually only done by neighbors) or boxes of foodstuffs as charity. Women go to houses in which they don't know anyone to campaign for their candidates during elections; those running for office will usually set up tents and men will meet there.

"Reading" houses: who is at home?

If you are standing in front of a Dhofari house, how would you know if there were people inside and what they are doing? You can't necessarily know about the wealth of the occupants, but you might be able to make some guesses based on lights, cars and shoes.

Unless it is a mini-palace set on four or five lots, you cannot tell the wealth of the inhabitants by looking at the house as it might not have been built by or for the people who currently live in it. Houses and land can move within family members as richer members help others. A man might build himself a new home and give his previous house to a relative. A woman might live with her husband and build a house for her mother and her younger siblings. A divorced or widowed woman and her children might live in a house built for her by her husband or his family. One informant's father built a new house next to his home, moved into the new house and handed over his previous home to his brother with all the furnishings intact.

Also, the house might have been built with (non-interest) loans, either from a bank or family members. Or a large house might have been built slowly over several years by siblings who paid for labor and supplies when they could.

A house that looks old or poorly kept up might be owned/lived in by people who are using their money in other ways, such as paying for college or treatment for a sick relative, or they might be waiting for a coming wedding or *Eid* to paint/refurbish. There might be reasons for the lack of maintenance such as the house belongs to a person who has died and the heirs are deciding what should be done with it. A very wealthy older man might refuse to move to a larger/newer house as he lived his whole life in that home.

It is important to remember that once the house is built, it belongs to the owner forever. There are no yearly land or property taxes in Oman. In extreme circumstances, the water and electricity might be cut off, but there is no way for a person to be alienated from their property and left homeless. If the government claims eminent domain, the person will be given land and a house or land and enough money to build another house.

To tell who, if anyone, is at home – you need to look at the lights, cars and shoes. All houses have outside lights near or above the two front doors. These are almost always turned on at night if people are in the house. They are sometimes left on all night or turned off when the household goes to sleep.

Indoor lights are usually turned off or down if there is no one in the room, and although most windows are heavily curtained, one can sometimes see light leaking out through a corner to know if there are people sitting in the *majlis* or *salle*. Or the *majlis* or front door might be open with light spilling out to show that people are in.

Houses have a series of lights that look like small lanterns along the top or sides of the walls surrounding the house and along the roofline. These lights are usually only on if there is a party. This is done as part of the understanding that lights = joy, to alert neighbors and to help guests find the house. If the roof lights are on, it's a happy party: graduation, someone returning from a long trip overseas, someone who has recovered from an illness etc.

Basically, the more lights you can see, the more people are in the house. If a house is completely dark, then you think about place and time. People usually go to sleep later in towns so if a house is dark at 10 pm in town, chances are everyone is out of the home; if a house is dark at 10 pm in an isolated place with structures for herd animals, chances are everyone is sleeping. One informant who lives in town has a sleep pattern that is five hours later than his brother who lives in the mountains.

In terms of cars, there is not usually space inside the *hosh* (courtyard) for cars, so there is often a parking space in front of the wall surrounding the house. This can be "read" by thinking about how the cars are parked, the time of day and which day it is.

If there is covered parking, it is for the senior man in the house, and seeing a car in that space means it is more likely that he is at home (of course, there is a chance that he was picked up by a friend). If there is a car parked slant-wise, blocking other cars on the road, it is probably a delivery, meaning someone is at home.

Working and school hours are usually Sunday–Thursday from 7 or 8 am to 1 or 2 pm, but if no cars are in front of the house during those times, it doesn't mean the house is empty. People who don't work, young children and older relatives, will be sleeping or in the *salle*. If you want to know how many people live in the house, look at the number of cars around 2 or 3 pm as it's usual for families to eat lunch together.

You can get a sense of the extended family by looking at the cars around 1 or 2 pm on Fridays as married children will usually have the main meal after Friday prayers with the husband's parents. Lots of cars means that there is a pater and/or materfamilias living there. No cars can mean that there is probably a nuclear family in the house who have gone to have lunch with parents and/or siblings.

When I asked one informant how you tell if someone is at home, the response was, "shoes!" Shoes do give you the most details about who is at home, but you have to have good eyesight as it is not acceptable to walk up to the front door of a house unless you are invited or you are from Dhofar and following local rules for visiting.

As shoes are not worn in the house, everyone slips off their shoes next to the door. Counting shoes, noting which door the shoes are next to and which type of shoes there are tell you a lot of information. If you know the inhabitants well, you learn who each pair belongs to and can know who is inside before you walk in.

Men usually wear thick-soled, black leather sandals. If the shoes are next to the *majlis* door, it means the man is probably visiting; men who live in the house will leave their sandals by the main door. You can tell children's shoes by their size, and, again, if they are next to the *majlis*, they are visiting with an older male relative and if they are by the main door, they live in the house. Women's sandals are usually colored and have thinner soles than men's.

Thus, if you put together information about lights, cars and shoes and some additional data, you can make reasonable guesses about what is going on.

For example, many cars and many pairs of men's sandals next to the majlis door means a lot of men are visiting.[11] If one sees lots of women's and kids' sandals next to the main door, this means there is some sort of family gathering. If there are lights on the roofline, it's a party. If it's good weather, a lot of people and there is a large courtyard, the men might be sitting outside on mats, so that women have the freedom to move throughout the whole house, including the *majlis*.

But if there are a lot of men's sandals by the *majlis* and only a few women's shoes, it means there is probably a meeting. In which case you need to think through football (soccer) schedules, it might be a group of young men watching a game or older men sorting through a serious family issue. Lots of women's and children's shoes but no men's shoes (and a few or no cars) means it's a women's gathering.

If there are lots of shoes and cars, the timing and the sounds can also help tell you about the gathering. The normal times for parties are weekdays after 7 or 8 pm, Fridays after noon prayers for families and Friday and Saturday evenings.

Neighbors might visit each other, but Dhofaris usually do not hold large gatherings during the day Sunday–Thursday or Friday and Saturday mornings. If there are a lot of cars and shoes during those times, it might mean that someone has died and people have come to sit with the family for three days of mourning.

"Reading" houses: the celebrating/mourning house

As I biked to grad school in North Dakota, I daily passed a house whose owners went all in on celebrations. The huge picture window in the living room started the year with paper snowflakes, then paper Martin Luther Kings, pink hearts for Valentines, paper top hats for Presidents' Day and on through St Patrick's four-leaf clovers, Labor Day, Flag Day, 4th of July, Memorial Day, Halloween pumpkins, Thanksgiving turkeys, Christmas trees and back to paper snowflakes.

Houses in Dhofar are not decorated for any reason except for weddings and, rarely, National Day. To anthropomorphize for a moment, houses are like *haklis*, you cannot tell from the outside what is going on in the inside. You can sometimes guess that there is an event by a sudden increase of cars, but that would require your knowing how many cars are normally parked outside as large houses often have 10–15 cars parked in front. Details such as time of day (women's condolences visits are usually in the morning, wedding parties are usually in the evening) and family knowledge (did someone just come back from a trip or a stay in the hospital?) might help you guess the kind of event, but you will not know from any house ornamentation.

An American friend who lived in an Omani neighborhood and I both had the puzzlement of trying to figure out if a neighbor's house was in mourning or celebrating when a lot of people suddenly started to visit. Asking informants "how do you know what is going on?" was answered with "the people will tell you." For example, many Dhofari women belong to a social-media group for the neighborhood and/or live exclusively near relatives so the news will travel quickly if a social visit is required, e.g. a new mother has just come to her mother's house or a child has just returned from studying abroad.

Sound can also be a factor as there is often music playing for a wedding and, during a party if the front door is open, one cannot hear distinct voices, but a general hum of chatter. However, if the house is in mourning, there will be no sound except perhaps a recording of the Holy Qur'an.

Weddings, however, are visible to all. The groom's family will usually rent colored strings of light which are hung in long loops from the roof or pulled in a straight line from the roof to the ground, like guy wires on a tent. These are lit for the night the bride is brought to the house and sometimes for a few days afterward. In addition, all the small electric lanterns that are placed at the top of the house's wall and around the roofline are turned on. The bride's house would not have lights but might, for example, turn on all the outside lights.

In the past there were two National Days, November 18th (the birthday of the previous sultan, Sultan Qaboos) and July 23rd (the day the previous sultan took office). Now only November 18th is celebrated and some people will decorate their house with green, white and red lights, the colors of the Omani flag.

The five senses and houses

First, the Middle East is not a good place for people with perfume allergies. Both men and women use scent every day, and in Dhofar this is extended to the house. Most Dhofaris place pieces of dried frankincense sap on small pieces of lit, odorless charcoal which produces a lot of perfumed smoke. Oud, small pieces of wood that is scented with oils, might also be used. As the charcoal/frankincense is placed inside a handmade, clay holder (*majmar*), a person can walk around the house bringing the smoke to the *majlis*, *salle*, hallways and bedrooms (see the discussion on smoke detectors in Chapter 4). Some people also do this at sunset, and it is usually done before parties and after eating.

The *majmar* can also be placed in a wardrobe to "smoke" clothes or a person can stand over the *majmar* to scent what they are wearing. An example can be seen in John Singer Sargent's painting "Fumée d'ambre gris." For *Eid* visits and weddings, there is usually a tray of perfumes in the *salle* and *majlis*; guests are sprayed when leaving.

The smell of cooking food is not regarded as pleasing. The kitchen door is closed while cooking, and the extractor fan is usually on full time. After eating in the *salle* and/or *majlis*, one must nullify the effect of food – dishes, kitchen, face, and hands washed, scent reapplied through air fresheners, incense and/or perfume. The result is that despite constant air movement from fans and the air conditioner (AC), the *salle* and *majlis* usually have a noticeable, heavy perfumed scent.

The omnipresent sound in Dhofari houses is the drone of air conditioners. As Smith notes in talking about houses in Muscat,

> the rendered [cement] block walls have no thermal insulation resulting in excessive heat gain for the interior. This in turn leads to the overworking of the inefficient and noisy wall-mounted, packaged air conditioners, themselves poorly located near the corners of each room.
> (1983 20)

Some houses have split ACs which are quieter, but there is always a background hum.

As all rooms have cement block walls with tiled floors, the noise reverberates through the space, especially as there are wide hallways. Although the *majlis* and *salle* often have carpets, there is seldom wall-to-wall carpeting or wall hangings to deaden the sound.

Another electrical sound is the high-pitched whine of small pumps to push water up to the roof-top tanks. In the last few years, many home owners have attached these motors to the main water pipe at the base of the house. In the past, people relied on municipal water pressure to force water up, but now most houses have a pump which, although barely noticeable, makes a loud buzz rather like having constant tinnitus.

Another common sound is children yelling. The topic of childrearing practices is too large to engage with here (see Chapter 3 in Risse *Community and Autonomy* 2019), but in general, Dhofari children are allowed to make noise in and near their homes as there is a general understanding that childhood should be a happy time and children should be able to express themselves. Visiting with women in the *salle* usually includes hearing a lot of commotion from children, even if the kids are not the center of attention or in the room itself.

In terms of touch, most houses are kept very cold, not to say arctic, at 16°C/60°F or lower.[12] As mentioned in the "AC and fans" section of Chapter 4, the cold air is needed in part because inhabitants are always fully dressed in the house, often with their heads covered. Also, some spaces such as hallways, kitchens and bathrooms often don't have their own AC, and therefore the main rooms are kept cooler so that the whole house is at a comfortable temperature.

Animals and houses

There are few pets in Dhofari houses. Some people have birds (small songbirds or parrots); cats or dogs as indoor pets are rare although it's usual for people to leave leftover food next to the municipal trash dumpsters which are placed every five to ten houses in town neighborhoods.

In the middle of towns, small creatures such as ants, spiders, cockroaches and mice enter through the water pipes, the drains, the washing machine out-take pipe and/or under the door. Lizards and snakes are occasional unwelcome guests, especially if there are plants near the property. Birds such as grackles nest in the AC covers; some people keep chickens.

On the edge of towns and in rural areas, camels and wild donkeys will saunter by, looking for plants and examining the area around dumpsters for something edible. If there are tree branches hanging over the wall, camels will tear at the leaves. Cows and goats do not usually eat household plantings or trash; cows, because they are not interested, and goats, because they are almost always with a herder. People who own herds of animals always have a low cement block wall around the house to keep animals out.

I have not heard of any of the dangerous animals such as wolves, hyenas, honey badgers, caracals or leopards coming close to houses.

Religion and spaces in houses[13]

A few months after I met one of the research guys, he said to me, "I want to see you pray." The men always did their prayers if we happened to be together at a prayer time, so he knew I had seen what they did and, as he had never seen a Methodist pray before, I recognized the same "how do you do that" type of question that I always asked them. I was sitting cross-legged, so I clasped my hands and rested them on my shins, took a deep breath, closed my eyes and said the Lord's Prayer and St Francis' prayer ("Lord, make me an instrument of your peace"). This elicited a lot of conversations over several weeks about what "doing prayers" means.

One awareness that came out of these conversations is that I myself understand two types of prayers: prayers which a person does at any time and any place with no preparation and prayers that are in a sacred space, i.e. when I walk into a church, I feel I am in an area set apart from all aspects of daily life as everything in the building makes me focus on my relationship with God.[14]

In my opinion, when the research guys pray, there is always some external support in that they will always make physical adjustments, such as doing the ritual washing, adjusting their clothing, facing Mecca and, if possible, laying down a prayer mat. If we are on a boat, lines are pulled out of the water, one man does the call to prayer, hands and mouths are cleaned and the man who will lead the prayers moves closest to the direction of Mecca as the boat temporarily becomes a sacred space. As I don't want to interfere with the moments of preparation or prayer, I huddle close to the side of the boat and look at the water.

Praying in a mosque is the best way to pray; as one informant told me "better in the mosque, all other places are the same." Thus, if they are not in a mosque, the research guys create the sacred wherever they are. In asking about the sacred in houses, informants answered the same way: the *majlis*, *salle* or bedroom were equally good, as was any "clean" space. Praying is not acceptable in the bathroom and not advised in a kitchen.

In Dhofar, Omani women do not usually go to the mosque to pray except in Ramadan, thus spaces in their homes become their sacred spaces, a change that is created by their intentions and actions. They usually pray in their bedroom, but none of my informants told me that they had a specific place for prayers. When the call to prayer is heard from the nearest mosque or a cell phone reminder, the person will wash, adjust clothing (for example a woman will make sure her *sheila* is tightly wound around her head), lay down the prayer mat and make the gesture to start the prayers. In the same way, if someone wants to read the Holy Qur'an, they will make sure they and their clothes are clean, set up the wooden stand to hold the book in a clean area and begin reading.

Further, it is always clear from looking inside Dhofari houses that the owners are Muslim because of the Qur'an on display on a wooden stand, wall hangings with excerpts from the Qur'an, photos or representations of the Ka'ba and often the absence of photos and representations of the human figure. Like the Shakers, religious belief permeates every aspect of one's material surroundings. In "Basic Principles of Islam and Their Social, Spatial and Artistic Implications," Bianca writes

> the distinctive feature of Islam is that it has given birth to a comprehensive and integrated cultural system by totally embedding the religious practice in the daily life of the individual and society ... it moulded the whole way of life by providing a matrix of behavioral archetypes, which, by necessity, generated correlated physical patterns
>
> (2000 22–23)

He further explains that "the notion of sacredness could be extended to social and architectural domains other than the mosque, and particularly to the family and its home" (2000 33). For example, it is normal in the USA for a hospital and airport to have a non-denominational reflection room, but in Oman, it is expected that every large structure (e.g. every office, government and university building, as well as hotel and mall) will have prayer rooms.

Safety and spaces in houses

In towns, the *majlis* doors are usually unlocked during the day. If it is left unlocked at night, the interior door (from *majlis* to the main hallway) will be locked. The main door might be locked, but that is often to prevent small children from leaving the house. Outside of towns, both doors are usually left open.

Ground floor windows are usually barred to prevent children from exiting rather than fear of opportunistic pilfering or to keep track of inhabitants. There might be a perception that windows are barred to monitor females, but if a female is going to have an illicit meeting, a man coming to her house or her leaving her house would be stupidly dangerous. There would be no possible justification for her being out of the house and several Dhofari men have told me that they have the right to kill any uninvited man who is in their house at night.

Also, the control is in force for boys as well as girls, albeit with different consequences. I have heard of many cases of boys being given a curfew, and if they come late, they have to sleep in the *majlis* or a relative's house unless a sister can get a door or window open for them to sneak in.

To me, barred windows can seem at odds with the fact that doors are usually open during the day. I read this as a perception switch from what I call a welcoming house when the inhabitants are awake and moving (*majlis* and front door open) to a fortress house when the inhabitants are sleeping and, while perhaps the *majlis* door is open, the door from the *majlis* to rest of the house and front door are locked.

As a related issue, I have not seen doors with "peep-holes" in them. If someone knocks, you open the door. If some of the research guys stop by my house unexpectedly and knock and I ask, "Who's there?" they will refuse to answer and pound on the door. The first time this happened I was very scared, but I had the presence of mind to run to the window to look at the place for parking. I saw a few cars and recognized one, so I answered the door and got a lot of comments about my rudeness. When I tried to explain that I was afraid, I was told there was nothing to be afraid of.

In the same way, if I get a call on my phone from an unknown number, the research guys encourage me to answer. There is nothing to fear from another person who is in front of your house or on the phone, i.e. communicating with you while you are awake. The necessity of trusting yourself, being polite to guests and the implied, ever-present available backup of living in a house with over 30 people means that having an open door or opening a door to a stranger is considered safe.

Care should be taken at the times when a person is asleep and not able to monitor the surroundings. While camping, this means a lit fire; at home, this means locked doors.

Cultural understandings of housing for expats

In other parts of the Arabian Peninsula housing compounds built by oil companies have influenced the design of buildings and domestic spaces. This has not happened in Dhofar as oil companies do not have a large, public presence in the region.

Only a few, small housing compounds were built during/after the Dhofar War (1965–75) for a foreign military, but they are currently rented by expats and non-Dhofari Omanis. These compounds are in the Dhariz (south-eastern) section of Salalah and have four, six or eight houses built almost at ground level with details which mark them as non-Dhofari such as the maids' rooms have their own entrance and only one main doorway. There is a dining room which is built open to the living room and kitchen, something that would never happen in a Dhofari house where the smell of cooking food should not be able to enter into sitting rooms.

Another difference is that the roof can only be accessed by a ladder. While Dhofaris don't necessarily use the roof space, it is always very easy to enter from an internal staircase. If one can only get on the roof by a ladder, the house is not Dhofari designed. Other design features that are not usually found in Dhofari houses include a low garden wall that gives visual access to a neighbor's garden, screen doors and built-in wooden closets in the main hallway.

These compounds are near land given by the government for the expat schools and Christian church complex. They are not compounds in the sense used in other Arabian Peninsula countries with hundreds of houses, shops, schools and extensive security procedures for entrance.

For apartments built in the last decade, there is a basic division between those for Dhofari Omanis and those for non-Dhofari Omanis. As explained in Chapter 4, there are "family" (for relatives or people vouched for/known to the owner) and "public" (open to anyone) buildings.

"Family" apartments would have fewer units without a manager, and it's important to limit sightlines for outsiders.[15] Whereas a "public" style apartment building would have one hallway on each floor and only one main entrance, with perhaps a small back staircase for fire safety if it was several stories high. Every time a person exited their apartment, they would be on display, so to speak, for all the other neighbors to see and everyone would pass through the main entrance.

Another difference is that for Dhofari-Omanis space is allocated between guests and family members with the intention that family members can move freely within the apartment, in addition to being able to come in and leave. Thus, most Dhofari-designed apartments have two doors so that, like houses, guests are secluded in one room, while family members have access to all other rooms and the main entrance.

There are other formats. In my (Dhofari-designed) apartment, the front door is not visible from the *majlis* so anyone can come and go without being seen. Or, for example, if the *majlis* is next to the door, the *salle* is placed so that it cannot be seen by a guest sitting on the *majlis* sofa, so family members can go into and out of the *salle* without being seen. Another type of design is one main door which opens into a hallway, with the *majlis* accessed by the first door on the left or right. Once guests are inside, the *majlis* door is shut and the family members have access to the hallway and all other rooms. For the moments of entry and exit, the host will be speaking loudly, welcoming guests or trying to convince them to stay/saying goodbye, so everyone will know the hallway is in use.

Rental apartments for tourists are usually built within a different framework, in which the section of the apartment near the front door is open to the back of the apartment so that if there are guests, there can be little or no movement or noise from other inhabitants.

An example is an apartment in which the front door opens directly into a small living room with six armchairs. Along the north wall is a guest bathroom. In the back north-western corner is a short hallway which ends in a six-sided open space about eight feet across with four doors. First door to the left is a small kitchen, second door (ahead, to the left) is a bedroom, third door (straight ahead) is a bathroom, then there is a small alcove with a washing machine and then fourth door (to the right) bedroom. Thus, guests can hear anything that is happening in the back of the apartment and those sitting along the eastern wall of the sitting room can see down the short hallway.

In this set-up the front "controls" the back of the apartment. This makes sense in terms of *khareef* rentals as tourists come as large groups of family or friends, and thus there is no need to worry about keeping guests separate. The housing space is family-only. If a male tourist meets a friend in Salalah, they will both understand that the housing is not set up to entertain guests and they will have a picnic or take a meal/coffee together in a restaurant (before Covid).

Notes

1 Doors are seldom if ever locked in the mountains or villages. If they are, it is almost always to prevent small children from entering the kitchen or leaving the house.

2 Men and women in the same house do not usually pray together. In Islam, men are encouraged (it is better) to pray in public and together with other men; there is not the same injunction for women.

3 For example, even after his father passed away and he inherited the building, one informant continued to refer to his home as "my father's house."

4 As discussed in Chapter 4, informants have repeatedly told me that whatever is locked in the house (the front door; the door to the *majlis*, store or a bedroom; a cupboard; the fridge etc.) is to prevent kids from creating havoc by leaving the house or creating a mess, not for fear of theft.

5 Where someone sleeps can also be the result of various kinds of assistance. As I explained in my first book, *Community and Autonomy in Southern Oman* (Risse 2019), within households of 30 or more people, everyone is trying to cover their own feelings while trying to figure out what everyone else is thinking. Thus people often refrain from making statements about where people are as they don't want others to discuss where they themselves are. For example, if a man is no longer sleeping in the same room as his wife, family members would notice but no one except perhaps a parent would make a comment.

There are some houses with tyrannical older relatives, but what I have seen most often is *haklis* trying to act as if they do not need help while trying to help others without calling attention to their kind actions. If someone, especially an older female, is perceived as being sad, lonely and/or having difficulties, many Dhofaris will make sure that someone is with her. Examples I have seen include a woman with several children visiting sisters with few or no children and encouraging her kids to stay overnight with their aunts. Sisters planning a schedule of who will go to stay at their mother's house when she was ill and sisters planning a schedule of who will go to stay at their mother's house when the youngest daughter got married and left the house. Another friend sent her daughter to stay at her mother's house after her mother had received sad news. In all of these cases, the person going or sending a child/children to a house made up an excuse for the visits and hid the fact that they were acting out of kindness.

6 In a similar way, a married man who visits his wife when she is at her parent's house might sit in the *salle* (if he is closely related to her family) or the *majlis* (if he is not). As most Dhofari women stay with their mother or an older sister for 40 days after the birth of their first child, a husband's behavior is on display. All the female relatives of the new mother will know how often he visits, how long he stays and what he brings with him. This information is passed on to the general community. For example, when a general question such as "how is the new mom doing?" is answered with, "fine, *alhamdulillah*, and her husband came every day to visit in the *majlis*," his reputation (and the reputation of his family) is increased. This is a man who respects his wife and takes his responsibilities seriously.

7 Cows and goats are not usually herded down; cows are kept inside during the day because of flies and graze at night.

8 For more examples, see the "House histories" section in Chapter 2.

9 For specific examples of births and marriages impacting housing, see "House histories" in Chapter 2.

10 There are many sad/amusing stories of husbands trying to figure out how to break the news to the first wife. One friend told me of a husband who took his first wife and their children to a hotel for a weekend to try to tell her in "neutral territory," but he never got the nerve. So after he dropped them back at home and drove away, he sent her a text message.

11 A meeting of ten male relatives who don't live in the same house will probably mean ten parked cars; a meeting of ten female relatives will mean fewer cars as they will be dropped off by male relatives, usually father, husband, brother or son. Women drive alone, but if there is a family gathering, they will often bring other women and children. For example, if one female informant visits her aunt, she will pick up her mother, an unmarried sister and a married sister so that they can chat in the car.

The fact that Dhofari men drop off female relatives for visits can be read as some Dhofari women are dependent on men and thus have no freedom/autonomy/agency. Some Dhofari women have this point of view, but my male and female informants (including women who don't drive) do not. Several Dhofari women have told me that having a husband drive her meant having a chance to talk to him alone. One explained to me that when living in a house with over 30 people and constant visitors, time driving to and from relatives was her chance to catch up with her husband. She did not want to learn how to drive as this would give him his freedom to spend evenings with his friends; driving would not give her her freedom.

For men, bringing women to visit relatives is not seen as a job, chore or imposition; I have never heard a Dhofari man complain about it. Keeping family ties is important, and a woman has the right to visit her family. Once a woman is married, the responsibility does not devolve solely on the husband. It's usual for a relative who drives to pick her up from her husband's father's house, bring her home for an evening and then return her. I know of one Dhofari woman who asked for a divorce partially because her husband refused to allow her brothers to bring her to visit her mother. Her family supported her as his insistence that only he could drive her was seen as unfair and unnecessarily severe.

12 Winter argues that the widespread use of air conditioning has significantly changed life on the Arabian Peninsula which I agree with, but not to the extent that he posits:

> The reasons for shopping, eating and playing sports in the evenings or early mornings are redundant once such activities move indoors. Similarly, work and leisure patterns change once the afternoon siesta is no longer required. AC enables the region's cities to be plugged into the global economy 24 hours a day, 52 weeks a year, rendering the traditional hot season retreat to cooler climes (such as Oman's mountainous region) much less important than it once was.
>
> (2015 5)

The afternoon siesta is still the norm in Dhofar, as is playing sports in the evenings, and the flood of tourists in the cool *khareef* season increases every year.

13 In this section I am deliberately avoiding saying "Christians" or "Muslims" as I don't want to make grand statements; I want to explain my perceptions of how Islam is connected to spaces within Dhofari houses on the concrete level of what I have seen and been told.

14 Some Christians might have a prie-dieu or "war room," but the space is a way to help people focus on prayer and could be used for other purposes such as writing, e.g. it's the concentration, not the location which is important, for example:

> You may have seen the movie, *The War Room* .... While it is nice to have a prayer space in your home where you can focus intentionally on developing your prayer strategy, this is not required. In fact, war room prayers can be prayed in your car on the way to work.
>
> (Ashley 2021)

15 One example is a small apartment building has four apartments, two on the ground floor and two on the first floor. Each ground-floor apartment is given control over the small *hosh* area near its entrance door, while each first-floor apartment is given control over half the flat, tiled roof. Thus there are two factors to heighten privacy. First, the inhabitants of all four apartments have their own outside area to use for drying clothes, growing plants in pots etc. The roof area is divided by a low wall, with the built-in drying racks built at opposite sides of the space. Second, the building design means that the apartment's front door is seen by very few people. If a person in the ground-floor apartment wants to leave and, while opening the front door, hears footsteps on the stairwell, they can quickly close the door, wait for the person (from the first-floor apartment) to leave and then go out. Thus the residents can limit or prevent being seen by anyone else.

References

For photos and a full bibliography, please see: *Come From Away*, https://mariellerisse.com

Ashley. 2021. "Praying the Scriptures: Create a Powerful War Room Prayer Strategy." *Undoubted Grace*. https://undoubtedgrace.com/praying-the-scriptures/

Bianca, Stefano. 2000. "Basic Principles of Islam and Their Social, Spatial and Artistic Implications," in *Urban Form in the Arab World*. London: Thames & Hudson. 23–48.

Risse, Marielle. 2021. *Foodways in Southern Oman*. London: Routledge.
———. 2019. *Community and Autonomy in Southern Oman*. Cham, Switzerland: Palgrave Macmillan.
Smith, John Alexander. 1983. "Desert Developments." *Building Design* 11: 18–21.
Winter, Tim. 2015. "Urban Sustainability in the Arabian Gulf: Air Conditioning and its Alternative." *Urban Studies*. 1–15. https://doi.org/10.1177/0042098015608782

6 Being "at home" outside of the home

Home as hotel/hotel as home

I was surprised the first time I heard "it was like a hotel" as a compliment about a home or room. To me, "like a hotel" refers to a bland, soulless space. To the Dhofaris I talk to, it means a clean, color-coordinated, well-organized space. After many discussions, hearing Dhofaris' reaction to my houses, and thinking about how my decorating has changed since living here, I realize there are three aspects at play.

One is the omnipresence of small children. As several generations usually live in one house, most houses have several small children which means a general tendency to have fewer decorative objects and/or put objects out of reach.[1] This connection between the presence of children and decorating styles is a good example of how spaces are shaped by beliefs.

In Dhofar, there is a general understanding that children should have happy childhoods which is manifested in several ways such as the rush to stop any child from crying (which is seen as harmful) and the pressure for older children to give in to the desires of younger siblings. One friend's young son did not want to eat what the family ate so she ordered dinner from a restaurant for him for several months; some parents will not force their children to brush their teeth or eat food that they don't want. However, children might be pressured into social skills, such as greeting a grandparent, and might not be taken to a store if they don't behave.

Babies are almost always held or set on blankets next to adults and children follow the daily rhythms of the family, without separate times to eat or a set bedtime. They play with other children in the *salle* or *hosh* (paved area surrounding the house); they are rarely alone in a room.

Thus the first aspect is that rooms, especially the *salle*, will often have nothing that is movable or breakable because people don't want to spend time and energy keeping something away from a child. The norm is to keep temptations out of sight.[2] The *majlis* will usually have food on display at all times to be ready for guests. Thus, the *majlis* door is usually locked so that kids can't eat or play with the items on the coffee table.

The second aspect is that for some Dhofaris, rooms and houses are not seen as having any fundamental importance beyond providing shelter.[3] One

DOI: 10.4324/9781003270317-6

hakli man I know didn't want the bother of building his own house so he bought one by parking next to it with the seller, looking at it from the outside and agreeing to buy it. He had no need to see the inside. One Dhofari friend's family moved into a new house and for more than two years this friend never ordered bedroom furniture. There were other places to sleep and creating a bedroom was not worth the time and hassle.

In North America, a bedroom is usually an expression and extension of one's personality but in Dhofar, a person might be in their 30s before they have any input into decoration and, by that point, perhaps have no opinion.[4] I want to be clear that this can be true for both men and women: as a small child sleeping in the parent's room, then sharing a room with same-sex siblings or cousins, then a new room after marriage that was decorated (for a woman) by the husband/husband's family or (for a man) by his sisters.

The third aspect is most Dhofaris follow the principle of "people, not things." When I look at a hotel room, I notice the lack of a personal touch, i.e. the items reflecting a person's travels, accomplishments and interests. But in a *majlis* or *salle*, there are few or no signs of the individuals who live in the house such as photos, books, souvenirs or knick-knacks. The window might be decorated with five kinds of fabric, tassels, pull-backs, swags and ruffles, but you won't be able to tell very much about the family.

When visiting, the *salle* is never the focus of the talk. If it's a new house, there will be compliments and a short discussion about where and how items were bought but that is only a few moments, not a main topic of conversation. It's good to have someplace to sit, lights, AC, drinks and snacks but the important element is the chance to have a nice, long conversation.[5] Thus a hotel room is the goal of decorating: a neat, clean space with marching colors and comfortable places to sit.

The idea of "people, not things" carries over to my second point, that hotels and rental homes are like houses in that it's who you are with, not where you are, that is important. As explained in Chapters 4 and 5, Dhofaris, especially *haklis*, will sleep in various rooms and houses; they are used to sleeping in new places. Also, hotels and rental homes are built and furnished in a manner similar to houses.

A rental house or hotel might have a pool, but most are plastered and painted cement block structures with tiled floors, AC, tinted windows and furnishings of only beds, nightstands, wardrobes, sofas and a TV. The direction of Mecca is clearly marked (usually painted on the ceiling), there are prayer rugs and all the food is *halal*. Unless you are in one of the few extremely expensive hotels, hotel rooms look like a slightly better (or more poorly) decorated and cleaned version of a Dhofari home.

This seamlessness between home and non-home means there is little adjustment between the two spaces which in turn means it is easy to travel. A man might decide on Thursday afternoon to go camping for two days or take his wife to a hotel. Since families usually travel with all the children and plans might change at any moment if someone is sick, vacations are often arranged at the last minute. All that is needed is to put some clothes in a bag and everyone is ready to go to a hotel, rent a house or visit a relative.[6] Dhofaris will decide to drive to Muscat or Dubai and within an hour or two are on the road; it's usual to book airline tickets a day or a few hours before the flight.

Renting houses

There are three types of house rentals: for a few days or weeks during the *khareef* (monsoon season, June to September), party or weekend rentals or year long. In non-COVID times, the cool, foggy monsoon weather brings thousands of visitors to Dhofar, most of who will stay for a week or more so they want all the conveniences of a set up home. Some Dhofaris build houses that are only rented during this time and stay empty the rest of the year; after years of rental, they might then be used as the owner's house or be taken over/sold to a relative.

To advertise, the owner might use a rental agency, post photos on social media or use the direct approach of painting the contact phone number in large numbers on the wall of the house. Between this practice and GCC house owners who only visit their property during *khareef*, there is a fair number of empty villas in neighborhoods that are near main roads and the mountains. For example, of the 24 houses nearest where I live, 4 are empty and 5 have been occupied about half the time.

Landlords of *khareef* rentals can charge high prices such as 50 OR per night but often have to pay for extensive repairs to the houses after the season. One landlord told me that what might happen is a man comes to a rental agency asking for a house for his family. Once he has the key and the manager leaves, the renter will call the rest of his group to come so that a landlord may think there will be 7 people in the house but in fact over 20 will be staying. I have seen several houses after the renters have left and the damage is beyond simple normal wear and tear: TVs broken, trash spread over the floors, curtains ripped and bedframes cracked.

The second kind of rental is a house specifically to be rented for parties or for weekends. Houses for parties are usually set at the edge of residential areas with a large parking/drop-off area in front of the house so they are easy to access. There are one or more large sitting rooms, a large kitchen and perhaps a few small bedrooms used for the bride to get ready. There is usually a high wall and a covered area in the *hosh* so partygoers can sit outside. The exterior decoration is often colorful, with mirrored tiles and a large portico while the interior is usually cream/ivory walls and furnishings to not detract from the decorations that the renter has brought. These houses are often used for women's wedding parties and may not have the typical *majlis* and *salle* division because it is expected that only women will be in the house as men's gatherings for weddings (and funerals) are usually held in rented tents, not the home.

Houses for weekend rental are usually built away from towns, sometimes sited for a view of the mountains or sea from the roof and often on more than one plot. There is a higher wall than usual (to ensure that women might walk around outside and not be seen) and a much larger *hosh*, often with playground equipment and flower beds or flowers in pots. The *salle* and *majlis* are huge and plainly decorated in dark colors which don't show stains/usage. There is a large kitchen and several bedrooms which are small and utilitarian. Often there is a covered space on the roof to enjoy the view and, sometimes, a small covered pool. These are rented by large family groups so that children have lots of room to play as the adults talk.

Given that these types of houses are designed so differently than regular homes, they will stay as rentals and not be taken over as family houses.

For year-long rentals, the occupants can sign a contract, which usually means paying an extra fee to formally register the contract or having a verbal agreement with the owner. Normally, renters have complete control of the house; they can repaint and change fixtures as they like, but they are also responsible for any plumbing, electricity and general repairs.

There are a few housing complexes, often with only 4 to 10 houses surrounded by a wall with a narrow, internal road. These are usually rented to expats, as well as Omanis who use the houses for informal get-togethers, not to live in. These have a more formal structure with written contracts and limits as to what the renter can change. The lack of control over the house is balanced by on-site managers who are on-call to do repairs.

A last factor in renting houses is age. Houses that were built in the 1970s to the early 2000s are often small, i.e. not built out to the size of the plot, and only one story. They usually have a distinctive look: square windows placed symmetrically on either side of one main door, painted in wide stripes of two tones of beige with a noticeable roof overhang or overhangs above windows and doors. The general appearance is more plain with fewer decorations, heaver lines and a roof wall that looks more defensive, less decorative than more modern houses, e.g. a parapet with thick crenellations. Sometimes the concrete is starting to crumble and the outside is not in good repair. Sometimes a family, having moved to a new house, will rent rooms in this kind of house to expat male workers. Thus, on a street on family houses, there might be one which is a boarding house for 10 to 15 expat men.

Renting apartments

A unique aspect of the housing market in Dhofar is that there is a large supply of furnished rental apartments and houses because of the *khareef* (monsoon) season. In other parts of Oman, unfurnished apartments and houses are the norm because the expectation is that people will rent for several months or years and landlords don't want to deal with the wear and tear on furniture from renters.

Another aspect of the huge rental market for *khareef* is that landlords will sometimes rent apartments and houses very cheaply for 9 or 10 months (September to May or June), then raise the prices during the high tourist season. For example, a two-bedroom apartment might be 150 OR per month for most of the year, and then 50 OR per night in July and August. This means some renters will, year after year, move their belongings into their office and leave for the summer, then move back in September first.

Being "at home" in the city: clothing, location and timing

After reading de Koning's *Global Dreams: Class, Gender, and Public Space in Cosmopolitan Cairo* (2009) I started to think how house and home could be seen as two separate concepts and that being "at home" while outside of one's house is an important topic. In "The Kabyle House or the World Reversed" (1972) Bourdieu makes several important, general statements about being inside and outside:

> The woman can only be said to be shut up in the house if it is also pointed out that the man is kept out of it, at least in the daytime ... A self-respecting man must offer himself to be seen, constantly put himself in the gaze of others, confront them, face up to them
>
> (141)

In Dhofar, it is true that men must be seen outside of the house. Only a man who is not able to walk well stays in his house all day. Men must be out and on display after work hours: playing football with peers, sitting in a café, smoking *shisha*, having a picnic dinner with friends. And as his face is never covered, he is known and seen wherever he goes.

Therefore, men are "at home" in the world, as their dress and demeanor are not significantly different in their *majlis* and their café. Their head might not be covered in the house, but their body is and they must be mentally prepared for anyone to stop by to talk or ask a favor. At a favorite café, he might be approached by someone asking for help as he might be at home.

Women's lives outside of the home run along different lines. First of all, women are not "shut up in the house" in Dhofar as a lot of time is spent in visiting. Similar to how Kotnik explains daily life in Sana'a, socializing is for entertainment as well "as a means of communication. Men depend on their wives and female family members for information about the reputations and activities of members of the community" (2005 477).

A second point is that Dhofari women who are going into public, i.e. not a relative or neighbor's house, usually wear a *niqab*, a black, cloth, face mask which "functions as a movable interior space that allows women to penetrate exterior space" (Kotnik 2005 480). In terms of architectural representation, the *niqab* might be seen as "movable *mashrabiyya*," the traditional, pierced wooden screens that cover windows, allowing breezes and light to enter while preventing anyone from seeing in (482).

Hadimioglu, referring to Iran, states that

> The chador is thus conceptualized as a mobile home that facilitates a woman's movement around the city and her dealings with men. It essentially describes an extended boundary that assures that she always occupies a private space ... within the particular Islamic society in which it is worn, the chador aims to act as a foil to the masculine visual regard.
> (2001 19)

Here the architectural comparison is to a "black tent" which is "perhaps also as a monumental architecture that supports a multiplicity of inscriptions" and a "prison" (2001 19, 20). It is "the curtain of physical separation. Use of the chador effectively limits the forbidden space to the interior of the tent" (24).[7]

As Abu-Lughod explains "Dress is an important part of the semiotics of space" (1987 168). Dhofaris make both spatial and clothing choices in public; for example a woman might choose to sit in a closed room in a restaurant and also pull the back of her *sheila* over her face to cover her eyes as she walks into the room, while another woman might choose to sit in an open area in a restaurant and pull her *sheila* back so her hair is showing. In the same way, a man might sit with his back to other tables when sitting in the family section so that he does not see other women, or sit in the open section while wearing a tight, brightly colored *dishdash*.

In general, being "at home" in public means making a series of choices about where to go, when and with whom. It is possible for women to shop, eat, have a picnic, go for a walk and sit on the beach without encountering any men.[8] It is also possible to do all those activities in close proximity to men. Thus Dhofar is not like Saudi Arabia where there are

> precise rules of who was allowed access to places and people at specific times of the day ... and visual, verbal and physical contact was highly regulated according to these rules with the aid of architectural elements, clothes and social practice.
> (Maneval 2019 63)[9]

In Dhofar, there are few "architectural elements" to segregate peoples and there is leeway in clothing choice and social practices. For example, in places where men cannot be avoided, such as seeing a neighbor by chance or in a shop with expat men as clerks, the site becomes "like a home" as the men will address the woman with the familial title of sister or daughter. All the male neighbors I have known called me "sister" no matter what the age difference was. As Abu-Lughod describes

> the family is simply written larger when it is impossible to achieve the physical and visual separation required between strangers. I am struck

> with the similarity of these rules in semi-private urban space to those that apply within an encampment of sedentarized Bedouins ... It is clear that when densities are high and houses too small to contain the manifold activities women are supposed to do in them, the spillover space becomes appropriated as semi-private space and co-residents who might inadvertently have visual access are appropriated into a fictive kinship relationship to neutralize danger.
>
> (1987 168)

AlMutawa has written several essays about how women do and don't feel "at home" in public in the Emirates.[10] In "Navigating the Cosmopolitan City: Emirati Women and Ambivalent Forms of Belonging in Dubai" (2022) she gives the example of an Emirati friend who felt out of place "in her own country" (67). This leads to a discussion about the "problematic binary discourse of supposedly 'authentic, local' spaces (or, at times, authentically cosmopolitan spaces) contrasted with alienating, 'tourist' spaces" (69). AlMutawa wants to "move beyond some academic narratives that implicitly or explicitly depict the cosmopolitanism in the new parts of the city as entirely segregated and impenetrable, a narrative that results in binaries of Western/Emirati or foreign/local spaces" (68).

AlMutawa argues that the same physical space can be embracing and unwelcoming to women at different times. For example, some Emirati women "describe feeling alienated in spaces associated with Westerners specifically seek them out when they want to get away from their community and experience a sense of anonymity" (71). Specifically,

> Emirati women who do not feel comfortable smoking *sheesha* in Emirati-dominated spaces choose to go to certain hotels or to areas of the city where many the people there are Westerners and/or tourists, and where they feel that no one knows who they are.[11]
>
> (78)

Salalah is not large enough to have areas to escape to, but there are a few locations where a woman can have certain freedoms not usually available. One, now closed, beach-side restaurant, had a women-only section where many women smoked *sheesha*. As the location was far from other shops and restaurants and was dimly lit, it was perceived as a safe place to smoke. Hotels and other restaurants also have *sheesha* pipes, but I have only seen expat women smoking.

In terms of the same space being both welcoming and not welcoming, in public areas in Salalah, this is predicated more on time than location. Parks and shopping festivals have women-only days, so a woman who wants to avoid men will frequent those places at those times. There are a few women-only restaurants and cafés. There are also women's markets, in which a large hall is rented for a few days and women with small businesses will rent a booth and sell clothes, perfumes, accessories, food etc. Only women may attend and some clothes designers hire non-Omani models to wear their dresses, a rare example of seeing a woman in public with uncovered hair, make-up and body-revealing clothes.

There is a big temporal difference in terms of the clientele between daytime and evening in malls. In daytime during the week, Dhofari women will have coffee in mall cafés usually with other women; however, women will seldom sit in a café at night. Weekend mornings and evenings are almost exclusively men, with women sometimes coming in the afternoon. But the anonymity AlMutawa speaks of in Dubai does not really exist in Dhofar. Even a Dhofari woman appearing in public in a loose *abayah* and *niqab* may be recognized by her walk, her purse, her eyes or her voice.[12]

Spaces perceived as "home" outside the city[13]

I have spent far more time with Dhofaris sitting outside than in enclosed spaces. One *hakli* man I have known for more than ten years and met with him in a room only once, when he came with several men to visit me when I was very sick. Another male *hakli* friend was talking to me about retirement and asked, "and what will I do then, sit at home?" as if there could be no worse fate. He is very attached to his family, but a man should be outside. When I ask him about his children, his answer is almost always about where they have been: he took the younger children for a ride, he took an older child shopping, he took them swimming, etc.

As I was working on this book and charting out which houses I have been in I realized that for the first few years I was here, I met several men in their houses and had picnics with women, but as I got to know people more, it was the opposite. Unless it's a formal occasion, men don't meet each other at their houses, so as I got to know the men, I was folded into their regular lives. Now I meet them for picnics or camping; if we are inside, it is at a restaurant or my house.

For Dhofari women, the house is just for family and very close friends, so in the beginning, it was better to meet me on a picnic or in a restaurant or café. It was a long, slow process for women to introduce me to their parents, siblings, spouses and their houses.

For both picnics and camping, all the general understandings of etiquette followed in houses apply although usually everyone takes on the role as host to some degree. For example, rather than the host pushing people to eat or drink, any person who opens the cool box will act like a host (asking each person what they would like) before they take something to drink. A person who opens a package of food such as cookies will pass it around before taking any themselves.

The man who is cooking might ask a man who comes late to bring fresh bread or more supplies such as water. No one would ever ask a "guest" to bring anything to one's house, but the cultural rules are slightly different when eating/camping away from towns. Men visiting relatives who live in rural areas will bring supplies with them as gifts, but do not usually call to ask what is needed. But for picnics and camping, men will often send a message before they leave a town to see if anything is wanted or they will be told what to buy.

Further, the cook decides when to eat, but unlike inside a home, in which the host must do all the work, all the people should share by clearing space on the mat, setting out a plastic cover, getting the hot sauce, cutting the limes, etc. And people should, of their own accord, help with the clean-up. I have only twice heard a man tell another man to cook dinner; I have never heard a man tell another man to clean the fish, cook rice, get the eating space ready, etc. Everyone knows the things that have to happen and people volunteer.[14]

Picnics: gardens and parks

In general, picnicking in open space means creating a private *salle*. Dhofaris on picnics see themselves as inhabiting a home space which is inviolate. The space is always clearly defined either by bodies (a group of women sitting in a tight circle) or by mats; if there are women, the space must never be approached unless there is a specific, immediate need. Men will approach other groups of men to ask for information or share food, but not a group of woman.[15] Cars are always parked to block the groups from view.

Green spaces for eating outdoors are at a premium in Dhofar as for most of the year the landscape is brown, dry and barren. Both Omanis and expats will picnic in the middle of roundabouts which are often decorated with trees and flowers or next to roads which have grass borders. In towns, groups of women will go to walled parks, usually one or two square blocks large, which are planted with trees and have amenities like toilets and food for sale. Natural features such as springs and "waterfalls" (usually a slow drip of a few drops unless there has been rain recently) also have picnic areas; some are set up with tables and shelters.

Picnics: open spaces[16]

Close to town and in open spaces with lights, men will drop women and children off and the women will sit closer together to create a defined space that is theirs. For example, groups of women at the beach sit shoulder to shoulder, reminding me of the Roman tactic of overlapping shields, *testudo* (tortoise). Small children run around the outside like satellites.

Outside of town, women will sit alone in areas formally belonging to their tribe or which is perceived as being under the control of their family, but usually there will be men with them some or all of the time but more to enjoy time talking together than as a protective element. Women from the mountains are able to cope with dispatching snakes and scorpions as well as building fires as protection from wolves and hyenas.

Hakli families will usually share one large mat; families from other groups of tribes might make two seating areas, one near the car for women and one at a slight distance for men. The two spaces act as *salle* and *majlis*; as in a house, small children will act as messengers and have the freedom of both mats and the space between them.

The exact amount of space depends on the landscape. The zone under temporary control of the family might be very large or, in crowded places like beaches on the night of the full moon, might only encompass a few meters more than the mat. One plain outside the town of Jibjat is famous for its park-like setting with trees and lovely views. One group per tree is the limit; the trees are spaced out enough so one can't overhear one's neighbors and everyone parks so that the group sits between the car and tree, with the car at an angle chosen for privacy. In open areas like the desert or near-desert open spaces, people should camp out of sight of others.

Hakli men are very aware of the space that should be respected and get annoyed when someone comes and parks too closely but rather than confront the person, they will leave and find another place. As with dealing with neighbors, the better person does not confront a rude person. With picnics and camping at least one can move and if someone is so impolite as to park within a few meters if there is a lot of open space, then just toss everything in the cars and relocate.

As Dhofari men are usually out of their houses every night, most men have a certain place where they meet friends. The group's favorite spot might be a cave on the side of a wide valley, a spot where a *wadi* widens, a hilltop, under a large tree, etc. The only rationale for how to park is to provide a wind block.

Government-built shelters and *straha*

Government- and hand-built *straha* ("hut") are important in that they are roofed; shade is essential in Dhofar for most of the year. Both kinds of shelters are first come-first serve. Even if a man made the structure himself, if someone has parked in front of it and set up camp, the builder has no recourse and must wait until that person has left. Sometimes, men will leave bundles of wood, their blankets and some supplies in a shelter and go fishing; no one will take the space or steal the provisions.[17]

In government-built structures, there is a poured cement floor, set a few feet above ground level, with cement pillars supporting the roof. Sometimes people tie ropes between the pillars above head height and hang lightweight fabric to block wind and/or sightlines.

Some *straha* made by local men have walls of plain (unplastered) cement block courses with a gravel floor and roofs constructed from wooden beams, plastic tarps, old blankets and/or fish nets. Others are less sturdy with wooden posts supporting a roof of chicken wire interwoven with palm fronds.

Once the car is parked in front; the shelter is treated like a person's house whether it is occupied for a few hours or days. As with picnics, the car acts as the *bab*, the gate in the wall around the house. No one will come nearer than the car without calling out loudly and waiting to be greeted. If the person is not known, even if they are invited to come closer, they will often stay on the far side of the car and explain what they want, for example, to give food. Since there are no internal divisions in *strahas*, the space is like a *salle* or *majlis* and a man will usually not accept to sit down unless he is a close friend.

Camping[18]

Camping is usually done in geographical areas close to one's home space; fishermen camp on beaches, men from the mountains camp in the mountains. If in an unfamiliar place, men will sometimes sleep in the car or in a parking lot. Twice on trips with the research guys we slept in parking lots as we were in areas away from beaches and they didn't know the *wadis*. Further, if a person is in an unfamiliar place, sleeping in the mosque is allowed. During some *khareef* seasons, for example, I have been told "they are sleeping in the mosques," meaning that so many visitors arrived in Dhofar and could not find lodgings right away, they would spend the night in a mosque.

While *strahas* and picnics have only the dichotomy of being outside (the far side of the cars, mats or circle of bodies) and inside (where the people are sitting), camping has three layers.

The first layer is where the cars are parked, an area that functions like a *hosh*. Anyone can walk on the far side of the cars without acknowledging/being acknowledged. On beaches, the area below the high tide mark is seen as a free passageway. It was frightening for me the first few times I was sitting by a campfire and I would suddenly realize a man was walking just beyond the glow of the firelight, but the research men explained that this was every person's right. The passer-by might lift his hand or call out, but a man walking by the water or beyond the cars is like a man walking on the other side of a house wall.

A stranger who approaches a camping area and needs help will not come closer than the cars. For example, he will stand on the far side and call out his request for a tow or a tow rope and the men will get up and walk over to help him.

The second space, like a *majlis*, is the public area for friends and family, usually delineated by mats in the space bounded by the cars and whatever natural features are used such as the ocean, *wadi* walls, rocks and drop-offs. Once a man has approached, called out and been invited "in," he may join the group and sit on the mat.[19] If he is older, younger men will offer him their chairs or pillows to lean on. The newcomer, as in a *majlis*, will be offered whatever there is to eat or drink.

The third space, corresponding to the bedroom, is the area used for sleeping. This can be all or part of the inside of the shelter or the area closest to the rock overhang and is delineated by either piled or set-out sleeping mats, pillows, bags of clothing, etc. This zone should never be acknowledged or approached by anyone who is not spending the night; sleeping bags, blankets and personal gear are treated as invisible. A man might reach over and take his blanket to use as a pillow to lean against, but no one else should touch it unless the owner offers it although food, juice, soda, water and the accoutrements for tea are available to everyone.

Sometimes the men who are camping simply fall asleep in the open/*majlis* area. There is no attempt to get them to move to another space and the men who are talking will not modulate their voices. A man might stand up, set up his padded sleeping mat in the sleeping area and lie down, but still listen to the conversation or take his mat and blanket and lie down further from the group, but still within the area delimited by the cars and natural boundaries.

Everyone follows the basic understanding of keeping an empty space of at least two feet between sleeping mats and, as it is culturally forbidden to step over a sleeping person, to set up the mat in a way which does not block access to parts of the sleeping area.

It was not difficult for me to go camping with groups of *hakli* men because there is so much privacy built into their understanding of camping.[20] No one touches or steps close to the personal belongings or bed of another person; no one examines or discusses another person's possessions unless that person calls attention to something they have. And everyone is fully dressed at all times. I would take off my head scarf only when I was lying down and sleep in baggy sweatpants, t-shirt and a sweatshirt. I envision the sleeping mats as beds in a hospital wing which are separated by flimsy curtains; you simply pretend that you are alone.

In the morning, as each person wakes up, they move from the sleeping area to the open area or near the fire to make tea. When everyone is up, the mats are rolled up, blankets folded on top and the sleeping area becomes an open space with equipment stacked against the far wall or rocks.

I assume there are Dhofari women who go camping, but I only know of one woman who did with her husband. The men I know have never been camping with their sisters or wives; when I ask, they explain their wives don't want to.

Long-term camping

Most of the men I know have done some type of long-term camping. For this discussion it's important to remember that the Dhofar War was from

1965 to 1975, and that it took several years after the war ended for schools and roads to be built throughout the Dhofar region. Thus a group of brothers born in the 1960s might have very different childhoods; for example, the oldest having no chance to go to school and learning to read and write after being hired by the military; the middle child leaving home to board at one of the first schools built in Salalah; the youngest living at home and going to a school near his house.

Men who are in their late 30s or older and lived near the coast would go in groups of four or more boys to beaches outside of towns when they were young. They would fish, talk and swim, sometimes staying for weeks at a time. If anything was needed, someone would walk to one of the rough roads that paralleled the coast and would start walking towards town, hoping an older fisherman would drive by and give them a lift. Once older, they would buy cars in decrepit condition and try to make them work. When they were in high school, they would often go fishing after school and on weekends and then camp during holidays.

This kind of lifestyle was possible on the coast when families did not need the work of young boys. Thus a ten-year-old might help his family by bringing back fish or money made from selling fish, but there were older brothers and/or male relatives to make sure the basic family needs were supplied.

The men I know who did this believe that the confidence they gained by being without adults is an important part of their personality and try to give their sons the same chances. Several times while driving I have come across two or more boys in their early teens without a car and miles from a paved road, so this tradition in some manner continues.

In the mountains, before schools were built, boys and girls worked to help support the family from an early age by herding animals, getting water, etc. (see Janzen 1986 and Tabook 1997). Men in their late 30s and older remember "walking with camels," practicing transhumance by moving across the mountains during different seasons and after rainstorms to bring their herd to good grazing. Some places had shelter such as the typical roundhouse or caves, but there were also weeks of sleeping in the open next to a fire. This kind of camping is still occasionally done while herding camels. Several mats are spread out under trees near good grazing, with the supplies being tied up onto tree branches.[21]

Another kind of long-term camping is done during the abalone season which is a few weeks in November or December. As it depends on the number of abalones, the season is not open every year, but if it is, men will temporarily move to be close to the best places for diving. Some will rent an apartment, but others will erect large tents outside of coastal towns. The cost is shared between the older men who will dive for the whole season; younger men and men who will dive for only a day or two will stay for free. Usually, the older men will pay a restaurant to bring meals[22] and the younger men will make tea when needed.

Camping for abalone season is different than weekend/recreation camping in that, while the hosts are very kind to guests, there is a very definite bedtime. Guests are not allowed to stay late, talk, make noise and expect attention. Men who are ready to sleep will tell people to be quiet or sit in another area. I have never heard of this happening in any other circumstances. Guests will sit in the *salle* or *majlis* chatting away while hosts are yawning and everyone knows that the hosts have exams or work in the morning, or that young children will wake the hosts up early.[23] Sleep is always seen as less important than being a good host.

But diving for abalones is dangerous work as men are free-diving down several meters in cold, sometimes murky, water for hours at a time. Serious divers will not invite friends to visit and anyone who comes on their own accord will be told in no uncertain terms when to leave or, if older, will find themselves sitting alone at the campfire.

Picnics and camping: issues of safety and privacy[24]

I was once camping with some of the men in my research group and my stomach rumbled. As I was embarrassed, I pretended that the sound was not from me and the men made some comments in Gibali but never teased me so I assumed they were being polite. A few moments later, they got up and began dragging pieces of scrap wood away from the campsite and made two large fires on the far side of the cars, in addition to the fire near the mat.

Later I realized that they had presumed the rumble was the growl of a wild animal and had built the fires for protection. Years afterwards I confessed and they told me that, yes, they heard the sound, thought it was an animal, confirmed this with each other and decided to light additional fires without telling me so that I would not be afraid.

Safety on picnics and while camping is first and foremost about wild animals: scorpions and snakes in sandy and rocky places, wolves and hyenas in unpopulated areas.[25] The site has to be chosen with care and a fire needs to be lit after dark. Foodstuffs need to be put in cars or well packed and placed near the fire/sleeping people to keep them safe from foxes. Animal attacks are very rare but keeping a fire going is essential in areas away from towns.

The danger from other people is also perceived as low, but not zero; there is the same sense of "of course nothing will happen, but it's better to stay careful" that motivates people to light fires to keep hyenas at bay.

If it is a women-only group, parks are preferred because there are women-only days which means there is no chance of men in the area. Beaches are also easy for women-only groups; while there are no other people close by, it's public enough that no man would dream of bothering a group of women.

For picnics in public areas, there are usually groups of men (either Omani, expat or mixed) so a group of women will usually include a male, even if it is a teenage boy. The boy is a kind of placeholder, a signal and reminder that the Omani women "have men," meaning they are part of a family which will retaliate if women are accosted in public.

Harassment in public is rare in Oman, but it depends on several factors such as the country of origin of the person who is harassed and the harasser. Omani women I know believe a strange man treating them badly is unthinkable. Some might feel that their family and tribe are a burden with expectations of certain kinds of behavior but there is also an understanding that the men of the family and tribe will take direct action (threats and/or violence) against any man who harms a female relative. Fights are very rare, but I have heard men speak of a few fights they have had and warnings they have delivered to both Omani and expat men on behalf of family members.

I have never been harassed by a stranger, in a public location or at a social event. I know that part of the reasons I can move about with ease are that I am older and have an effective stare-of-doom.

I have heard first- and second-hand from other expat women, e.g. wives of professional men and single women who work as nurses and maids, speaking of, for example, refusing to use taxis out of fear of being annoyed.

A final comment is that privacy is very much connected to age. As I have said in my previous books so much of what is written about the Arabian Peninsula concentrates on the rights of men in opposition to the rights of women and there is little on the rights of older people in opposition to the rights of younger people.

A man who approaches a picnic or campsite of older men who he knows/ is related to should greet everyone politely and then listen. He should stay out of the talk, try to be helpful (peeling fruit, making tea) and not ask questions. Young men who come to sit with the research group when I am there will look at me out of the corner of their eyes, but never demand to know who I am. They will not comment on decisions such as what to do, when to leave or what/ when to eat.

If the man is of a similar age, he is treated like he is coming into a *majlis* by being offered food and drink and not expected to do any work. To show his in-group status, the research men will explain who I am without him having to ask.

If the man is older, then the perception of the area changes so that he is both host and guest. He treats the campsite as if it was *his majlis* and the other men are his sons. He will drive or walk up, call out and immediately come in to sit down and stay as long as he wants; he will dominate the conversation by asking questions and talking as long as he pleases. Yet he is also a guest, which means the men who are camping will offer whatever food or drink is there. This double status can be seen in that an older man can request that something be made for him, something a man would do in his own house, but a polite guest would never do.

Thus if a man is younger or of a similar age, the group dynamics will not alter greatly. Certain topics might be discussed or not discussed, but the body language does not change. An older man changes everything; people sit up straight, hold their bodies still, speak less unless trying to politely force the guest to eat or drink. Side chatter stops and the older man sets the topics and tone of the group conversation.

Although I have never heard a man express relief when an older man leaves, sometimes sites are chosen in difficult-to-get-to-locations far from paved roads so that "no one will come." For *haklis*, a picnic or campsite is like a house, anyone may approach at any time and they should be welcomed. So if people want privacy, the only guarantee is to be in a place where they can't be seen.

Notes

1 Another factor is that Muslim men may have up to four wives. Some men will marry a second wife ten or more years after the first wife so that a man could have a daughter (from the second wife) who is the same age as a granddaughter (daughter of son or daughter from the first wife).

2 Other examples are discussed in Chapter 4. First, adults keep their clothes in cupboards in their bedrooms but children's clothes are sometimes kept in a storeroom so that they can't use them as playthings, e.g. scatter clothes around the room. Rather than keeping clothes within reach or sight, parents can control access until the child is old enough to be responsible. I have heard many stories of small kids getting into an older sibling's bedroom and wreaking havoc, but not being punished as it was the adult's fault for not locking the door. Likewise, counters in kitchens are high, stoves are placed up on platforms and extra food is locked in a storeroom so that children cannot see or reach items.

3 This does not mean a house is not or should not be protected by the owner. Yet the meaning of "protection" varies widely between cultures. In North America it can mean, among other definitions, "no one comes into my house without my permission." But among *hakli* families, it's normal for men to walk into the *majlis* of a family they don't know. I discuss this further in Chapter 5.

4 When a female Dhofari friend told me that she had refurbished her mother's bedroom without any input from her mother, I could only shudder with horror at the thought of what would happen to me if I decided to repaint and install new furniture in a relative's bedroom without telling them beforehand. Being covered with honey and tied next to a fire-ant nest would be the least of it.

5 As I was working on *Foodways* (Risse 2021) and thinking about the topic of houses, I realized that I had picked two topics to write about which do not receive concentrated attention in the form of intense, daily discussions. The Dhofaris I know do not talk frequently about menu planning and discovering new dishes, nor do they talk about new trends in house design or decoration. People focus on food for parties to make sure there is enough for everyone; they focus on the house they are building to make sure the space is fairly divided and the rooms are a good size.

It is not a coincidence I write about food and houses; these two topics are easy for Dhofaris to talk about with me as the subjects do not directly relate to sensitive topics such as politics or family problems. Also, they are easy to photograph; no one ever objected to sending me pictures of food or houses.

6 A small, but important, point is that if there is a maid at home, being in a hotel in which someone cleans the room and food is delivered to the room is very similar to being at home.

7 In footnote 19, Hadimioglu notes that "if a camera is used in a harem [women-only space], the women are likely to put on their chador. The forbidden space, once extended to the bounds of the entire room, is effectively contracted into the space of each woman's tent" (2001 24). The same holds true in Dhofar. At wedding parties, for example, one of the duties of the groom's female relatives who are hosting the party is to make sure female guests are not taking photos. If the groom arrives, his relatives say "men coming" loudly over and over so that women cover their faces. At several weddings I have been to, I have also covered my face to blend in and, with only my eyes showing, it's allowed me to have a good, long look at the groom and his brothers as they walk by. Mohammed Al Murr's "The Wink of the Mona Lisa" (1998) has an excellent fictional, but realistic, description of a man's point of view while walking through a wedding party.

8 Sometimes the choice of which places to go and how to dress are in the hands of the woman in question; sometimes older (both male and female) members of her family will push for certain types of behavior. This is usually read by outsiders as husbands, fathers and brothers oppressing wives, daughters and sisters but the reality is much more complex. I know both male and female Dhofaris who have female relatives who have decided to act much more conservatively than the rest of the family; Dhofari women who asked for and were given a divorce when their husbands tried to tightly control who the women visited; and male relatives who overruled conservative female relatives to allow young women freedom of movement.

9 Another difference is that Maneval states, "Public squares and gardens which are open to everyone simply do not exist" in Jeddah, while there are many in Dhofar (2019 164).

There are public gardens in most sections of Salalah, temporary public spaces such as Ittin Festival, the outside seating area at Gardens Mall, many government-built shelters at beaches and scenic overlooks in the mountain, as well as public spaces in small towns such as the circular, stepped mini-stadium at Quirun Heriti. Further, Maneval argues that "vacant land, roundabouts and median strips are not supposed to be used as public space. None of these places was designed for the purpose of outdoor sociability" (179); while in Dhofar it is very normal to picnic on the grass-covered areas in roundabouts and next to roads.

10 This point reminds me of my trying to find a good café in Dubai in the late 1990s. Some were "too local" with low ceilings, no sightlines and only male customers; some were too intimidating with expensive menus and glaring waitstaff. I finally ended up "at home" at La Gaufrette in Deira City Center which had a very mixed clientele.

11 There are two other points which are somewhat beyond the scope of this work. One is that there are "people of different ethnicities and nationalities in places such as DIFC [Dubai International Financial Centre] but those without sufficient economic (and cultural) capital are directly or indirectly excluded from such spaces" (AlMutawa 2022 67). Thus a space might be non-segregated in terms of country of origin but segregated by wealth.

Secondly AlMutawa argues that

> while critics of Gulf cities oppose the so-called mass consumerism of Dubai, they seek an 'authenticity' that they can easily consume (by consuming 'local' food bought in a small 'authentic' shop or 'experiencing authenticity' in an old market). They reject the globalised nature of a city like Dubai, wanting it to conform to their idea of what a Middle Eastern city *should* look like. They are disappointed to see that many Emiratis regularly eat and drink in cafes and restaurants like Starbucks or Texas Roadhouse, rather than opting

for 'traditional' food, or that shopping malls are ubiquitous in place of small, local shops ... Thus, we must question to what extent 'authenticity' is another form of Orientalism, an expectation for people to live, eat, dress, and behave in a certain way and for urban spaces to look a certain way; to be 'different' from other globalised cities.

(2018)

This is true for Dhofar as well as I discussed in chapters 7 and 8 of *Foodways in Southern Oman* (Risse 2021), some expats have told me with pride that they would never eat at KFC as they want to only have "local food"; but KFC is "local" to Omanis.

12 For myself, there is simply no escape. When I visited a brand new hotel more than an hour outside of Salalah which had only ten other guests, one walked up to me and told me where I worked and what my job was. When I once apologized to a sales clerk for having to take an extra plastic bag, she said, "It's ok, we all know you" and proceeded to say my name. Baggers at the large grocery stores will simply push the cart to my car without me having to say which one it is; a fact made more amazing because there are usually at least five other cars of the same color and style in the lot.

13 The information in this section is gleaned from over almost 400 documented picnics, over two dozen camping trips, interviews and years of observations of how and where people arrange themselves and their immediate environment when they are outside their house.

14 Some people never do work, but that is not commented on. Either you are happy to have the person with you, whether they help or not, or you don't invite them. Similarly, usually people wait until everyone is present before eating, but a few times I have seen a man make a plate and start to eat, without any criticism. Trying to change peer group members is not a *hakli* trait.

15 When I was doing an interview with a *hakli* man about picnicking, I asked, "Have you ever gone up to a group of women you didn't know who were sitting together?" "No," he said emphatically, "they would want to talk!" He then imitated what he considered women's "talk": What is your name? What is your tribe? Where are you from? What are you doing here?

16 For a plan of a picnic site, see my essay https://mariellerisse.com/2021/10/30/houseways-homespaces-away-from-home/

17 For a photograph of a fishing shelter, see Blue, Al-Jahwari, Staples, et al. 2014 65.

18 For plans of camping sites during the day and at night, see my essay https://mariellerisse.com/2021/10/30/houseways-homespaces-away-from-home/

19 I have seen photos of some men camping with coffee tables, large folding tables for food preparation, trays, benches, rugs and other such supplies. Gatherings with the research group are very simple: a plastic mat, a few pillows, a cooler for soda, a tea kettle, some small tea cups, a pot for cooking, a long-handled spoon and a few large metal platters.

20 There is a link between camping and knowing me. Many *hakli* men in their 40s and older had a lot of responsibility as children and learned to trust themselves. The men in my research group sometimes explain me as a tourist who they were taking around for money but it takes enormous trust in themselves, their place in the community and me to go camping on a beach where any number of relatives and friends could potentially stop by.

I cannot emphasize enough how unusual it is for a single American woman to go on picnics and go camping with groups of Dhofari men. I was driving once with a *hakli* man in a barren *wadi* when we passed a pickup. He made a soft *humph* sound which in American cultures would mean "slight problem" and among *hakli* men means "major disaster." "What?" I asked.

"My wife's brother and his family," he said.

"Will you be OK?"

He shrugged and I did not mention the topic again. To ask, "Are you going to face major tension at home because I wanted to see an ancient site?" is too intrusive.

From being around Dhofaris for more than a decade, I know the right thing to do is NOT ask, but wait until the next time I have an idea to go somewhere. If he comes up with a reason not to go, then I know there was blowback. There are men who have made it clear that they got a talking-to from a relative about picnicking with me; others have introduced me to their wives and children as a matter of course. A few do not speak about their families' reaction to their knowing and spending time with me.

21 There are many photos of this on social media, almost always with several large, metal bowls full of frothy camel milk in the center of the photo.

22 As diving is exhausting and starts as soon as the sun creates visibility in the water, breakfast is usually just tea and a little bread. Water, drinkable yogurt, bread, and packaged leftovers from breakfast: oatmeal and/or *attriya* (or *balaleet*, a dish made with vermicelli; usually it is very sweet, flavored with cardamom and rose water and served with an omelet on top but for the season it is made with made with milk, and without eggs) is put in bags for the boat. There is a late lunch around 5 pm, dinner at 8 or 9 pm.

23 Sometimes the issue is that a female guest is waiting for a brother or husband to pick her up, in which case the women might soldier on keeping up conversation or everyone lapses into a rare period of silence.

24 I talk about safety in houses in Chapter 5 and privacy for houses in Chapter 8.

25 Another consideration is the presence of *djinn*, who usually live in uninhabited places. When picking a place to sleep, they will pay attention to what they and the people with them see, hear and feel. As is usual in *hakli* communications, a person doesn't need to say every detail; an "I am not comfortable here" will lead to the whole group getting up and moving without comment or complaint.

References

For photos and a full bibliography, please see: *Come From Away*, https://mariellerisse.com

Note: Social media in Oman is full of photos of men camping, or at least having a cup of tea next to a fire, but I have not found any academic work on the current habit of camping. There are often mentions in social media of wealthy men from the Arabian Peninsula camping with dozens of tents, ACs, TVs, etc. This kind of create-a-house-in-the-middle-of-the-desert is reminiscent of Marie Antoinette playing a shepherdess and not similar to the usual weekend camping in Dhofar. There are several texts which discuss camping, not in terms of vacation/amusement, but as a way of life more than 20 years ago. Dawn Chatty has several texts about a vanishing type of nomadic life in the region north of Dhofar (2013a, 2013b, 1976, 1997, 1998, 2000). Miranda Morris has two articles about Dhofar, one gives information about lifeways before and during the war (1987, 1997). The other article gives information about camping during the frankincense harvest season which seems similar to camping during abalone season, i.e. people camping away from their homes for a short time to earn money. Tabook's (1997) unpublished dissertation is a treasure of information about Dhofar in the 1990s and earlier including details about transhumance (see also Tabuki 1982).

So although I have not cited these texts in this chapter, I include the details of their work below.

Abu-Lughod, Janet. 1987. "The Islamic City: Historical Myth, Islamic Essence and Contemporary Relevance." *International Journal of Middle East Studies* 19.2: 155–76.

AlMutawa, Rana. 2022. "Navigating the Cosmopolitan City: Emirati Women and Ambivalent Forms of Belonging in Dubai," in *Migration in the Making of the Gulf Space Social, Political, and Cultural Dimensions*. Antia Mato Bouzas and Lorenzo Casini, eds. New York: Berghahn Books. 67–85.

———. 2018, Dec.4. "Challenging Concepts of "Authenticity": Dubai and Urban Spaces in the Gulf." *London School of Economics Middle East Blog Posts*. https://blogs.lse.ac.uk/mec/2018/12/04/challenging-concepts-of-authenticity-dubai-and-urban-spaces-in-the-gulf/

Blue, Lucy, Nasser Said Al-Jahwari, Eric Staples, Lorena Giorgio, Paolo Croce, Alessandro Ghidoni, Ayyoub Nagmoush Al Busaidi and Luca Belfioretti. 2014. "Maritime Footprints: Examining the Maritime Cultural Landscape of Masirah Island, Oman, Past and Present." *Proceedings of the Seminar for Arabian Studies* 44. 53–68.

Bourdieu, Pierre. 1972. "The Kabyle House or the World Reversed," in *Algeria 1960*. Cambridge: Cambridge University Press. 133–54.

Chatty, Dawn. 2013a. "Rejecting Authenticity in the Desert Landscapes of the Modern Middle East: Development Processes in the Jiddat Il-Harasiis, Oman," in *Anthropology of the Middle East and North Africa*. Sherine Hafez and Susan Slyomovics, eds. Bloomington: Indiana University Press. 145–64.

———. 2013b. "Negotiating Authenticity and Translocality in Oman: The 'Desertscapes' of the Harasiis Tribe," in *Regionalizing Oman: Political, Economic and Social Dynamics*. Steffen Wippel, ed. Heidelberg: Springer. 129–45.

———. 2000. "Integrating Participation into Research and Consultancy: A Conservation Example from Arabia." *Social Policy and Administration* 34.4: 408–18.

———. 1998. "Enclosures and Exclusions: Conserving Wildlife in Pastoral Areas of the Middle East." *Anthropology Today* 14.4: 2–7.

———. 1997. *Mobile Pastoralists: Development Planning and Social Change in Oman*. New York: Columbia University Press.

———. 1976. "From Camel to Truck." *Folk* 18: 114–28.

Hadimioglu, Çagla. 2001. "Black Tents." *Thresholds* 22: 18–25.

Janzen, Jorg. 1986. *Nomads in the Sultanate of Oman: Tradition and Development in Dhofar*. London: Westview Press.

Kotnik, Toni. 2005. "The Mirrored Public Architecture and Gender Relationship in Yemen." *Space and Culture* 8.4: 472–83.

Maneval, Stefan. 2019. *New Islamic Urbanism: The Architecture of Public and Private Space in Jeddah, Saudi Arabia*. London: University College London Press.

Mohammed Al Murr, Mohammed. 1998. "The Wink of the Mona Lisa," in "*The Wink of the Mona Lisa*" *and Other Stories from the Gulf*. J. Briggs, Trans. Dubai, United Arab Emirates: Motivate Publishing.

Morris, Miranda. 1997. "The Harvesting of Frankincense in Dhofar," in *Profumi d'Arabia*. Alessandra Avanzini, ed. Rome: L'Erma Bretschneider. 231–50.

———. 1987. "Dhofar: What Made it Different," in *Oman: Economic, Social and Strategic Development*. B. R. Pridham, ed. London: Croom Helm. 51–78.

Risse, Marielle. 2021. *Foodways in Southern Oman*. London: Routledge.
Tabook, Salim Bakhit. 1997. *Tribal Practices and Folklore of Dhofar, Sultanate of Oman*. Unpublished PhD thesis, Faculty of Arts, Exeter University.
Tabuki, Salim Bakhit. 1982. "Tribal Structures in South Oman." *Arabian Studies* 6: 51–6. (same author as above)

7 Situating and comparing Dhofari houses

The "Islamic city"

The Arab and/or Islamic cities which appear frequently in architectural and/or social research are either centuries old (Amman, Casablanca, Cairo, Jeddah, Tunnis), created within the last 30 years by wealthy governments (Abu Dhabi, Doha, Dubai, Kuwait City), war-torn (Aleppo, Baghdad, Damascus, Sana'a) or religiously significant (Mecca). There is some work on Muscat (see Chapter 1) but little on Salalah.

First, Salalah is much younger and smaller than the cities usually used as examples, such as Alexandria and Riyadh. The government of Oman has less disposable income and fewer expats in countries such as Qatar. Although the Dhofar War (1965–1975) effected the whole region, it was not fought in the city of Salalah. Almost all engagements occurred in areas with few or no inhabitants except the pitched battle at Mirbat Fort on July 19, 1972.

For more than 30 years, "Islamic city" has been used to refer to certain characteristics of cities and I would like to engage with the term to explain how Salalah does not fit most of the definitions and why.

Abu-Lughod's article "The Islamic City" (1987) succinctly goes through the past scholarship of how an "Islamic city" was conceived of in "Orientalist scholarship" (155). For example, William Marcais stated that Islam is an "urban religion" and that an Islamic city needed a Friday mosque, market and public bath (156). His brother George Marcais stipulated that "residential quarters are often specialized by ethnicity" (156) and importance of the "rights of neighbors" (157) were essential characteristics.[1]

Her reasons for looking at the historical definitions are both to note the colonial/imperialist tendencies of such accounts, as well as to warn current city planners about the impossibility of using modes and designs created in the 1400s and earlier for modern urban planning. In her conclusion, she writes that the creation of the ancient cities

> were deeply influenced by such non-Islamic factors as climate, terrain, technologies of construction, circulation, and production, as well as political variables, such as the relation between rulers and the ruled, the general level of inter-communal strife, and fluctuations in the degree of

DOI: 10.4324/9781003270317-7

> internal and external security ... one does not have the capacity to re-create Islamic cities by edict
>
> (172)

This is a specific rebuttal to anyone who wishes to re-create a mythologized construct. Specifically, she argues that "Only a view of the Islamic city such as that held by earlier Orientalists would allow one to even entertain such a notion" (173).[2]

A few years later, Raymond's "Islamic City, Arab City: Orientalist Myths and Recent Views" (1994) takes up a similar argument. First, he explains why and how previous critics viewed the "Islamic city" as a negative construct, for example

> Having found nothing in the theories of Weber on the evolution of Western cities that could be applied to the cities they had before them, the specialists, in particular Sauvaget in Syria, had to admit that they were dealing with a type of urban layout that could only be defined by a morose enumeration of all those elements it obviously lacked: the regularity and institutions of the antique city and the charts and communes of the medieval town
>
> (4)

His conclusion is that "Whatever the uncertainties that remain, or gaps in our information, it seems that one cannot speak of an 'Islamic' city such as the one the Orientalists thought they could define. The characteristics mentioned have nothing Islamic about them or are not relevant" (16). Further, like Abu-Lughod, he states both that the Orientalists were wrong in their definitions and that cities grow within specific frameworks of place and time, hence cannot be duplicated or reinstated:

> In this vast, 'Muslim', domain we are certainly faced with an urban system whose reality reveals the great weakness of the Orientalist description: its conclusion, explicit or not, of so-called ' urban anarchy', is quite obviously devoid of any meaning, since a city, that is to say a geographical concentration of a large population, can only subsist or develop within a system of coherent relations between its society and the space in which it expands
>
> (17)

In a more recent article, Andraos (2016) uses "Arab" instead of "Islamic" but has the same argument that outsiders/Orientalists are creating and writing about architecture using a

> mélange of symbols and metaphors — the medina, the oasis, the souk — [which] all too often produces reductive meanings and experiences; it can encourage, albeit unintentionally, the sort of essentialism which,

> as Edward Said so eloquently argued, is not only offensive in its representations but also instrumental in perpetuating forms of colonialism.

In addition,

> All too often an idea of "Islamic architecture" is promoted in an effort to unify a region that extends from Turkey to Syria to Iraq to the Emirates – to advance the strange concept of a cohesive Islamic people, nation, empire. The predictable result is cultural displacement.[3]

Yet, within these discussions, a few conventions about the aspects of an Islamic and/or Arab city become clear. Abu-Lughod argues that

> The three Islamic elements that set in motion the processes that give rise to Islamic cities were: a distinction between the members of the Umma and the outsiders, which led to juridical and spatial distinction by neighborhoods; the segregation of the sexes which gave rise to a particular solution to the question of spatial organization; and a legal system which, rather than imposing general regulations over land uses of various types in various places, left the litigation of the neighbors the detailed adjudication of mutual rights over space and use.
>
> (1987 172)

Raymond's view is

> The fundamental feature of the structure of the 'traditional' Arab city is the very clearly marked separation of its economic activities and its residential functions ... the central area of the markets is strongly linked to the main mosque [and] ... Around this centre there spreads an area devoted above all to residential housing, in which economic activities only appear in the form of local, non-specialized markets
>
> (1994 12, 13)

Wirth saw the definitive features as including a

> disintegrated city layout, dead-end street structure, courtyard house, and (ethnically) separated quarters. In addition, there is the defensive function of the city...The social, political, and religious rules and norms are reflected in the design of large architectural complexes (e.g. bazaar, mosque with bath and oven) that are considered a characteristic feature of the Oriental-Islamic city.
>
> (Escher 2019 124)

In a review of the scholarship, Maneval states that the key attributes of Islamic cities "include dense and irregular settlement patterns with tortuous streets, a division between commercial and residential quarters, a subdivision of the residential quarters into smaller neighbourhoods, blind alleys and dead-end courts shared by the residents of adjoining houses" (2019 132).[4]

Whether or not the term is useful, the concept of "Islamic city" refers to several characteristics which are not applicable to Salalah. Of the definitions mentioned, only segregation of sexes and a main mosque can be found in Salalah. To further explore the role of gender separation in Salalah, I will use Bianca's essay "Basic Principles of Islam and Their Social, Spatial and Artistic Implications" (2000). He starts with the idea that

> architecture and urban form can be seen as a natural expression of prevailing spiritual values and beliefs which are intimately related to the acknowledged cosmic order of the world ... there is a close interaction between what people build and what they believe.
>
> (22)

Like some of the Orientalists cited by Abu-Lughod, he believes that Islam is an "urban religion" as the edicts that men pray together daily, the male community gathers on Fridays and the *Haj* be undertaken if possible necessitate certain types of physical spaces, buildings and community organization (28). But he goes into more detail by explaining that

> the distinctive feature of Islam is that it has given birth to a comprehensive and integrated cultural system by totally embedding the religious practice in the daily life of the individual and society ... by providing a matrix of behavioral archetypes, which, by necessity, generated correlated physical patterns.
>
> (22-3)

I want to focus on these "correlated physical patterns" as keeping a male/female separation in public is a factor mentioned by most texts about the physical/built environment in a conservative Islamic country. This partition can be arranged through laws/government regulations, how buildings are designed and constructed or people's individual choices about placement, irrespective of the building's layout. In Dhofar, people's choices are the main factor as there are not many laws and not all public buildings are set up to maintain gender privacy.[5] For example, there is nothing in the Salalah airport that shows that the space is in a conservative Muslim country except for the prayer rooms.[6]

Commercial and public spaces that are set up to prevent genders from mixing include restaurants, cafés, banks, hospitals and universities which have women/family-only areas. Some places also have time limits, such as women-only days at a shopping festival or parks.

The kinds of spaces with the most built-in divisions are restaurants/cafés and parks: places that are centered on eating and resting, where women might be lifting their *niqab* (face covering) and relaxing. Some restaurants have the family area upstairs with the entry through a different door; the family section might be a group of small closed rooms or separated by a low wall.

But even physical barriers such as placards and walls which create separation in public are easily and often overcome. In Salalah, men will sit in the women-only section of a café if the male area is full while women can sit in the open/male area if they want to.

I saw another example of the disregard for external divisions when COVID vaccines were given in two large, adjacent sports halls: one for men and one for women. As I walked by the male hall, I saw two women walking out hand in hand with a disabled man. To me it was a very typical Dhofari scene. Rather than bring the man into the female space with all female clerks and nurses or give their male relative to male attendants while they waited outside; the two women brought the man into the male space, knowing that they would be allowed to enter. In talking about what I had seen with a Dhofari woman, she agreed with my assessment stating that, "they had to respect him as a man [by taking him to the male hall]" but in doing so the women would not be judged as acting inappropriately.

Further, even if one place is women only, there are nearby places in which genders can mix. For example, one college in Dhofar has a "women-only reading room" in the library, a women-only computer lab and a women-only cafeteria. But students who wish to work in gender-mixed groups can do so by studying in a classroom, sitting in the open computer lab, eating lunch together on the lawn.

In general, whether or not there are physical barriers to prevent genders from mixing, it is the actions of individuals which create divisions. One example of how Dhofaris create a personal sphere of privacy while circumventing stated rules can be seen in hospitals and clinics where you can often find the "wrong" gender in a waiting room. Several times I have seen a man sitting with his mother or wife in the women-only area so that the two are not separated and she does not have to sit in the male-only area. In the times that I have seen this, the man sits in the chair closest to the door and looks either at his phone or at the floor if not talking to the woman. Thus it is not the built environment but his behavior that creates his segregation from other women.

A second example is that several years ago my bank started an initiative to have a "women's only" teller complete with a long, narrow, pink carpet for women to stand on while waiting. Before this, women wearing black *abayahs* would often cut to the front of the line or stand in line and then men would gesture for them to go to the front. Women who were not conservatively dressed would wait in line but there would be a little extra empty space ahead of and behind them.

The "women's only line" initiative fizzled out fairly soon (I never saw a woman in the women's teller space although there are female tellers) and was eventually replaced with a ticket system in which each person would take a numbered ticket when they arrived and wait for the number to be called. The chairs in the waiting area are not marked in any way but are always divided in some fashion with women in one part and men in another.

In areas with no built-in segregation, such as the airport, stores and beaches, Dhofaris sit/walk in ways to create boundaries. When you walk into the gate areas at Salalah airport, there are no signs about who should sit where but the space is always divided into sections where Omani men are sitting, families are sitting and expats are sitting. You can sit wherever you like, but if you break the unwritten social understandings of space management by, for example an expat woman sitting next to an Omani man, you will be stared at and the people near you might move.

The overarching rule of public space usage in Dhofar is the more conservatively dressed a woman is, the more space she is given to maneuver. A Dhofari man will not enter a narrow aisle in a store if there is a conservatively dressed woman already in the aisle.

I once pulled up to order takeaway from a restaurant with large plate glass windows allowing a view into the interior which had about 10 tables set up, 2 occupied by pairs of men, and about 10 kitchen- and wait-staff. After I ordered from the runner who came to the car window, a car pulled up to my left and I glanced over. There was an Omani man in the driver's seat and a woman who was exiting the passenger side wearing an *abayah*, *shelia* and *niqab*. As she walked between the two cars and across the front of my car towards the restaurant entrance, I thought: there is no way this woman is walking into that restaurant. If she wanted food, she would order from the car from the runner. If she needed the bathroom, she would not pick a place with a line of cars facing the windows of a large, well-lit restaurant; she would use a mosque or the bathroom along the back wall of a gas station. She is not going in there. And she didn't; she walked past the entrance and went into the clothes store to the right of the restaurant.

She had every legal right to have a meal in that restaurant and, being fully covered, she had every social and moral right as well. But 15 years of watching, asking questions, having meals in public and trying to recognize cultural understandings, taught me that she was not going to go in. Hence my argument is that Salalah is an Islamic city because of the small, daily choices that Muslim Dhofaris make, not because of laws, how buildings are designed or where buildings are located.[7]

Movement: who goes where

I remember (but can't find the quote) a discussion of Oscar Wilde's trial in which the author argued that the prosecution did not need to explain or verify what happened at Wilde's late-night meetings in hotel rooms. What was important was that they proved Wilde had been in a certain place at a certain time with certain people. His physical presence was so damning, no other details were needed because there could be no purpose of being there unless it was for illegal activities as defined under the law at that time.

That reasoning obtains in Dhofar. The *hakli* I know are very slow to condemn and are careful to articulate what they know from personal experience and what someone told them, but placement is vital. Why would a person go to X place unless there was Y reason? Men, for example, will tell me whether or not there are female, Moroccan waitresses at the cafés they go to. Some say with a laugh that they do; they like talking/laughing with the women who are pleasant in order to get bigger tips. Some make it clear that they don't.

There is a deliberateness about most *hakli* lives that is difficult to explain and catch examples of. I have gradually learned some contours because I am occasionally called out for actions which are coded as purposeful but weren't. This leads to a lot of discussions along the lines of "of course, you meant X because you were in Y place"; when I protest, I am often not believed. These difficult discussions helped me to see how important location is, even to the level of where you choose to sit within a circle of friends.

One example of placement is that I was at a picnic dinner with a much larger group than normal and one man (X) got up after the meal and changed his position. When I mentioned this to another man (Y) later because moving places within the circle is rare, even rarer when it is a large group, Y castigated X's actions thoroughly and with heat. This stands in stark contrast to Y's reaction to other events such as someone being an hour late or losing $500. When I found out a friend lied to me for over a year about something important, Y advised me to be calm and forgive the person. But moving places at a picnic brought down the full weight of his censure and disdain. A real man did not do such a thing and X should "hold himself."

Part of the significance of placement comes from religion. For example, in Islam, a woman should never be alone with a man who is not *mahram* (proscribed from marriage; these include father, brother, uncle, son and a man who was breastfed by the same woman). By chance, I ended up sitting alone on a beach with a man who was friends with men in the research group and he told me that he was not comfortable to be sitting alone with me. I said, "But I am old!" trying to give him a way to frame the situation.

"No," he said, "Not allowed."

I stayed silent as he wrestled with this dilemma. He had known me for years, knew men who knew me, knew that other men were coming soon and that it would be rude to go but also he felt uncomfortable sitting alone with me. I told him that it was fine if he left as I have often sat on beaches alone. He shook his head. I repeated that it was totally ok to go to another location and come back when the other men arrived. He responded by getting up to build a fire to make tea so that he was not leaving, but also not with me.

Certain places belong to different groups of people in different ways. For example the grassy sides of roadways are the location for expat workers who turn on and off the water, trim the grass and trees and weed during the day.[8] The same spaces belong to groups of young boys who play football in the late afternoons, while expats often use open, sandy spaces to play cricket or beaches to play volleyball. Roadside space has a religious use for people who are traveling when the call to prayer sounds, as they stop and pray on the grass. In the evening, the space is used by families for picnics.

Being near the side of a road in a sandy/rocky area is construed differently. This type of area is often used for selling food as it is easy to leave and reenter the roadway. Women will sit near a small table and sell prepared food or different types of bread. Men will sit near a truck and sell fruits and vegetables. Young boys will stand and sell camel milk during the *khareef*. Usually, the milk is given away for free, but in the monsoon season, there are so many camels in a small area, Dhofaris have more than enough and thousands of tourists are happy to buy.

Standing next to a road is only done by street sweepers or those looking for a ride. If a man is standing near the road raising and lifting his hand, palm down, he is asking for a lift.

Movement: who wears what where

Another example of cultural understandings of movement within towns is the connection between clothes, location and movement. Depending on what you are wearing, where you are and what you are doing, a person can create a type of invisibility.

One example is bicycles. In Dhofar, only three types of people ride: young children of either gender and any nationality, expat male workers and serious athletes in specialized gear with specialized bikes. And for each of these groups, there is a particular relationship between bike riding, location and/or clothing. Young children ride in the *hosh* or near their house; expat men ride on any street while going to and from work, always fully clothed with long-sleeved shirts and long trousers.

However, Omani men in biking clothes do not usually ride near their houses. They put on their gear, get in a car and drive to a neutral place, for example, a parking lot near a gas station. Then either alone or with a group, they begin a trip on main roads. It is acceptable to wear very tight, form-fitting clothes only during the activity.

Similarly, men will not leave the house wearing football clothes but have at least a *wazar* (sarong) tied around their waist over their shorts. At the parking lot or side line, they take off the *wazar*, play and then put it on again when they leave the pitch. The same holds true for horseback riders.

When walking for exercise, Muslim women wearing an *abayah* and any kind of head/face covering are treated as invisible force fields. Men do not greet or look at them and will move to the opposite side of the path or off the path to avoid passing close by. Women in pants/skirts might be treated the same way, might be greeted or might be nearly run over by a man intent on "not seeing" her to the point where he walks straight towards her and forces her to move aside.

Movement: driving and public transportation

When discussing Jeddah, Maneval (2019) discusses cars as a "bubble" of freedom and "a private living room on wheels" (180, 181). He states that

> a private vehicle ... has much in common with the screened and isolated contemporary Saudi home ... it serves as a physical barrier protecting the privacy of a family from undesired contact with strangers ... If it does not provide enough visual protection, speed helps passengers to escape other people's control
>
> (181)

This is true in Dhofar as private cars are the only truly acceptable means of transportation.[9] I was once in a taxi in Salalah which pulled up next to one of the research guys' car at a light. He insisted I get out and get into his car. I protested that I had several errands to run and he said he would take me. Another time I asked a research guy to send a taxi to my house; he arrived driving a school bus, took me to a shopping center, waited while I shopped and brought me home. A third research guy told me how a friend of his was arriving in Salalah by bus from Muscat so he drove an hour to pick him up at 4 am, then drove him home. Having the friend take a taxi or wait until a decent hour was out of the question. When a mutual friend's bus broke down in the mountains, a Dhofari man called me and we drove 45 minutes to "rescue" him rather than allow him to wait for the repairs or a replacement bus.

For expat men, there have always been little vans that take people to different parts of Dhofar. Perhaps women use them as well but I have never seen a woman in the minibuses. There is a fairly recent, inexpensive municipal bus that has two routes. One goes from the port on the southeastern side of Salalah to the airport on the northwestern side; the second serves the main downtown area of 23rd July Street. Women sometimes use these buses as they are large so that enough people can sit separately, but the vast majority of riders are expat. Oddly, there are no shelters at the bus stops, simply a metal pole with an image of the bus and the route timings.

The most difficult aspect of driving in town is women walking out into the middle of traffic, often with small children. The first time this happened a woman wearing an *abayah*, *shelia* and *niqab* stepped off the curb directly in front of my car. I screamed, swung left, slammed on the brakes and by the grace of God, the on-coming car swung to its right into a parking lot as I went into its lane. The woman did not break stride or look at either car. I smashed the horn for a good 15 seconds but there was no reaction from her.

So I learned that in town I always needed to watch women who were standing near the edge of the road. It has happened several more times, including once as I was writing this book. A fully covered woman with two small children walked straight into a stream of cars which braked and pulled off to the side. I (the only female driver) was the only one who honked as she and the kids slowly walked across the four lanes without any acknowledgment of the havoc they caused.

The most entertaining aspect of driving is that it is virtually impossible to keep Dhofari drivers, myself included, out of places they want to go to. For example, about ten years ago the municipal government decided to improve 23rd July Street, the main east-west shopping street. It was about ten blocks long with one lane of tarmac in each direction, then about three lanes wide of hard-packed sand between the road and the line of storefronts. The whole width (about eight lanes total) was torn up to make a divided street with two lanes in each direction. During construction, all the stores stayed open but there were dirt barriers to keep people from entering.

The general reaction was that a dirt barrier should not be treated as a serious impediment to driving. As one of the research guys asked me, "Were you raised by small people?"[10] We all went up and over the dirt pile, along the expanse of hard-packed sand, weaving between mounds of rocks, heaps of broken tarmac, workers digging, bulldozers plowing, trucks dumping gravel and men in hard hats trying to take measurements. Graders, front loaders, tar trucks and rollers were all doing a slow-moving *pas de quatre* amidst the stacks of concrete blocks, deep ditches for electric lines and huge, round water pipes.[11]

Lastly, placement of cars is as important as placement of persons, as was discussed above. Because it is a communal culture, everyone knows the standards and what the implications are of being in A place at B time. A man who sits alone in his truck at the beach at night is probably talking to a girl, probably a girl he "should not" be talking to.

I once went through a McDonald's drive-thru late in the afternoon during Ramadan. I noticed that the pick-up ahead of me was the type usually driven by men who live in the mountains. I thought: no man who drives that kind of car would ever eat McDonald's food to begin with and certainly not during the day in Ramadan. I stared at the pick-up as the single man leaned over to order food and pay. Then I realized: the only way what I was seeing could make sense is if the driver was getting food for a child who was so small, their head did not show above the seats. So I watched very closely when the order window slid open and the worker handed over the food: a kid's meal which the driver took, then his hand moved down and to the right. It was a child's meal for the child in the front seat.

Placement: who designs the space

Dhofaris are usually in complete control of their house so it fits their purposes. One Dhofari friend walked around for months with a tape measure in her purse so that she could measure the size of rooms to help her decide how large to make the spaces in her house. Of the ten Dhofaris I know best, eight have planned and built the house they live in, one is renting and planning to build within a year and the tenth bought a house sight unseen.

As I was writing this book I gradually realized how well houses are suited for Dhofaris in opposition to how poorly planned so many other types of buildings are. I am constantly amazed at commercial and public structures which appear to have been designed by people who have never visited, much less lived in, Oman or the Middle East. Large projects designed by outsiders are often so badly conceived they appear to be made with malevolent intentions. One mall has an outdoor seating area facing north, the least desirable direction as southern winds (coming from the ocean) are preferable being soft, cooling and moist; northern winds are hot and often carry sand. One development outside of Salalah is infamous for its narrow, dangerous roads.

One institute of higher learning is comprised of several large buildings built around a large open area that has no shade or benches. None of the buildings are connected by covered walkways, in a climate that is hot and sunny nine months of the year and drizzling for the other three. The buildings aren't oriented to protect walkers or windows from the north wind and the parking is disconnected from the buildings. If the architects have spent even one day in the Middle East, the buildings don't reflect it.

There are two main foreign hypermarkets (X and Y) in Salalah. X has many stores in the Middle East while Y's experience is limited. The disconnect between what architects plan and the on-the-ground realities can be seen in the differences between the two approaches to parking. X has parking directly connected to the building, with the main roads on the far side of parking lots. Y has main roads between the stores and the parking lots, which means people trying to get into and out of the building are traversing busy streets full of drivers trying to get into or out of the parking lots.

At one of Y's locations, the most convenient entrance is located opposite the entrance to the parking lot. Anyone who has lived in the Middle East can guess the result. A car will pull up to the entrance and stop for a few moments as everyone in the car gets out, while the cars waiting to turn into the parking lot are unable to move, causing a long tailback of traffic. Or a car will stop and various people will converge, putting bags and themselves in the car as a line of 10 to 20 cars wait for their turn.

X's parking lots have wide entrances, exits and aisles, with wide parking spaces. Y's parking lots are made for shoppers with VW Bugs and Morris Minis in a country full of SUVs and pick-ups; the entrances and exits are dangerously narrow, clearly designed by people who have never driven here and have a deep hatred of cars bigger than a Kia Rio. The predictable result is that in Y's parking lots people simply drive their SUVs up onto walkways and the raised platforms designed to keep cars away from the entrance.

I was stunned to see a development prospective for an area outside Salalah in which every design element was referenced to a European city.

The large project, put together by trained architects, had maps of the existing buildings so the authors must have visited the location at least once but their suggestion was the creation of large, Italian-style piazzas surrounded by cafés. Having places for people to gather is a wonderful idea, but not in towns with howling winds for several months of the year. Huge open spaces will not work both in terms of the weather and in terms of cultural understandings of space. Dhofaris want open sightlines, but they like to be grounded by some kind of anchor object. In wide open spaces, Dhofaris will sit huddled next to their car or in a tight circle. For example, they prefer to sit next to the side of a *wadi*, a tree, a group of rocks, etc.

One example of a useful project is in the beach area at the southeastern edge of Salalah. When the area around Haffa souq was demolished for a forthcoming development, the government created a new picnic area. Although many people prefer to sit on Haffa beach, the new recreational area is always full. Situated between a road and the beach, it has a winding walkway interspersed with seating areas, some with sail cloth-type shades and some with BBQ pits. One parks by pulling off the main road directly into slanted parking spaces, so there is no danger of having to cross a road. Men often sit in chairs next to their cars under the streetlights to talk while families can walk a very short distance to one of the shelters which have clear views of the ocean but are semi-protected from outsiders' gazes by palm trees, low walls and nonlinear paths.

In talking this point over with informants, they agreed with me and gave examples. One mentioned a building designed for offices, small stores and a restaurant which was built open plan and did not have adequate ventilation so that the whole building smelled of cooked food. Several Omanis have told me that they avoid the place as it makes them feel sick. A Dhofari woman gave the example of how several cafés built in the last five years do not have a separate section for women, so she feels she has fewer choices for where to have coffee. I want to point out that she does not mean complete segregation, i.e. separate rooms, blacked-out windows or women-only spaces, but that cafés should have open seating areas as well as some tables that are placed for privacy such as booths at the back of the space or shoulder-height screens.

Placement: houses and cars

Maneval mentions that "streets in contemporary neighbourhoods in Jeddah have been designed for cars and not for pedestrians ... Except for a few streets in the old town and its adjacent neighbourhoods, there are no pavements" (2019 180). The same holds true in towns in Dhofar. Homeowners will often pave the section between the house wall and the street to use as a parking space, but there are no sidewalks. To move from one house to another, either you are constantly moving between different types of paving stones, gravel, parked cars, dumpsters and rocky open land, or you walk in the street. Similarly, while a row of shops with aligned storefronts may have a short, common sidewalk, walking between stores means navigating many different types of paving materials, open spaces and parked cars, with the additional hazard of dripping air conditioners. Outside of towns, the area outside the house wall will usually be flat open land, perhaps graded or scattered with gravel.

Some houses have covered parking of either stretched fabric on a metal frame embedded in cement blocks or a temporary tent-like structure that will not survive a winter windstorm. As it is socially expected to have a clean car unless it is a vehicle for transporting animals or feed, men often clean their car when it's in front of the house or they will pay a male, expat worker to wash it every morning.

Sometimes the house takes up all of the land and the house wall is so close to the street that the owner must park in the street. While this isn't legal, it's also not complained about and no one would suggest tearing down the house wall to get the cars out of the streets, so although all residential areas are designed with two-way streets, practically speaking many only have the center of the street open for driving.

The pattern of streets within residential areas is usually made up of "two types of streets: the first is the open ended, publicly owned through street; and the second, a narrow dead end street which is the property of homeowners" (Alkhalidi 2013 290). This in some way mirrors the pattern of doorways in cul de sacs, which lead to larger alleys which lead to public streets seen in towns built before automobiles. However, the Dhofaris I interviewed have told me that they would prefer to be on or near a main street, not on a dead-end street.

Placement: houses and neighborhoods, mosques and stores

This idea of a neighborhood as a group of houses and a few small shops centered on a mosque is explained as

> The land use pattern consists of residential zones ... a local Mosque and shops serve these zones The mosque is located around the social square, which acts as a connecting link between the mosque and the entrance of the housing cluster. A common element, at the level of city planning, is the minaret of a mosque seen clearly from a crossroads of each quarter. This becomes a landmark, and a guide of the mosque's location.
>
> (Alkhalidi 2013 290)

When I interviewed Dhofaris about what they would like located next to or near their house, the response was always a mosque and small stores nearby but not adjacent.[12] Parks and gardens were rarely mentioned and when I asked about them the answer was, "we will go far," meaning that if the family was going to have a picnic, they would go to a distant place, not near the house. One friend lived about a block from a large municipal park but never visited it.

Within towns, the mosque is seen as the center of the neighborhood; men walk to it for the five daily prayers if they are in the house at prayer time.[13] This walking is the only time I have seen men walk within neighborhoods. The area around a mosque is usually paved with flagstones where men stand and talk before and after prayers. During Ramadan, this space can be used for *iftar*, the sunset meal to break the fast, with dates, pastries, fruit with water, juice and/or buttermilk (*laban*), etc. given free. The space is also used to collect goods during charity drives.

Many mosques share a side wall with a shop. There might be only one small grocery store or a few shops including a bakery, vegetable store and/or dry cleaners.[14] Men can stop and pick up necessities for the house on the way back from prayers and children are sent to get last-minute items for meal preparation or to buy sweets.[15]

The small stores often have signs saying that they sell "Luxuries," but the wares are basic necessities such as fresh milk, canned milk, tea, sugar, instant coffee, Kleenex, diapers and formula with a large selection of inexpensive candy, soda and chips for children.

Placement: houses and public spaces

Any open lot within a town that is not enclosed by a wall is perceived as open space where children may play, people might sit, cars can park, etc.

A second type of public space is that which the municipal government has improved for recreational purposes. For more than 15 years, the government has created well-lit, well-kept walking paths next to main roads. Some of the walking paths have exercise equipment installed next to them. More recently it has heavily invested in public health by building football stadiums and sports arenas, for example, a larger-than-Olympic-sized pool with inexpensive swimming lessons and open-swim timings twice a week for women. There are also walled parks with family/women-only hours and leisure areas, such as a newly built zone on a beach in southern Salalah as explained above.

Many neighborhood mosques have small playgrounds near them and there are larger playgrounds in the parks and on a few beaches. Some residential areas in Salalah are built with lots in a wide oval surrounding an open space which is not yet developed but which might hold a park or playground in the future.

Thus most Dhofaris in towns have a way to enjoy fresh air within walking distance of their house if they want to. Being "trapped in a house" is usually a function of weather, not the inability to move. In residential areas, children play in the *hosh*, the street and open lots. Boys who are too young to drive will play football near houses in the late afternoons and might gather under streetlights to chat in the evening. Women, usually not alone but with other women or children, stroll around their neighborhood on cool nights for exercise and to talk privately. Sometimes women will sit at the top of the front steps after dark.

The above description is for towns; in rural areas, Dhofaris often sit outside the house in the *dekka*, a seating area adjacent to the house which might be roofed and/or have furniture. Walking is done much more frequently: to visit relatives and neighbors and/or check on gardens or animals.

A third type of public space is the narrow alleys between houses which are marked in city plans but reality does not always match the policies. Many homes have a second door from the kitchen which opens into an alley for ease of access and some alleys are in constant use. However, some homeowners build a low wall across the space to keep anyone from using the lane. This is done either to create an extra parking space for the house or simply to prevent the noise/disruption of cars moving close to the house.[16]

The specific part of an alley that is between two houses is seen as "belonging to" the houses and the usage can affect neighbor's relations. In one case I know of X built a house with the *hosh* slightly raised, which meant it was a high step from the alley into the *hosh*. X's family did not build steps to make the height difference easier to traverse as they perceived it rude to put steps in the alley, intruding into public space. X's neighbor, Y, brought up the issue, asking why they hadn't made a short staircase to ease entry. When X explained their position, Y insisted that they make steps. X brought a cement worker to make one, narrow step. Everyone had behaved well and this mutual courtesy was perceived as reason to be proud that X and Y were "good neighbors."

An opposite case I know of was when a man (A) paid to have the alley between his house and B's house set with bricks. Normally this would be seen as a generous act as he had to pay for the alley to be graded with a small bulldozer, then pay for the workers, paving bricks and sand. However, he instructed the workers to not pave four rectangles of the area (two feet wide, six feet long) next to the wall of his house. These sections of dirt were for "flowers" but it was actually to keep cars away from the wall of his *hosh*.

B figured this out as the grading and preparation were done, so when A asked to attach a water pipe to B's water supply to wet the sand before the paving bricks were placed, B refused. To refuse water to a neighbor, especially one who was paying a lot for the project, is not only bad manners but ridiculously miserly; but B was angry that A had used the project to take over some of the alley space, forcing cars to drive close to B's wall.

Placement: houses and commercial spaces

Overview

When I visited Al Guratha in 2005, I tried to figure out why this Yemeni city looked so different than Salalah and the answer was there were no plate glass storefronts. Modern cities grew because of the invention of elevators (pax fitness fanatics) as there is a limit of stairs humans are willing to climb; prosperous and peaceful cities are marked by how much breakable glass there is on display. Many stores in Dhofar still have metal screens which roll down or slide across the front of the store at closing, but newer stores simply have sheet glass windows. In the same manner, older stores have painted signs, sometimes lit with a spotlight at night; newer stores have electric signs.

These cosmetic differences belie the continuity of commercial spaces. Except for hypermarkets and large stores for furniture, building supplies, etc. most stores in Dhofar are rectangular with the short end facing the street, a long narrow selling space and usually a blank back wall with no separate storage space or rear door. The counter for paying is almost always at the front of the store, near both the door and a window. The lighting is from florescent tubes, the floor linoleum and often cooled by an AC placed over the door.

Most stores have the goods displayed on the walls with few or no aisles; if there are aisles, they are either wide enough for two people to pass without touching or someone will not enter an aisle if a person of the opposite gender is standing in one. Muslim male and female workers take care not to stand too close to each other or customers.

Shops are usually available from the street they are situated on, i.e. one parks directly in front of the store, not in a separate parking lot, requiring only a few steps to enter. For many shops (such as car repair/supplies, restaurants, small grocery stores) it is normal for a driver to call a runner to the car to discuss what is wanted and prices. Along some of the streets with many small shops selling the same items (such as the western end of As-Salam Street), a person might walk to a few different shops but only a person with no other choice would walk several blocks given the dust, heat and lack of sidewalks.

The opening/closing times for stores in Dhofar are varied. They can open at 8, 8:30 or 9 am, with a lunch break at 1, 1:30, 2 or 2:30 pm, to reopen at 4, 4:30 or 5 pm and close for the night any time between 9 pm and 1 am. Restaurants might be open all day, or closed at 3 pm and reopened at 6 or 7 pm and closed again at midnight or 2 am.

As is normal in the Middle East, stores selling similar items are often found next to each other. These are sometimes identified as "souqs" (such as the fish, meat, vegetable and gold souqs), streets or sections of streets (such as the parts of As-Salam Street with items for cars, phone stores, perfume and women's clothing/ fabric/accessories;) or parts of town such as the southeastern sector of Salalah with farms and farm stands and the northwestern *saniya* (industrial workshop) sector with subdivisions for car repair, car painting, iron-mongers, cabinet makers etc.

Traditional shopping areas

The traditional shopping area was Haffa Souq located next to the beach in the south-central part of Salalah. It was famous for frankincense, frankincense burners, clothing stores, tailors, perfumes, restaurants/coffee shops and a cinema. Most of the shops and nearby houses are now destroyed as the government has planned a large, multiuse development in the area, but a small section is still open and there is a tented section set up with tables. There were houses near, but not adjacent to, the souq area.

Another shopping area is As-Salam Street, running east-west north of the beach. At the main intersection with the Al Nahdah street is the Gold Souq. Along the whole street, there are shops on the ground floor, a few of which are big enough to continue up to the first floor, but the first and second floors are usually small apartments. In the past, there were single-family detached villas, but they have been torn down or converted so that there are only a few houses left on adjacent streets.

One of the malls has an ersatz souq with wooden beams, a dropped ceiling, narrow aisles and fake lanterns. As most of the shops sell Dhofari frankincense and perfumes, the area is redolent of *oud*.

Malls

Within the last 15 years, a few malls have been built, with several new ones about to open.[17] The most popular are Al Isteqrar, LuLu and Salalah Gardens which are anchored with a large grocery store and have cafés, restaurants and a pharmacy. Grand Mall has opened within the last year. Each mall is usually referred to by the name of the grocery store, so Salalah Gardens is almost always referred to as Carrefour; someone will say "let's meet at Carrefour," meaning a café in the mall, not inside the store. All have a similar selection of stores selling perfume, *oud/bukhor*, jewelry, décor, clothing, phones, shoes, glasses/contact lens and health supplements.

There are also several other malls, such as Gallery Mall (which has two cafés, small stores and a smaller grocery store) and Oasis Mall (anchored with two housewares/clothing stores, a cinema and a small grocery story), as well as strip malls such as Al Nadha which have a variety of restaurants and cafés.

The first mall-type space was Istaqrar, which opened in 1978 and then a second, two-story hypermarket in the 1990s. Only this store is close to houses; the rest are set off on large plots of land which make walking to them very difficult.

Opened in 2011, Lulu Shopping Centre was built along the same principles as Isteqrar, i.e. one large store selling groceries and housewares that dominated the space, with a few non-chain fast-food and small stores selling perfume, jewelry, clothes, shoes and purses.

Salalah Gardens Mall opened in July 2012, built along the lines of an American-style mall with a large grocery and housewares store (with small computer and clothing sections) anchoring the shopping areas with a large selection of stores and a cinema. The upper floors of the U-shaped structure are a hotel and the empty inner area has tables situated around palm trees and shrubs. There is not a café, but runners from various fast-food places walk around with menus so four people sitting together can order from four different places.

The two newest are Salalah City Mall which opened in 2020 and has several floors of apartments over the anchoring grocery store on the ground floor and Salalah Grand Mall which opened in 2021.

Thus going to a souq or mall for almost all Dhofaris involves getting in a car and driving. Except for Istaqrar Hypermarket, shopping areas do not have villas nearby, only apartments which are usually rented to expats. As explained above, there are often small stores in residential areas and near apartment buildings, but not large stores, malls or souqs.

Comparisons of cultural ideas of houses on the Arabian Peninsula

As discussed in Chapter 2, Dhofar in particular and Oman in general have a different history and population than countries such as Saudi Arabia, the United Arab Emirates, Bahrain and Qatar. Oman had less external influences and has fewer expats. Also, as most Dhofaris practiced transhumance until during/after the war, many people lived seasonally in caves, temporary shelters and houses with stone walls only to shoulder height, topped with branches. The weather in Dhofar means that two popular Arabian architectural styles, courtyard houses and wind towers, were not frequently built. Finally, in contrast to Yemen, there was no need to build defensible houses.

Throughout this book I have used comparisons with Saudi Arabia based on Maneval's *New Islamic Urbanism* (1997); in this section, I will briefly look at how houses in other Arabian Peninsula countries are typified to further understand Dhofari practices.

For example, in "A Chronological Exploration of the Evolution of Housing Typologies in Gulf Cities" (2016) Remali, Salama, Wiedmann and Ibrahim divide the development of Doha, Dubai, Abu Dhabi and Manama into four stages: Post-Nomadic Period (until 1763), Traditional Period (1763–1945), Modern Period (1945–1990) and Contemporary Period (since 1990).

The Post-Nomadic Period is defined by "line" houses, i.e. an enclosed area with rooms along the perimeter wall, usually on only one or two sides. In the Traditional Period, rooms were along all sides of an enclosed area, sometimes two or more rooms deep, with open space in the middle. In the Modern Period, houses were rectangular or square structures with a main entrance at the front, rooms of similar sizes, usually off of one main corridor. The Contemporary Period has houses which are irregularly shaped with several entrances, rooms of different sizes, several corridors and little or no sightlines between interior spaces. According to these phases, Dhofar was Pre-Nomadic until the 1960s/70 and then went through the first three periods between the 1970s and the early 2000s, beginning with the Contemporary Period around 2010.

As examples of the ubiquity of courtyard houses, Fletcher and Stepney explain the typical Qatari house, the *bayt sha'bi*

> can be simply divided into the private, family area comprising the courtyard and spaces around it, and the public area of the *majlis*. It follows that the doorway, which gives access to both, is of some importance and may be considered the fourth element of the *bayt sha'bi*. This doorway would usually be constructed with a sharp angle or dogleg, presenting a wall to the external viewer and preventing any sight of the internal, private space of the courtyard.
>
> (n.d.)

While Eddisford and Carter describe that

> The key features found in an idealized Qatari domestic compound were the majlis (pl. *majālis*), colonnaded veranda (*liwan*), bathroom or toilet (*masbah*, *hamam*), a room set aside as a kitchen and a well, sometimes in the courtyard or within a room. Other rooms arranged around the edge of the courtyard were mostly multi-functional, and living arrangements and room use were often modified seasonally.[18]
>
> (2017 106)

The few courtyard houses that were built in Dhofar in the 1960s–1970s were replaced by single-family dwellings. The few remaining or newly built courtyard houses are in the northern and/or eastern areas which are less effected or outside the range of the summer monsoon season.

Yemen: house as citadel

The traditional mountain house in Dhofar which is round, one-story and made of rock courses topped with sticks, is very different from traditional houses in Yemen which are often tower houses made of

> stone and sun-dried mud bricks with stone foundation walls up to 1 meter thick and about two stories high, often without any window openings at ground level. Above its foundation walls, brickwork takes over. On the inside of the building, the structure is covered with a layer of clay and gypsum plaster, sometimes finished with face stones or packed earth. An internal staircase serves as circulation space around which the five to nine stories are arranged.
>
> (Kotnik 2005 475)

The first two levels are usually windowless or have small windows and have animal pens and storage rooms.

> Above these two levels are the domestic areas. A carved door opens from the staircase at each upper level, giving access to a generous lobby around which the rooms are grouped: usually one main room, a bathroom with lavatory, a small kitchen for the preparation of beverages, and a storeroom. On the third level, the main room is called the diwan and is reserved for special functions such as weddings, births, funerals, or discussions of tribal matters. When not in use, it is unfurnished and may function as a storage room or seasonal bedroom The rooms in which the family lives throughout the day begin above the third floor ... The top floor is reserved as an afternoon reception room, the *mafraj*.
>
> (475)

A few older (pre-1970s) houses in Salalah have a slightly similar style: the ground floor is used for livestock and storage, with living rooms in the upper stories, but they are lower and broader than tower houses, not common and not purpose-built for protection. Whereas,

> For centuries, tribal warfare and the threat of raids were omnipresent in Yemen, leading to an architecture of defensive character. Tower houses as an architectural type derived from watchtowers...They were often strategically placed on slopes or long lines down the middle of wadis. Isolated farmhouses were rare. More commonly, buildings were clustered for mutual protection to form small villages. In general, these villages were unfortified, placing the responsibility for defense on the individual households.
>
> (Kotnik 2005 474)

The fighting in the Dhofar War (1965–1975) took place mainly in the mountains and was primarily engagements on open land. When the fighting was concentrated in one place, it was at forts and fortified bases, not in towns among residential properties so a defensive architecture did not develop. Some houses built in the 1970s and 1980s had more protective elements, such as small windows and heavy, metal sliding gates, with castellations on flat roofs but this is mainly stylistic decisions, not from a need to secure the house.

Another difference is that in courtyard and modern Dhofari houses, visiting men may only enter the *majlis* or the front part of the courtyard and are effectively contained in small areas (relative to the whole footprint of the house) with limited viewsheds. But in a Yemeni tower house, visiting men must walk up through all the floors of the house to enter the *mafraj*.[19]

Two similarities are that men cannot see who is entering or leaving and that the purpose of spaces changes during the day. Yemeni men sitting in the *mafraj* at the top of the house, have no view of the house's doorway or the street. While the tower house is a formidable place of defense, in day-to-day life, men cannot visually keep track of who is coming or leaving. In the same manner, Dhofari men in the *majlis* do not have clear sightlines to the front door. In both types of houses, one would need to be on the roof to know who was entering and departing.

Further, as in Dhofar, who controls which space can vary depending on the time and day. As Kotnik explains,

> It is a man who must defer to the female guests in his home. When a man returns home in the evening, he always pauses before entering the interior of his house and calls out "*Fi nas?*" [Are there any people here?] ... In other words, male members of the household can be excluded temporarily from their own homes.
>
> (2005 477)

Further, the rooms themselves can change:

> The multifunctional use of rooms points to a crucial difference between the Yemenite and the Western understandings of space. Architecture in the Western world developed out of a scientific paradigm characterized by rational separation and classification: Absolute space is divided into functionally defined compounds, the rooms. In Yemen, however, space is not absolute but relational, because it is always constructed anew on the basis of changing activities; that is, space is defined by the people present and their behavior.
>
> (Kotnik 2005 478)

In Dhofar, a *majlis* can be a schoolroom with children listening to a hired tutor, café-like with boys watching football games and drinking tea, a place for serious family discussions, the seating area for senior women during a wedding, empty, a bedroom for male cousins or newly decorated and over-brimming with guests on *Eid* morning.

Qatar: connections between and sizes of houses

As explained in Chapter 3, the Omani government gives land to unmarried citizens for a nominal fee. This practice is in contrast to Qatar, where land and house are given together and "to qualify for a land and building grant, one must be a Qatari citizen and the 'head of a household' [i.e. married]" and the plot is "900 square meters, walled, linked to public utilities" (Nagy 2004 46). These

> land distribution policies can make it difficult for family members to live near each other ... they [a group of brothers] are usually granted lands in newly developed areas at a distance from each other. Nonetheless, some families have found ways to build homes near each other. The

> simplest solution is to purchase land on the private real estate market. But, this costs more
>
> (49-50)

Qataris, like Omanis, will buy and sell plots to get land next to or near family members, and will sometimes join several plots together to make a family compound holding several houses. Further, Nagy writes that

> both Qataris and others commonly assume that the new styles of housing in Qatar will encourage nuclear family households, neolocal residence patterns and the demise of extended family values. However, this does not seem to be the general pattern of change in Qatar ... I consistently found that Qataris are able and willing to expend effort and resources in order to establish residences within proximity to their extended family. It is incorrect to assume that villas only house nuclear family. Many of them are occupied by extended families, including three generations of kin, more than one husband and wife pair and their offspring
>
> (2004 56)

This also holds true for Dhofaris, particularly for mountain dwellers, many of whom practiced transhumance until after the Dhofar War. The change from transhumance to settled living which took place in the 1960s and 1970s did not result in the break-down of tightly-knit family connections as they still usually live in houses with not only different generations, but a changing roster of family members.

In their writings about Qatar both Nagy (2004) and Al Mohannadi, Furlan and Major (2019) discuss how a house can be both conceptually bigger and smaller than it first appears. "Bigger" in that a Qatari will not see the house they live in as their only house but feel connected to all the places where their family lives. "Smaller" in that few people ever see all of another person's house.

Nagy argues that "the social boundaries of the family do not necessarily correlate to the physical boundaries of the house" (2004 47). Thus

> During a family's development cycle, new family members will be added to the existing house, and others will leave to form houses of their own or join existing houses. Consequently, some individuals identified as family members may not reside in one's house, such as a married son who has established his own house with his spouse and their children. In some cases, individuals maintain residence in more than one house. For example, newlyweds frequently shift residences between their natal and marital homes and men with multiple wives may maintain separate houses for each wife.
>
> (48)

Al Mohanndi, Furlan and Major (2019) affirm that "While a woman is not expected to live with her family in her father's household after marriage, she could maintain a room for occasional use." In terms of segregation, Al Mohanndi, Furlan and Major explain that

> certain spaces are classified based on the user's gender. The outdoor *Majlis* unit is mainly a designated space for male users and the indoor *Majlis* area is for female guests. In some cases, the *Majlis* room is embedded within the villa where male visitors could utilize it while women gather in the family's living spaces. As a general trend, female guests can utilize the private rooms of the villa with more flexibly than male guests, who should not travel unaccompanied through the household.

Both of these housing patterns are similar to Dhofar, where women often return to their parent's house for 40 days after the birth of a child and non-resident men cannot leave the *majlis* to see other areas of a house.

One difference is that the Qatari government gives more assistance to citizens, allowing for a larger house and more household help to be the norm. Having larger plots of land and several live-in workers means that the *hosh* outdoor space is used differently. In many Dhofari families, especially in the mountains, women often sit on the steps or the *dekka* to watch children playing to talk and enjoy the view. Whereas in Qatar,

> outdoor yard space is not utilized by women due to their exposure to the outside and the fact that drivers or domestic assistants (often male) use this yard. If the main gates and garage doors are secure, then it is acceptable for women to use the yards especially for outdoor events and social gatherings when the weather is mild.
>
> (Al Mohanndi, Furlan and Major 2019)

Further, having a larger piece of land means that it is normal in Qatar for the *majlis* to have

> its own extended block outside of the main household either as a concrete built room or a modern tensile structure resembling the old tent. Modern tents are used as extended guest rooms where men gather occasionally for special events such as festivals, Eids, weddings and funerals. Most of the modern tent structures in Qatari neighbourhoods are air-conditioned and furnished with high-class amenities.
>
> (Al Mohanndi, Furlan and Major 2019)

In Dhofar, a separate *majlis* is rare and tents are not permanently placed next to houses. A tent for a wedding or funeral would be rented and set up in a flat, empty area that might be near the house, but not next to it.

Kuwait and Qatar: gatherings in houses

Both Stephenson (2011) and Asmi (2016) discuss two traditions of weekly meetings in houses for personal and political discussion. Stephenson discusses the Kuwaiti dīwāniyya which is

> is at once an institution and the space where the institution is manifested ... through which Kuwaiti men conduct business, settle disputes, give and receive information, connect with the family, and freely express their opinions on any matter of life, including politics.
>
> (2011 184)

The dīwāniyya as a place is different than the Dhofari *majlis* in that it is "formally seen as the territory of adult men" (187) and while politics might be discussed in a *majlis*, men do not hold an all-night, weekly gathering.

Writing about Qatar, Asmi starts with an example of a weekly family and friends *majlis* organized by Johara, who "wanted the space to be a place for Qatari and non-Qatari women to share their concerns, ideas and thoughts about Qatari society" (2016 18–19). *Majlis* here does not refer to the room, but a weekly meeting of either just female family members or female family and friends that some Qatari women organize to discuss personal, educational and political topics. Asmi explores how these get-togethers are a space of "kinship capital," "women's expanding cultural capital" and "the ways in which cultural capital can come to enhance a women's role in the family" (20).

In examining these articles, there are two main differences with Dhofari. One is that while some Dhofari families hold weekly gatherings, for example, a tradition of all the sons of one set of parents having lunch together on Friday, they are less formal and less outward focused. The purpose is for family to be together, tell stories, relive memories, ask questions and enjoy private time.

The second is that *hakli* gatherings are often less gender segregated. A *hakli* man might sit in the *salle* with his wife, mother and female neighbors; a *hakli* woman might bring tea to her husband and one of his friends who are sitting in the *majlis*.

There are times and places of strict segregation, for example, a man's wedding party held in a tent would be strictly male only.[20] But within a house in everyday life, women's lives are intertwined and not separate from a man's, with men sharing information about male movements with women, but women not speaking about other women to a man.

Notes

1 Abu-Lughod's personal observations in walking through Hindu and Muslim neighborhoods in India were that "ratio of men to women on the street and in public was higher in Muslim than in Hindu areas" and that she considered that

main differences to be "gender segregation and social patterns of proscribed foods" (1989 161).

2 To try to re-create the former model of city life would mean: "(1) juridical distinctions between Muslims and/or citizens and outsiders; (2) segregation by gender and a virtually complete division of labor according to it; and (3) a fully decentralized and ex post facto system of land use and governmental regulation over space. In today's world, these three are considered retrogressive" (Abu-Lughod 1989 172).

3 Against this understanding that "Islamic" and "Arab" are unhelpfully vague adjectives in discussing certain types of cities, there are authors such as bin Zayyad and Sinclair who want to encourage architects, city planners and government officials to center urban design on the religious context to Islam. They argue that

> there is no dichotomy between *din* (faith) and *duniya* (material world) in the Islamic faith. The present researchers see the unification of this approach as most pertinent to the quest for a contemporary Islamic design expression.
>
> (2017 2)

4 In terms of the Jeddah, Maneval notes that

> hardly any characteristics of the Islamic City paradigm apply ... the highly diverse population of Jeddah did not have segregated neighbourhoods of different ethnic or religious groups ... Jeddah's residential architecture and street pattern – tower houses instead of inward-oriented courtyard-houses, and thoroughfares instead of cul-de-sac streets – are not in accordance with the Islamic City paradigm. Neither is the existence of residential houses in the market area and the integration of commercial functions in residential buildings ... Finally, since the specific forms of sociability framed and enabled by dead-end streets in other cities in the Islamic world did not exist in Jeddah.
>
> (2019 133)

5 This section is a reworking of my presentation "Private Lives in Public Spaces: Perceptions of Space-Usage in Southern Oman" (Risse 2021). I am grateful to Robert Flahive and Ingy Higazy for the helpful panel discussion.

6 It's important to note that while Dhofaris act in ways to keep themselves divided from strangers of the opposite gender, they don't legislate/demand that expats follow the same rules as long as the expat males are not next to Dhofari women who are attempting to be apart. Thus you can have Dhofaris self-segregating in the same spaces where expats are mingling, e.g. at cafés, there are Dhofari groups which are women only, family and male only, as well as expat male/female friend groups.

7 As I was working on this section, I asked one female informant "Why is your town [Salalah] 'Islamic'?" She answered "because women work, and they help children, help people and the community. Islam is not sitting in a mosque, it is working." To me, she was answering the question to speak through me to potential readers who either believe that Islam is oppressive towards women or that Muslim women should not work. She continued, "Islam is not living a closed life" and that people who did not allow female relatives to work are stupidly afraid that "the people will eat your wife."

8 Grass trimmings are gathered in heaps and sometimes taken by Dhofaris to use as fodder. Ornamental date palms are sometimes planted but because the weather is not hot enough for long enough, they usually do not produce fruit. Coconuts often litter the ground but I have never seen anyone taking one; perhaps the type is not the best for eating.

9 Pascal Menoret's (2014) discussion of car culture among young men in Saudi and Gardner and Zakzouk's "Car Culture in Contemporary Qatar" (2014) are not directly relevant to Dhofar. Young men race, spin their cars, etc. but this is fairly limited. With Qatar, there are three points of difference. First,

> Many of the other interviewees talked about street racing, a risky and illegal activity that takes place late at night on roads far from the eyes of the police. All of this suggests that being seen in appropriate vehicles, as well as performing in those vehicles (as in racing), provides Qataris with a venue for establishing and negotiating their social identities ... In Qatar and the other wealthy Gulf States, all of which have small and socially interwoven indigenous populations, reputations are a potent form of social capital that is readily translated into economic capital (in the form of, say, a public sector job).
> (2014 141)

In Dhofar, car racing might improve a young man's standing among his peers, but would not spill over as a type of social capital within his family or tribe.

Secondly, in Dhofar the main type of playing with cars is driving up steep sand dunes. Gardner and Zakzouk mention this as a way of differentiating locals from expats

> the desert recreation areas of Qatar are a performative space. They are important spaces in the sense that it is here that Qatari citizens articulate and perform their difference from the legion of foreigners present in the city-in cars they establish some modicum of a cohesive and collective identity distinct from that of the foreign population.
> (2014 140)

As previously discussed, Oman has far fewer expats than Qatar, the Emirates, Saudi, Bahrain and Kuwait. I have never heard anyone state that they were doing or not doing anything to distinguish themselves from expats. And expats can buy or rent cars to go dune-bashing so driving a car to the top of a sand dune does not create a distinct identity.

Thirdly, Gardner and Zakzouk state that "In a small society that's highly focused on appearances, owning an appropriate vehicle is directly connected to one's social possibilities" (2014 140). This is not true in Dhofar where the price of a car will not necessarily tell you anything about the wealth or job of the owner. A very wealthy person might drive an older car and a person with little money might have a very nice car bought with loans or given as a gift.

10 My favorite driving quote is when a group of us were in the mountains and I balked at driving up a steep hill, one of the research men said, "You think that is a hill? You think you cannot do that? Go home, stay home, sit on your chair, give me your car."

11 When the government was building the long mountain road between Hasik and Shuwaymiyah, I drove the road with various research guys as it was being built, gunning up steep hills with powered limestone flying to thickly that it was impossible to see the road and being stopped by workers as they were about to ignite explosives. And I have lovely memories of the new road east of Taqa before the streetlights were put in and the roadway was painted with markings; three lanes of gorgeous, new tarmac and you could drive wherever you pleased. Another great memory is driving cross-town, from the south-east corner of Salalah to the north-east corner on the night when the entire power grid went down. In Dhofar, it's not the type of car you have, it's your trust in your driving ability that's important.

12 As I mentioned in Chapter 1, one male informant told me that the best placement for a house was "500 meters from mosque, 200 meters from main road, 500 meters from stores." The house should not be *next* to these places because then small children might play in the mosque, be close to fast-moving cars and bother the storekeeper.

13 Graveyards are not usually attached to mosques nor located in neighborhoods; they are often very large and walled.

14 Similarly, large apartment buildings built in the last ten years have small shops on ground floor so that while driving through some sections of town one sees the same collection of stores for every building: dry cleaner, coffee shop, small grocery store, fruit and vegetable store etc. There is endless duplication so that the clerks in the store can bring whatever is needed up to an apartment and an apartment dweller can pick up whatever is needed on the way to or from work. Thus most people in Dhofari towns live within walking distance of a place to buy everyday essentials.

15 After reading "The Little Store" by Eudora Welty students wrote many lovely essays about trips to the small store near their house; Welty's essay reminded them of their experiences as a child and how their understanding of the store and the person who ran it changed over time.

16 I see this as an example of what Abu-Lughod argues "Islamic property rights" give "precedence to the rights of proximate neighbors over the rights of the community-at-large" (1989 203).

17 See Abdelghani (2013) for a discussion of shopping and malls in the Muscat area.

18 See also Al-Mohannadi, Saleh and Furlan (2019).

19 A third difference is that "In Yemen, working as a stonemason or bricklayer is regarded as an honorable pursuit, and only members of the highest social class are engaged in these skilled handicrafts. This is another indication for the importance of the tower house in the affirmation of reputation" (Kotnik 2005 479). Dhofari men now supervise, but do not engage in building houses, although they did in the past. Older men might help construct and/ or supervise the building of rock walls, animal pens and wind breaks.

20 There are *hakli* men and women who choose to self-segregate, for example a woman who declares that she will not see her husband before marriage although in many families, a man might see and talk to a woman he wants to get engaged to while sitting in her family's *majlis,* chaperoned by her family members. I have one Dhofari friend who has a brother-in-law who refuses to look at the faces of his wife's sisters. This sort of behavior is accepted, but not championed as the way every person should behave. Most of the *hakli* men I do research with have introduced me to their wives as a matter of course; I have met brothers of all of the Dhofari women I know and, in most cases, their husbands.

References

For photos and a full bibliography, please see: *Come From Away*, https://mariellerisse.com

Abdelghani, Montasser. 2013. "The Impact of Shopping Malls on Traditional Retail Stores in Muscat. Case Study of Al-Seeb Wilayat," in *Regionalizing Oman.* Steffen Wippel, ed. New York: Springer. 227–47.

Abu-Lughod, Janet. 1989. "What Is Islamic about a City? Some Comparative Reflections," in Urbanism in Islam: The Proceedings of the International

Conference on Urbanism in Islam. Tokyo: Middle Eastern Culture Center: 193–217.

———. 1987. "The Islamic City: Historical Myth, Islamic Essence and Contemporary Relevance." *International Journal of Middle East Studies* 19.2: 155–76.

Al Mohannadi, Asmaa Saleh and Raffaello Furlan. 2019. "Socio-cultural Patterns Embedded into the Built Form of Qatari Houses: Regenerating Architectural Identity in Qatar." *Journal of Urban Regeneration and Renewal* 12.4: 1–23.

Alkhalidi, Abdulsamad. 2013. "Sustainable Application of Interior Spaces in Traditional Houses of the United Arab Emirates." *Procedia: Social and Behavioral Sciences* 102: 288–99.

Andraos, Amale. 2016. "The Arab City." *Places Journal.* https://doi.org/10.22269/160531

Asmi, Rehenuma. 2016. "Finding a Place to Sit How Qatari Women Combine Cultural and Kinship Capital in the Home Majlis." *Anthropology of the Middle East* 11.2: 18–38.

Bianca, Stefano. 2000. "Basic Principles of Islam and Their Social, Spatial and Artistic Implications." in *Urban Form in the Arab World.* London: Thames & Hudson. 23–48.

bin Zayyad, Sabeen and Brian Sinclair. 2017. "Culture, Context + Environmental Design: Reconsidering Vernacular in Modern Islamic Urbanism." presented at the 10th EAAE/ARCC International Conference. https://www.researchgate.net/publication/314218959_Culture_context_environmental_design_Reconsidering_vernacular_in_modern_Islamic_urbanism

Eddisford, Daniel and Robert Carter. 2017. "The Vernacular Architecture of Doha, Qatar." *Post-Medieval Archaeology* 51.1: 81–107.

Escher, Anton. 2019. "Eugen Wirth (1925–2012) - Geographer of the Oriental City in North Africa and the Near East." *Middle East: Topics & Arguments* 12.1: 122–6. https://doi.org/10.17192/meta.2019.12.7940.

Fletcher, Richard and Erin Stepney. n.d. "Morphologies of Housing in Doha: from Bayt Sha'bi to Suburban Villa." 1–23. https://www.academia.edu/41429399/Morphologies_of_Housing_in_Doha_from_bayt_shabi_to_suburban_villa

Gardner, Andrew and Momina Zakzouk. 2014. "Car Culture in Contemporary Qatar," in *Everyday Life in the Muslim Middle East*, third edition. Donna Lee Bowen, Evelyn Early and Becky Schulthies, eds. Bloomington: Indiana University Press. 133–42.

Kotnik, Toni. 2005. "The Mirrored Public Architecture and Gender Relationship in Yemen." *Space and Culture* 8.4: 472–83.

Maneval, Stefan. 2019. *New Islamic Urbanism: The Architecture of Public and Private Space in Jeddah, Saudi Arabia.* London: University College London Press.

Menoret, Pascal. *Joyriding in Riyadh: Oil, Urbanism, and Road Revolt.* New York: Cambridge University Press, 2014.

Nagy, Sharon. 2004. "Keeping Families Together: Housing Policy, Social Strategies and Family in Qatar." *The MIT Electronic Journal of Middle East Studies* 4: 42–58.

Raymond, André. 1994. "Islamic City, Arab City: Orientalist Myths and Recent Views." *British Journal of Middle Eastern Studies* 21.1: 3–18. https://sci-hub.se/10.1080/13530199408705589

Remali, Adel, Ashraf Salama, Florian Wiedmann and Hatem G. Ibrahim. 2016. "A Chronological Exploration of the Evolution of Housing Typologies in Gulf

Cities." *City, Territory and Architecture* 3.14: 1–15. https://doi.org/10.1186/s40410-016-0043-z

Risse, Marielle. 2021. "Private Lives in Public Spaces: Perceptions of Space-Usage in Southern Oman," presentation at Middle East Studies Association Annual Conference. Montreal, Quebec. December 2.

Stephenson, Lindsey. 2011. "Women and the Malleability of the Kuwaiti Dīwāniyya." *Journal of Arabian Studies* 1.2: 183–99.

Welty, Eudora. n.d. "The Little Store," in *The Eye of the Story: Selected Essays and Reviews*. New York: Vintage Books. 326–35.

8 Privacy and houses

Privacy in everyday life

I thought that this book would concentrate on the physical aspects of houses, i.e. what they looked like and how the rooms were arranged, but while reading articles I came across the concept of space syntax and started to think about houses in terms of who sees what and why. In turn, this led to my interest in the topic of privacy, a theme that shows up often in writing about Middle Eastern lifeways, often paired with the topics of modesty, hospitality and Islam as discussed below in academic terms.

In this section, I want to about privacy in personal terms. When researching this book, I found two major disconnects between the (mostly male) writing about daily life on the Arabian Peninsula. One was men writing about how privacy is so important without giving nuanced examples of how it works.[1] Specifically, while most writing talks about houses being divided into public, semipublic and private zones, in Dhofar the divisions are based on issues such as time, belongingness and need, not only gender and physical location. Maneval has a similar point about this mixing of public and private domains in his book about Jeddah:

> I gradually understood that these categories [public and private] do not necessarily denote two distinct spheres, which are spatially divided... these spheres should be regarded as intertwined, because our notions of privacy determine the way we construct public spaces, and our perception of the public realm shapes the architecture of private space
>
> (2019 2)

I have visited one female Dhofari friend's house more than a dozen times and either there were over 50 people and it was teeming with the sounds of a party or it was silent. If we were in the *salle* or *majlis*, only her parent or a small child under the age of five would come to chat. There are ten men living in that house and I have met several of them, but I have never seen any of them by chance when I visited. The *majlis* and *salle* are in what is called the public zone, but the members of the house do not randomly

DOI: 10.4324/9781003270317-8

walk into them; by listening in the hallway, messages on the family group chat, being warned ahead of time, etc. house residents know who is where and will act accordingly. When my friend and I sit in the *majlis*, it is not a public zone.

A second point I want to emphasize is that Dhofari houses for men are not really a place of privacy. When interviewing fishermen for a different research project, all of them mentioned the quiet and peace of fishing.[2] I said that I found Dhofar homes very peaceful and they explained noise at home both in terms of children's voices echoing off cement walls (as children are not usually told to be quiet unless important guests or strangers are visiting) and the "noise" of being asked to participate in running the house: getting gas cylinders for cooking or jugs of water, dealing with repairmen, and/or driving people for medical appointments, visiting relatives or shopping. There was also "noise" in terms of social obligations, e.g. sitting and listening to relatives who were visiting. This was not said in tones of complaint, but a recognition that in home spaces they are on call to fulfill a variety of functions.

Dhofari couples who work in tandem function exactly the same way as American friends I know, huddling together quickly when one comes home to figure out who needs to be taken where and what needs to be done in the house. The biggest difference is that men are usually out of the house and their privacy, per se, works by time, not location.

A man who returns to his house at 1 am, after several hours of having tea with friends, is fairly certain that he will not be interrupted and, since children are usually awake at the same time as adults, this is his time to be with his wife and kids. Similarly, Friday mornings are family time.

Another way to look at this issue is that a phone call from home (i.e. wife, mother or sister) at 11 pm on a weekend night will cause a momentary alarm as this is usually a man's "private" time with friends; women would only call if there was an emergency. A call at 1 pm during the week would be welcome and expected; this is the time to be told what to pick up on the way home from work.

Whereas in talking to Dhofari women, they explained to me that the whole house can be or not be a private space. Depending on the relationship, living in their husband's father's house might feel like living continually in public. One Dhofari friend told me about the enormous lengths she went to make sure she and her children were always presentable; the pressure of feeling always on view eventually led her husband to move her and her children into a rental house.

On the other hand, "Freedom is my parent's house," said one informant, "Everyone knows me." Many informants explained that their parent's house was the place where they were understood, accepted, excused and welcome in every room. None of the women interpreted the place where they lived as having go and no-go zones; a house, as a whole entity, was theirs or not theirs.[3]

If they had their own house, there might be visitors at any time which means they might be interrupted in their work or sleep, or they might not be able to leave the house, but these visitors are family and they might go visit them (and interrupt them) whenever they wanted to.

Lastly, *hakli* informants explained that they would not go into a *majlis* or *salle*

if there were people of the opposite gender or older people of the same gender unless there was a specific reason out of their own self-respect, not fear. The question they asked before entering rooms was "do I need to be in there?" Where to go within a house depended on motive/goal, not set rules.

For example, in asking informants if they went into the kitchens of relatives, they would answer with the question, "Do I have a purpose to go in?" *Hakli* women will go into the *majlis* to bring tea to visitors if there are no men in the house; *hakli* men who walk down the stairs and hear women's voices in the *salle* might exit the house by the kitchen door as there is no need to walk by the *salle*. This is not experienced as exclusionary/inclusionary zones within their home space but that, while the entire house is theirs, some particular space at some particular time may or may not need their presence.

Lessons in being private and public as an expat researcher

The Merriam-Webster definition of privacy is "the quality or state of being apart from company or observation." I have talked about being "apart from observation" in Chapter 7 (being at home outside of the home) but I would like to give three personal examples here about being and not being private in public spaces.

After lunch with an expat researcher, she and I both stated that we needed to go to the nearby grocery store. We grabbed shopping carts and began strolling through the store, but after a few aisles, she said she only needed a few more things and walked off on her own. I wanted to call out to her. It seemed ridiculous to say, "stay and shop with me" yet I felt bereft, a nonsensical, over-sized emotion.

In thinking about that moment later in the context of our conversation, I realized that we were at opposite ends of the spectrum. She was slightly worried about doing research in Dhofar, something I really enjoy, but she walked blithely through the grocery store, a task that for me requires thinking, care and a game face. Several times while I have lived here I have decided not to go into a store as I didn't have the energy to deal with the hassle of being a public spectacle.

Even while wearing the most boring clothes imaginable, women openly stare at me; children point and call their parents to look at me. People walk by and examine what is in my cart; I have to constantly be aware of my surroundings so that I don't accidentally stand close to a man. Sometimes former students come up to say hello so I have to be ready for chitchat. When

I check out, the person in front of me or behind me, the clerk and/or the person bagging the groceries will often pick up objects and examine them, asking me or others what they are. As I walk through public spaces, I often hear people telling each other who I am and where I work.

This scrutiny is not invasive or dangerous, but it is omnipresent and the staring at my clothes is so pointed, I often feel that there is something wrong with my appearance. Since living here, I have developed a tick of constantly checking my clothes by smoothing down the front of my dress. It is women, not men, who are examining me so closely and when I am back in the States, I often say to friends, "Your mall is so fun! No one looked at me!" I love being invisible.

On the other hand, I grew up in a planned community in which houses were minutely examined in a way that people were not. Both my parents were active in the homeowner's association which had control over every house's appearance including paint color and additions such as a deck. They were the "gate-keepers" for the community; something that does not exist in Dhofar where, as long as the house plans pass architectural and structural muster, no one has any say about the house. Several Omani neighbors have made significant changes to their houses without any type of permission.

A third point I would like to make is about land ownership. One of my most memorable days as a teenager was landing in St. Thomas and being horrified at the grime and shabbiness of the town of Charlotte Amalie. I have spent a significant part of my life in the British Virgin Islands and could not understand why St. Thomas was so different (worse) in comparison. Walking around Charlotte Amalie made me feel that I was in hell. My father, who was an urban planner, explained that the people of St. Thomas had lost control of their land; anyone could buy property so that expats had taken over and destroyed the natural resources.

People from non-GCC countries can't buy land in Oman; so expats are confined to renting or buying in a few, small planned communities. Many GCC landowners in Dhofar only visit during the *khareef*, leading to a small, but noticeable, collection of empty houses which are sometimes left to fall apart. There are two within a block of my house which are in terrible condition as the owners haven't visited in several years and don't pay for upkeep.

Another aspect of this is that owners of large, strategically placed pieces of land have their names entered into public discourse in a way that is brutal by Dhofar standards as Dhofaris will seldom say the name of a person who is not part of the conversation. If I am talking to Dhofaris who work where I do, we might say the name of a co-worker, but anyone who we do not both know is simply "a neighbor," a "friend," "my cousin," etc.

But when I mentioned a large hotel being built next to a *wadi* (i.e. in a precarious setting), one of the research guys stated the full (first, father's, grandfather's and tribe) name of the owner. It was like hearing my mother say curse words.

"DID YOU JUST SAY HIS NAME?" I asked.

He shrugged and said, "he knows he does not have the right to build there." This has happened several times and it is always a shock to hear a man who calls the co-worker who shares his office "my colleague" for more than five years come out with the full name of a man who has acquired public land.

Thus, there are alternating levels of expectations of privacy. The contents of my shopping cart and my clothes are up for public discussion, but how I might choose to alter my house is not under the control of anyone but myself. However, if a person acquires land that was zoned to be public or should not be developed, their full name will enter public discourse as, by taking a resource perceived to be public, they are no longer protected by rules of civility.

Privacy: Islamic houses[4]

Othmann argues that

> traditional Islamic homes involves four main layers of privacy: (a) privacy between neighbors' dwellings, (b) privacy between males and females, (c) privacy between family members inside a home, and (d) individual privacy. Such privacy requirements are usually met through careful design by ensuring the safety of the family and separating the private life from public associations.
>
> (2015 15)

The point about Islamic houses being divided into male and female spaces is a frequent motif, for example, Al Thahab, Mushatat and Abdelmonem state that "the socio-cultural notion of the private/public segregation refers to the meaning of the private realm and its different spaces. The female domain provides a high degree of desired privacy, secrecy, concealments and isolation from the attention of the public" (2014 240).

Writing about Yemen, Kotnik explains that "Women move freely even through exterior space by veiling their bodies, allowing only their social class to be identified ... Thus, the veil functions as a movable interior space that allows women to penetrate exterior space" (2005 480).

To keep the interior space private, there should be "various external design interventions, such as the location and design of entrance doors, the placement and sizes of windows and openings, the control of building heights and balconies, and the incorporation of internal courtyards and gendered spaces" (Othman, Aird and Buys 2015 15). The careful work on designing the home is important as the home has to simultaneously fulfill the both personal/private needs of "a safe and private place for personal and family's sanctuary" and the need "to extend hospitality to neighbors and enhance relationships with the society" (2015 15). A house cannot function simply as a private retreat because "Hospitality is integral in pre-Islamic

Arab culture and its value has been approved by Islamic divine sources as it supports the creation of a tied, faithful community" (Al Mohanndi, Furlan and Major 2019).

Hegazy states that

> In the traditional Omani architecture, the main apparent principle which affects the house design relates to Islamic conventions of privacy. The introverted character of the dwelling, the arrangement and the orientation of rooms and viewing windows, towards the interior courtyard, the bent entrance (*majaz*), the exterior screened windows and the combination of the covered interior courtyard and the wind catcher (*malqaf*) are all distinctive characteristics of the Omani house. All these features are representing the response to the needed high level of privacy.
>
> (2015 190)

This idea obtains in Dhofar with a slight difference in that much of what I have read makes the public/private barrier at the second threshold (the wall around the house) or fourth (the *salle*). For example, Ghannam's excellent "Mobility, Liminality, and Embodiment in Urban Egypt" (2011) about the adjustments an Egyptian brother and sister make, and have made over time, before leaving the house.

Whereas in Dhofar, I see the public/private barrier at the last threshold (interior of the house/bedrooms) as from the moment a person walks out of their bedroom, they are on display even within the confines of the house because it is impossible to know who might be in the hallway: a son's wife, a cousin, a repairman, or a neighbor's child. At every place in the house except for the bedroom, a *hakli* must be completely clothed in a *wasar* (sarong) and t-shirt (and perhaps *dishdash*) for men and a *dhobe* (long, loose Dhofari-style dress) and *lossi* (matching light cotton headscarf) for women.[5]

One key difference between Dhofari women and Yemeni/Saudi women is that in women-only gatherings in their own home or others, Dhofari women continue to wear their *dhobe* and *lossi* or *abayah* and *sheila*. At wedding parties, female relatives of the groom might wear sheer, net *sheilas* and body-hugging dresses, but almost all other women will be in highly decorated but very loose *dhobes*. In the *salle*, a woman will not remove her head covering even if there is no chance a man might interrupt the gathering and a female past puberty will never leave her room in small, short or tight clothing such as a miniskirt. This is in contrast to Yemen and Saudi Arabia where women will take off the *abayah* and *sheila* at women-only parties.[6]

This to me is an echo of the previous lifeways of transhumance and living in open shelters and/or closed round houses in which all who came had to be welcomed and invited in. It can also be seen in the designs of the first cement block houses in which the open space (either large room or wide hallway) had visual access to every door inside the house. Being in a house meant more privacy, but never complete privacy.

Thus in Dhofar, Othman, Aird, and Buys' list of privacies are conflated so that "(a) privacy between neighbors' dwellings, (b) privacy between males and females, [and] (c) privacy between family members inside a home" are all handled at the wall/*bab*, door and *salle*/*majlis* thresholds, while individual privacy may only be found within a bedroom (2015 15). For example, a man's dress and demeanor in his *majlis* will not be different than that in a neighbor's *majlis*, his office or his café.[7]

Privacy: thresholds

"Threshold" is a useful term for thinking about privacy in houses as it can mean both the beginning and the terminus, marking the places which distinguish where different sets of people are allowed to be. The first threshold is knowing where a person's house is. Most streets in Salalah aren't sign posted with names; I don't know the names of any of the four streets where I lived or the name of the street any of my friends live on. Some houses have numbers, but that's rare and people navigate by landmarks, usually mosques and schools. When asked for address, most Dhofaris write the name of the area they live in and/or the post office box from their work.

Thus a Dhofari won't know/have any way to know where another Dhofari lives unless they are specifically told. A man might be friends with another man for five or more years and never know where he lives; this lack of knowledge is not necessarily seen as a sign of emotional distance, but that knowledge is given when it needs to be given, not before. The jump, so to speak, from not knowing to knowing between friends is done for a reason. For example, if a friend's father has died and he must go to the house to pay his condolences. As unmarried girls in their late teens/early 20s are usually not allowed to visit friends, best friends for ten years or more might not know each other's house, but a visit is usually allowed on the day of a wedding.

The normal way to tell someone where you live is to "drop a pin" using WhatsApp or another social media platform so the person uses an online navigation system. This is how food orders are delivered.

The second threshold is the wall around the house which is the limit for strangers. The *hosh* and house are seen as inviolate. Several Dhofari men have told me that they have the right to shoot any person within the walls of their yard who has not been invited.

There is usually a bell next to the *bab*, the door in the wall, which strangers will use.[8] Even if they are bringing food from a restaurant and have been called to the house, delivery men will not enter the *hosh* until the front door is opened and they are either called to come closer; more often a child is sent out with the money to bring the food in. During Ramadan, sometimes packages of food are distributed through neighborhoods. The *bab* will be opened and the box set on the ground next to it. Young men coming to pick up friends will honk, but not drive into the *hosh*.

The *hosh* is perceived as part of the house and a space for in-group members only. It is where children play, women work (e.g. hang clothes to dry, water plants) and relax (sitting on the steps in the afternoon or evening) and men wash cars. If the sliding gate (for cars to enter) is open, passers-by can see in, but they should not be seen to be looking. If a stranger is too obviously staring, women might cover the bottom half of their face with their *lossi* and children might yell or throw stones.

In the mountains, the wall around a house is much lower as it is used to keep animals out, not to block sightlines, but a stranger must approach with respect: parking away from the wall, greeting anyone in sight and calling out loudly if there is no one visible. Usually, a visitor will be given a place to sit in the *dekka* with everyone already there sifting so the visitor has the best place.

Doors are the third threshold; "entrance doors in traditional Muslim homes are placed away from the main street and not directly facing the opposite neighbors" (Othman, Aird, and Buys 2015 15–16). As explained above, no one comes to the door leading to the front hallway and *salle* unless a relative, neighbor or invited and one should step back away from the door (definitely off the "welcome mat") after knocking; close friends and relatives might knock, then open the door but would immediately call out to alert the inhabitants.

A man coming to the *majlis* door would be less formal, assuming that the interior door (to the house) was closed and that he was in a semipublic area. *Majlis* doors are usually open, in which case he would knock and immediately walk in, calling out a greeting. If the door is closed, he would knock, wait a moment then open it and walk in.

Once in a *majlis* or *salle*, a guest is free to stay anywhere in the room, with the caveat that the best seating is usually given to older people. They may use the attached bathroom but not stray any farther afield. A man in the *majlis* should never touch/go near the door to the house and a woman should not walk down the main hallway past the *salle*'s bathroom. Even close female relatives and neighbors would normally not go into the kitchen, for example, to drop off a dish.

Any person bringing something to the house by the kitchen door would follow the same rules as coming to one of the front doors: knock and step back if not the person is not well-known to the inhabitants, knock, enter and call out if known. Once in, they should not attempt to leave the kitchen.

Bedrooms are the most private area. Only the people who sleep in the room, their children, parents or siblings normally may enter. Visiting male relatives usually sleep in *majlis* (sometimes in male relative's room); visiting female relatives sleep in a female's or guest bedroom. House tours are usually given only for new houses or a close friend/relative is visiting for the first time.[9] During wedding parties in which a bride sits in her new room in her finery, female relatives from the bride's and grooms' side can come to see her and the room.

A female live-in servant may go anywhere in the house but would knock and wait before entering a bedroom. Her own room, usually near the kitchen or on the roof, has the same privacy; no one should enter without her permission.

Male servants never live in the house; if it is a large property, they might have a room in a separate building but this is rare. They usually come to cook and clean in the late morning or afternoon/evening, entering and leaving via the kitchen door. If employed long term and known to the family, they can walk from the kitchen to *salle* without calling out, but would never enter the bedrooms. Men coming to do repair work must call out when entering the house and be escorted/supervised within the house.

As many men (sometimes families) spend weekends camping, I want to briefly mention that these cultural understandings of thresholds are valid also for temporary living quarters as discussed in detail in Chapter 6. First, only the group of good friends will know the place they usually drink tea/camp. If anyone else approaches, they should be respectful, meaning dim headlights, not drive or park close to the campsite and call out before getting out of the car. If it is a stranger asking for help, a person sitting by the fire will stand up and walk over to the car; the stranger should not immediately walk up to the fire. If the person knows the group, they should park and, as they approach, loudly call out greetings. In over 15 years of having picnic dinners with Dhofari men, I have never seen a man quietly approach a campfire.

Usually there is a mat by the fire, with the sleeping bags and foodstuff set back on another mat further away. Newcomers should greet every person, sit by the fire and show no interest in any other part of the campsite. The area around the fire is the *majlis* and the only accepted pathways are to/from cars and to/from the sea if on a beach. If sleeping bags are set out, even if there is no tent or cover, that area is treated as a bedroom and should not be walked near or commented on.

Privacy: sightlines and space syntax

"Obviously, there is a relationship between how human beings organize their lives and how they shape spaces for their activities, such as the way the spatial setup affects the opportunities for and creates limitations to human activity" (van Nes and Yamu 2018 3). One theory of explaining "spatial setups" is space syntax which was

> Developed by Bill Hillier and his colleagues at the University College London, it has been applied in urban studies since the 1980s. This method consists of calculating configurative spatial relationships in built environments ... Space syntax measures the two primary all-to-all (all street segments to all others) relationships. Firstly, it measures the to-movement – or accessibility – potential of each street segment

> with respect to all others. Secondly, it measures the through-movement potential of each street segment with respect to all pairs of others. (1, 2)

In other words, space syntax is focused on the connectivity and sightlines within cities. Although it was conceived for use in urban environments, I think the theory is also helpful for thinking about how houses work, as exemplified in Al Mohannadi, Furlan and Major's "Socio-Cultural Factors Shaping the Spatial Form of Traditional and Contemporary Housing in Qatar: A Comparative Analysis based on Space Syntax" (2019). In this article, the authors discuss types of integration within houses such as

> gradual connectivity in which the intensity of connective spaces ranges from the least connective private rooms to the most connective central courtyard ... The second scenario is balanced connectivity, revealing an ideal situation of the traditional house ... The third scenario is intermediate connectivity achieved via entrances, porches, corridors, arcades and other intermediate architectural forms

This is helpful for thinking about Dhofari houses by asking: what connects to what? Looking at a floor plan, one might state that the *majlis* connects directly to the main hallway, but in terms of daily usage, the door is far more of a barrier than might be first apparent. Only children between about six and ten might approach the door at speed without adjusting clothing and/or attitude. Young children are kept out of the *majlis* unless supervised as they might create a mess, older girls and boys approach with decorum in case there are visitors, men will call out to announce themselves to women in the *salle* and women will knock to announce themselves to men in the *majlis*.

On the other hand, the two main doors (to *majlis* and front hallway) might be seen as significant barriers but they are often partially or completely left open in *hakli* houses as the house is designed so that when looking in the door to the front hallway an outsider can only see a blank wall or part of an empty hallway.[10] It is the door in the wall (*bab*) that is the barrier to strangers. Relatives and close neighbors have the right to walk to the doors, knock, call out and enter.

In the same way, a floor plan showing a long main hallway might be interpreted as a house with easy access to all parts of the building but even if there is no visual signal, guests may not walk the length of the hallway. A kitchen or side entrance might look inconsequential as they are not decorated with porticos or other prominent design features, but they might be the most used as those living on the first or second floor might regularly bypass the main entrance.

Thus one has to pair a blueprint with a cultural understanding of how Dhofaris live so that the reading is complete. For example, the "best location" for a bedroom depends on several factors. A suite of rooms on the ground floor might be given to the oldest relative (for ease of walking to *majlis/salle*) or a young married son (so that he is the first bothered if anyone comes to the house). A couple might want more connectivity and take a suite near the head of the stairs at the front of the house or less connectivity and live on the top floor at the back for more privacy.

Privacy: viewsheds

The term "viewshed" (derived from "watershed," often used interchangeably with "isovist") is also helpful to conceptualize space inside and outside of houses. It means what can be seen if one is standing at X point, i.e. the line-of-sight for people living in and visiting a house. I would like to discuss four issues regarding viewsheds in homes: male/female, hallways, ground/first floor and viewsheds of individual rooms.

The first point is that men and women have different viewsheds. In Salalah and Dhofari towns, it is normal for a group of women to sit on the steps of the house in the afternoons and early evenings in good weather to watch children playing. They have free visual access to the adjoining houses and street as the top step is often above the level of the wall. Women visit and are in touch with female neighbors far more than men are with male neighbors.

However, men will not sit outside their houses in towns; they will go to an outdoors café or scenic spot with male friends. Thus, in towns, women have more knowledge about the area and people directly around their house than men. Whereas in more rural areas men usually have more information about their houses' surroundings as they will sit in the *dekka* with women and often walk in the area around their house to look after animals or supervise shepherds.

In terms of other people's houses in towns, a man approaching a house will often park outside the *hosh*, so he might glance at the house and greet children playing in the *hosh* as he walks to the *majlis* door. A woman entering a house will often be driven right to the front door so she will have less chance to see the house as a total entity. When she opens the car door, she will be too close to see the entire façade and won't have time to notice details of the *hosh*. If the *majlis* door is open, she might glance inside to see the space, decorations and most of the men sitting whereas the men would only be able to see a black-clad shape. If the men are relatives, she will know who the men are but they will not know who she is.

Once inside a house, a visiting woman will see more than a visiting man as a man can only see the *majlis* and who comes in or out of the *majlis* door; a visiting woman will see the main hallway and *salle*, as well as anyone who lives in the house who is entering or exiting unless that person uses the kitchen door.

As Stephenson argues about houses in Kuwait "women are extended greater flexibility of movement in the home and move in and out of the household spaces in ways men cannot" (2011 21). For example, men may only know the *salle* of their own house, their parent's and perhaps a sister's. A groom will only know the *majlis* of his wife's relatives' houses but the new bride would have the chance to see the *majlis* during parties at her husband's relatives' houses.

A second issue is that hallways in Dhofar are much wider than the arm span. Thus, although houses aren't built "open plan," from certain vantage points, you can see many different spaces. Standing in the main, ground-floor hallway, one can usually see the front door, the entrance to the kitchen, the main stairs and into the *salle*. From the top of the stairs one can usually see down to the main ground-floor hallway, the open space (sometimes used as a *salle*) at the top of the stairs and the doors to most or all of the first-floor bedrooms.

Further, stairs to upper floors are usually not visible to someone standing at the front door; they are inset from the main hallway and sometimes hidden behind a (non-load-bearing) wall so that one has to be almost directly in front of it before it is seen. If the stairway is visible from the door, it will always have a landing so one can only see half the flight of stairs. There is never a direct view of the upper stories.

Lastly, sitting rooms, bedrooms and kitchen all have empty space in the middle of the space: the *majlis* and *salle* have stuffed chairs and sofas around the walls with coffee tables next to them and an open space in the middle; bedrooms have the bed and cupboards/dressers against the walls and open space in the middle of the room and kitchens have counters set around the walls.

Furthermore, all rooms are built square or rectangular; there are no nooks or closets. Books, dishes, clothes, beddings, etc. are stored in pieces of furniture that are placed next to a wall. Dining and kitchen tables are placed close to one wall or where two walls meet. To look at this from a child's perspective, while playing hide-and-go-seek, it isn't possible to fit behind furniture and there aren't any closets. The only places to hide are behind doors or inside kitchen cabinets or bedroom clothes cupboards.

The effect of this pattern is that when you walk into a room, you can see everyone and everything immediately, especially if people are sitting down as Dhofaris always try to keep everyone in the group in view whether sitting on sofas placed next to the walls in a *majlis* or on a mat near a fire for a picnic.[11]

One consequence of these building and furnishing conventions is that for some Dhofaris, "privacy" refers to their personal thoughts and emotions as they are almost always in actual or potential sight of other people when in a house. Privacy might never be found in a bedroom as children might share a room (once close to puberty, in single-gender groups) and young children stay with their parents.

Another consequence is that housing design and living patterns create the necessity of always being modestly dressed as explained above.

For example, a man leaving his bedroom might see the live-in maid, a repair person, his brother's wife who lives across the hallway, the teenage daughter of another brother or an older female relative who is staying for a few days.

Privacy: creating seclusion in public spaces within houses

A *majlis* and *salle* are usually large enough to seat at least 20 people and are square/rectangular with all the furniture pushed against the walls. Houses are built from concrete blocks and have tile floors, sometimes only partially covered with an area rug, thus everyone in the room can see and hear each other. In a sizable, echoing space, how do people manage to have private conversations?

Having a large sitting room with a perfect view of every person combined with the cultural need for adults to always show a calm and positive expression means that Dhofaris develop communication codes, work at never showing emotion and sometimes deliberately tune out conversations.

In American families, there can be family-only codes such as saying "FHB" (family hold back) at a party, meaning there might not be enough food so family should eat less so the guests can have as much as they want, but it is more common for family members simply to make verbal requests/demands in front of visitors.

In Dhofar, it is usual for older relatives to direct younger people with quick eye movements (such as looking at the AC unit to tell someone to make the room cooler) or hand gestures. When I taught a cultural studies class and asked students to come up with examples of non-verbal communication, many explained the signals for "bring fresh tea" and "bring more food" that older siblings and parents used.

The cultural understanding is that a guest should have a seamless and stress-free time so the hosting family try to create a calm atmosphere through private gestures and self-control. For example, if a guest catches that the host is asking for more food to be brought, the guest has to protest that they don't want more food, leading to, for the host, an unwanted discussion. It's better to give the signal without anyone noticing.

Several times at weddings, I have sat next to women who were part of the hosting family and often another woman would come over to, almost inaudibly, ask a question or give information. The two would discuss hosting emergencies (not enough food, the bride will arrive very late, etc.) with no visible sign of agitation so that the dozens of women who could see them had no idea that there was a problem. While writing this book, I attended one wedding in which one of the newlyweds' siblings received shocking news in the middle of the party. This person had no visible reaction and when talking to the person who caused the problem, gave no sign of distress.

There is also a cultural norm of tuning out, turning away from and/or politely ignoring visitors. This behavior means that people can have private conversations, after the requirements of hospitality and respect have been met, and that a person who is new to the group has time to adjust.

A female Dhofari friend (A) lived outside of Dhofar for several months where she met an Omani woman (X). When A's brother (B) came to visit A, he met X's husband (Y). So when X, Y and their children came to visit Dhofar, A invited them to dinner at her house with the understanding that B would host Y in the *majlis* with A's male relatives and A would host X in the *salle* with A's female relatives. I was invited as I had also met X previously.

When X and Y arrived, they were greeted by A and B who stood outside the door then brought the guests to the respective sitting rooms. When X walked into the *salle*, all the women (X's mom, sisters, sisters-in-law, and nieces) greeted X and she was led to a sofa in the middle of the south wall, a few spaces down from A's mom. A sat in the middle of the east wall and I was in the middle of the north wall.

The first 20 minutes was the necessary polite, general conversation in which X asked about everyone's health and everyone asked X about her health, her family's health, her trip to Dhofar, where she was staying and if she liked the hotel while A was offering drinks and snacks to X and her children. The first round done, the second round started in which more specific questions were asked about X's health, the health of X's children and female relatives, their trip to Dhofar and X started to ask about how A's mother was doing and who were the other women in the room. A's mother was included in all the questions and responses; X looked at her more frequently than anyone else and the other women, including me, listened to everything with polite attention.

Then we moved to the dining table (on the south side) to eat dinner, then back to the sofas and plates with desserts were passed around. A few minutes later, there was a gradual change in that A's mother and other female relatives turned their attention away from X by saying prayers using a *misbaha* (prayer beads), looking at their phones, talking to children or each other. A and X, more than $1\frac{1}{2}$ hours after X had arrived, were able to talk freely about people they knew/experiences they had had in common.

There were the same number of people sitting in the same places as when X had arrived, but instead of one person talking at a time with X and A's mother as the twin focal points, now A and X were a dyad. A's female relatives and I sat quietly, sometimes listening, sometimes talking to each other. As the time to leave grew closer, the talk again became more general with people offering X suggestions about where to go sightseeing and what restaurants to visit. X was invited back to the house, which she parried with how short their stay was and how they had relatives to visit.

In thinking about this visit beforehand, I had thought that it was too bad A and X would not get time alone (such as meeting at a coffee shop) to catch up. But what happened was that A's family created that conversational freedom for them, without changing the space or their locations, by shifting their attention away. In a room with ten women and five children, A and X were able to share reminiscences and catch up on mutual acquaintances for more than an hour.

To look at this issue from another angle, I was once visiting a Dhofari friend when an older female relative (M) stopped by. I had not met M before and was surprised that the younger women (N) with her was wearing elaborate make-up, a lot of jewelry and a highly decorated dress, shorter in front than usual for normal visiting. My friend looked at me and said "bride" in Arabic; women who are newly married usually dress up for visits in the weeks after the wedding, especially when meeting their husband's family. N had recently married M's son and M was bringing N to meet her new relatives. N sat silently, looking bored, as we spoke; I felt kind of sorry for her as she must have had several of these types of visits with her new mother-in-law.

But about two years later I saw that situation differently. A female Dhofari friend invited me to her wedding; I agreed with some trepidation as I had not met any of her family before. I arrived at the house for the party and her mother took me into the *salle*. I could hear quiet comments of women "placing me" (telling each other who I was) as I walked around to greet each woman. Once I sat down, all the women ignored me.

This might sound negative, but it was very freeing. I was in a tightly packed room with every seat taken. All the women were in pretty, loose dresses with lots of perfume, children ran in and out, maids came around offering tea, coffee, juice and water, as well as snacks; there were lots to see and do. Women who came in shook my hand and the women next to me encouraged me to eat and drink so I did not feel any hostility, just a sense that everyone had collectively decided to leave me alone. After about an hour, the woman next to me asked me a few simple questions, I think to test both my level of Arabic and my willingness to engage. When I answered readily, other women joined in with questions and we ended up having a lovely time, joking about husbands, travel, driving cars and studying.

As I drove home, I thought about the silent bride (N) and wondered if perhaps what I had marked as boredom was relief that the women in my friend's house had given her the same sort of emotional/psychological break by ignoring her so she could be with a lot of unfamiliar people without having to make conversation. These were women she would know and visit for the rest of her life and rather than perhaps making a misstep at the start of the relationship, she had the chance to look around, listen to the talk, and start to form ideas/opinions about the women before being expected to join in.

The spaces within a house for visiting are few and large, thus Dhofaris have created a series of behaviors that make accommodations for others. In certain circumstances, everyone will tacitly ignore people who want to talk about something that is of interest only to them and/or people who they feel might not want to or be able to join in the conversation. Being able to see and hear others in the same room does not automatically mean it is necessary to engage with them, so privacy is possible even in a crowded room.

Finally, sometimes family members will make sure a room is empty for people who need to have a confidential conversation. For example, women usually return to their mother's house after they have their first child and one family I know lives in a house with a mother, several unmarried daughters and several married sons and their families. When a married daughter came back to stay for a few weeks with her new baby, she and her husband met in the *majlis*. The husband was not a close relative so it would not be appropriate for him to spend a lot of time in the *salle* and it was not possible for him to come to her bedroom as this would mean entering the private area of the house. The men in the house willingly did not use the *majlis* at certain times so their sister's husband could visit her and the baby alone. I have heard of similar examples of a husband coming to visit his estranged wife at her parent's house and her male relatives leaving the *majlis* so they could talk in private.

In one house I lived in, my bedroom window was opposite the kitchen door of a neighboring house and for a terrible series of nights, a man and woman stood outside the door and had long, anguished conversations. When I asked one of the research guys, "Why are they talking THERE at 2 am?" He answered, "If they are divorcing, he can't take her in his car and that house is small, probably there is no other place to talk."

Privacy: windows

One of the hardest concepts for language students to grasp is to rethink common metaphors. In the Middle East, the full moon is seen as a time of safety and peace because you can see everything without the heat of the sun, unlike the negative connotations of danger (werewolves, vampires) found in North America.

It's the same way with architectural details. Someone from the UK might argue that windows should be used to look out of, thus a window should be made of clear glass, uncovered during the day, often uncovered at night and, in good weather, left open to let in fresh air. However, the front door should be closed all the time.

None of this obtains in Dhofar. Windows are either made of opaque glass (in bathrooms and the kitchen) or are completely covered with treatments which usually have several layers, such as a heavy or lined, light-blocking fabric with a tulle/sheer overlay which is sometimes tied back or swept to one side [jabot] with a fringe and/ or beading. There are usually heavy frame elements with a valance or pelmet/cornice with swags.

Drapes seldom have a simple, open style such as tabs and if there is a visible rod, there is almost always a finial. Café curtains are rare; usually, the whole window is covered at all times. Ground-floor windows and the window at the first landing of a stairwell are frequently barred. However, depending on the weather and the neighborhood (how close are the other houses and whether the neighbors are 'known' and/or family) the front door might be left open during the day.

As Dhofaris are always fully dressed in their houses, sometimes an upper story window in a public part of the house (for example, a family *salle* at the top of the stairs) will only be covered with sheer fabric if there are no direct, near sightlines. Driving around at night, one can sometimes get a glimpse of an indistinct shape moving, but there is nothing like the large, uncovered, picture windows in the living rooms of most American mid-western towns.

Another way to explain the non-use of windows is that before the infrequent, severe rainstorms, Dhofaris often cover the house windows with blue or gray/opaque tarps, which are sometimes left up for weeks or months after the storm. Some houses are built with no windows on the side that is facing another property. The only *majlis* in a house in the city which I have been in with open curtains was located next to the high wall surrounding the house so you couldn't see anything except the wall.

If someone needs to see something outside the house, they go to the front door and look out. In over 15 years of visiting Dhofari homes, I have never seen an adult pull back a curtain to look outside. Small kids will sometimes do so and then tell an adult in the room what they see, but usually grown-ups don't show their faces in a window.

There are two exceptions to this rule. The first is betrothed women; as vom Bruck explains about Yemen

> When the groom comes to the bride's father's house in order to make arrangements for the celebration, the bride might get a glimpse of him from an angle of a window or through a curtain slit. The bride's curiosity is interpreted as interest in her future spouse and is not discouraged. (1997 153)

Several Dhofari women have told me about either peeking through a window to see their groom or female relatives who have done so. One male informant joked with me about this tradition and how men feel walking into the house knowing they are being observed.

The second exception is rental houses usually have sitting rooms with sheer curtains as such houses usually have higher than normal surrounding walls and are located outside of congested areas. The understanding is that no one can see in and everyone in the house is related, so window coverings are not necessary. Rental houses sometimes also have larger windows because there are often small jungle gyms/playground equipment and/or pools; with floor-to-ceiling windows, adults can easily sit inside and watch the children.

The information above is for houses in and close to towns; outside of towns, as there are either no neighbors or the neighboring houses belong to relatives, there is less concern about privacy. The surrounding walls are low (waist-high) and serve primarily to keep livestock away from the home. Houses often have a *dekka*, an outside seating area accessible from the front door. Sometimes it is covered and furnished; sometimes it is simply clean swept mats to sit on. If the house is built up and there is only a small landing in front of the main door, people will sit on the front steps in cool weather. Thus, although windows are similarly covered with fabric, people have far more visual access to their surroundings.

Privacy: neighbors

The four main ways I gather information are what informants tell me, what I read in books and ask informants to comment on, what I see and what I am told not to do. Regarding neighbors, most of my data is from what informants told me not to do as to talk about neighbors is not acceptable in *hakli* cultures.[12] "We have good neighbors *alhamdulillah*" is only appropriate statement; the correct behavior is to try not to see and, if something is seen, never discuss any speech or actions done by neighbors.

To say that a person "looks out of windows" is the only negative comment I have heard from informants and friends about a neighbor. I have heard that expression three times and always with a sense of exasperation. The issue is not simply the "looking" but the interest in other people's lives and telling others what was seen: two very unattractive traits.

In all three cases, I was told about the neighbor because circumstances warranted my knowing. For example, a Dhofari friend (X) asked me to be sure to wear Dhofari clothing when I visited her because she had a neighbor (Y) who "looks out of windows" and if Y saw a Western person enter X's house, Y would tell people and insist on knowing who I was and why was I visiting. In the other two cases, when asking Dhofaris if they were free for a visit, the friends told me that there was a problem within the family because of a neighbor who "looked out of windows," misconstrued something seen and told other people causing a "touch" (problem) that needed to be fixed.

What I have learned through living as the only non-Omani in different neighborhoods and being admonished about proper neighborly behavior is that one must always conduct oneself with respect and restraint no matter what the people next door are doing. When I asked, what can I do about the neighbor boy who is throwing stones at me? The answer was, "nothing" (although I did finally go to talk to his mother). What can I do about my neighbor who has workers that start drilling holes in concrete at 6 am on weekends? Nothing. What can I do about my neighbor who is drilling a well and, as he does not want anyone to notice this activity, drills from midnight to 5 am while, of course, staying at another house to avoid the noise? Nothing. What can I do about a neighbor who paves the alley way next to my house with cheap tiles which break, making walking and driving hazardous? Nothing.[13]

Another example of the understandings that good Dhofaris never try to see what the neighbors are up to is the fact that although almost all people in Salalah have easy (indoor staircase) access to flat, usually tiled-floor roofs, people seldom use them. I happily discovered the fun of leaning over my roof parapet so I could see down into the beautiful garden in the *hosh* of my neighbors' house, only to be told that this was completely unacceptable behavior. I had the right to stand on my roof as I pleased but I do not have the right look down over the edge. One informant told me a neighbor's *hosh* is "not for you," it is "for the people so they can take their rest." If you want to see people, you must go "by the door."

This reminded me of a fact I learned when I was working on food issues: no culture eats all of the available food resources. For example, Dhofaris don't eat sea turtles. In the same way, cultures with similar physical structures will use them in totally different ways. Some Arab cultures use flat roofs as extra living or sleeping space and, to me, sitting on the roof would seem a useful option in good weather. A few informants told me about sleeping on the roof in hot weather in the past, but now with air-conditioners, they no longer do. One informant told me, if you want to see sit outside, "rent a house or go to the mountain."

When I put a tent on the roof of two houses I lived in to enjoy the night air, my Dhofar friends/informants treated me with the same strained politeness that I would use on a person who wore a ball gown to the beach: my best wishes to you doing something that makes you happy which I would never think of doing.

Privacy: acoustical and olfactory

While the societal expectation is that to avoid drawing attention, Dhofaris will not make loud noises in public, at home whatever noise is produced is no one else's business.[14] When I walk into friends' houses in Dhofar, I feel like walking into a museum on a Tuesday morning: windows covered so no sunlight, very clean floor without any clutter, cool air, decorated walls and, most importantly, no noise, no sense of any other people. Even in houses where I know there are more than 20 people living and several cars are parked outside, unless there are small children playing the *salle*, there is utter silence.

However, if someone wants to make noise, that is their right. For example, kids playing/screaming in the *hosh* or outside on the street are not asked to/expected to be quiet even at 1 or 2 am. If there is a wedding party, it's fine to blast music at high levels until 3 or 4 am. Boys coming to pick up friends will blast the car stereo and honk repeatedly in the middle of the night.[15]

Within the house, children are usually free to make whatever noise they would like except if there are important guests. Further, the noise from the *salle* should not be heard in the *majlis*, but there is usually a TV on and a closed door, so people are not hypothetically tip-toeing around in their own homes. Shouting in anger, for example, a mother yelling at a child and between siblings, is accepted but might cause an older person to intervene.

Discussing Jeddah, Maneval explains a similar cultural understanding

> While much emphasis was placed on shielding bodies from view and on the regulation of physical access to people, the permeability of walls to sound did not seem to pose a problem. The close proximity of neighbouring houses and the large latticed openings in the facades hardly prevented the spread of sounds between buildings or from a building to the street
>
> (2019 74)

Smell is a very important factor as, unlike some cultures, the smell of cooking food is not perceived as positive. Kitchen doors are closed during meal prep and the extractor fan is turned on. While there are almost always snacks and/or fruit on display in the *salle* and *majlis*, cooked food is taken away as soon as everyone has finished eating and *luban* (frankincense) or air freshener is immediately used. Women burn *luban* almost every morning and often at sunset.

Dhofari informants have repeatedly told me that people should make "a good smell for neighbors," by being careful to not have anything that produces a bad smell in the *hosh* but that sounds are "not your business."

Privacy: photos

In general, there are three times in which photos of decorated home interiors are sent to friends or relatives and/or posted on social media: newlyweds rooms, "we are ready" and "good words." Thus while parts of the house are never exposed to public view *in person*, they may be shown through images which are sent without identifying names.

As visiting other people's houses is usually only done between relatives and neighbors and is almost always confined to the *salle* or *majlis*, sending out photos of the room prepared for newlyweds means that Dhofaris can share images of a bedroom and bathroom (sometimes also sitting room) that normally only the bride and groom's close relatives would see.

What I call "we are ready" photos show the preparations in a *majlis* or *salle* for a happy event such as a party for a birthday, graduation, promotion, award, special person visiting, wedding or an *iftar* meal during Ramadan.[16]

"Good words" images are commonly sent between friends and relatives in Dhofar. Sometimes a person, usually female, will take a decorative photo of the *majlis*, *salle* or object, such as decorative lamp or teacup, and write "good morning," an uplifting message, words of encouragement or a religious maxim and send this to friends/relatives. [17]

These types of photos circulate widely and allow others to see parts of the house that are usually not visible. Those who received the image directly from the photographer might know that this is from the sender's house but most will think it is a pretty image and send it on to others. Thus, many people can see the interior without knowing whose house it is so privacy is protected as either the artist's name is either not attached, or only the first name or a teknonymy/paedonymic, i.e. *Umm* (mother) with the name of the oldest son is given.

The primary purpose is to increase bonds of friendship but these kinds of pictures can also be used to help gather design ideas. Home- and food-styling magazines are not common in Dhofar, so people use the circulating images to get inspiration for their own homes.

People who are building a house will often take photos of the construction stages, but these are usually only sent to close friends and relatives who know not to forward or post them on social media.

There are two other kinds of house photos which are often posted on social media: houses for rent and for sale. The owner will take photos and superimpose a name and phone number so that whoever is interested can call.

Coda

I would like to end with two personal reflections. First, I would like to thank the Omani government for taking the coronavirus seriously, implementing lockdowns and mask requirements to keep people safe and providing free vaccine shots and boosters. Living alone in a foreign country during a pandemic was very stressful. I am especially grateful for the team responsible for the information graphics; having information explained in clear and simple terms was very helpful. There are many samples of their work on my website.

Secondly, given that my academic background is literature and travel writing, it might seem odd that I decided to write about houses, but I grew up in a home in which everyone had strong opinions about how to live and an active interest in building decks, planting gardens, finding a rug in exactly the right shade of blue and putting the sofa there, no, not there, there, a little to the right, no, now forward a little.

The root of this problem was that when he was in his early 20s, my father walked into Louisburg Square in Boston and thought, "everyone should live like this." That collection of houses changed his life; he became an urban planner and spent more than 60 years thinking, talking, writing and teaching about how to create better-organized houses, neighborhoods and cities. My mother plans gardens and both siblings have planned renovations of their houses down to the trim on the underside of cabinets.

I thought I had escaped this legacy until I got interested in how Dhofaris designed kitchens as part of my foodways project. I realized that I am not interested in decorating or remodeling, but I love listening to people's stories about how they live in their houses, what choices they make and why.

It was odd spending two years researching and writing about houses at exactly the time that I was stuck in mine; for a few months in the spring of 2020 I left only once a week to get groceries. I didn't leave Salalah from July 2019 until June 2021 and only visited a few other houses during that time. I am grateful for my informants' kindness and willingness to take and send photos, do phone interviews, answer quick questions on WhatsApp and trust me with so many details of how they live.

Notes

1 The second was male academic writing decrying the shallowness of shopping malls, a topic I hope to discuss further after this book is published.
2 Except in the *khareef* season when the waves are 2–4 meters high.
3 Too much should not be read into the fact that a woman call the house where she lives "my father's house." This does not imply that she feels like a guest or is lacking agency; in the same manner a woman might refer to her son as "[the name of her husband's] son" or say "my husband and his son."
4 Cazacova and Yapicioglu address issues relating to privacy with two surveys of Dhofari women in "Residential Architecture: Evaluation of Tenants' Satisfaction in Private Culture" (2021). As our backgrounds, points of view and experiences are very different, I choose not to engage with this essay.
5 A man in a clean, white *dishdash* and sandals is ready for any possible occasion – work, funeral, wedding, visiting; if he is going camping or doing physical labor, he will simply take the *dishdash* off as a *wasar* (sarong) and t-shirt are always worn underneath.

Some Dhofari women prefer a housedress with a slightly different cut and/or decoration than the traditional Dhofari *dhobe*, but it would still have sleeves past the elbow and length at least past the knee. If a woman is leaving the house, she will cover her head with a large, square, black scarf which trails down past her shoulders or wear an *abayah* (long, loose black cloak) with a *sheila* (silky black headscarf).
6 See Pyburn (2003) and Le Renard (2014).
7 This is not directly related to privacy but it's important to note that, except for who leaves to go arrange for meals in the kitchen, if a group of women are sitting in a *salle*, it is difficult, if not impossible, to tell who lives in the house, who is a close female relative and who is a neighbor. In contrast to a culture in which, for example, the senior woman is in charge of the tea tray, in a Dhofari house, the tea tray might be placed closest to a guest. A woman might pour a cup for herself and a guest might pour for someone who lives in the house. Many times while visiting one female friend, one of her sisters (who don't live in her house) would hand me a cup of tea and I would pass it on to another guest.
8 There is no home mail delivery in Dhofar. People either rent a Post Office Box or have mail delivered to the Post Office Box for their work.
9 When houses are being built, friends might be brought in to see or photos of the progress might be shown. Since the Dhofaris I do research with kindly let me walk around their houses and/or share photos with me, I give a full tour of my house to them because I know the 'how do you live?' interest is mutual.
10 The same holds true for larger houses with a side entrance. The door is often left open but the passerby can only see a small, empty space with a door into the house (which is kept closed) and a few steps going up.
11 One way to keep a more rounded shape in a square or rectangular room is that instead of sectional sofas meeting at a 90° corner angles, either the corner section is angled, or a triangular arm rest is placed at the corner.

12 This is similar to the section in Chapter 3 about repair people. To speak badly about someone or to put someone's name into public discourse are both seen as shameful; it is even more shameful to speak of someone in whom one should have no interest. The *ne plus ultra* example is that a Dhofari man should never speak about a brother's wife.

13 I was taught another type of lesson after the water pump (controlled by a switch in my neighbor's *hosh*) was mysteriously turned off three times within a month in the hot season, meaning I didn't have running water in my apartment. When I hired a plumber who walked into the neighbor's *hosh* to turn the pump back on, my neighbor screamed at the plumber. I got mad and screamed at my neighbor. In telling the story later to the research guys I was told in no uncertain terms that the fault was mine. I should have called my landlord and let him deal with the neighbor as I clearly lacked the ability to handle the situation.

14 To be more specific, most Dhofaris choose to be circumspect in public to avoid being under observation but some use "look at me" behavior by talking loudly, gesticulating, wearing a lot of perfume and/or tight-fitting clothes. Some Dhofaris also signal "look at me being virtuous," i.e. preforming conservative beliefs in public in a way that attracts attention. For example, in an airplane, some Dhofari women and men make a very public controversy about refusing to sit next to opposite gender when boarding a plane, by talking with a raised voice, blocking the aisle, refusing to sit where asked, arguing with a stewardess, etc.

15 When asked "what's the hardest part about living in Dhofar?" My answer is always, "loud neighbors." I am not always able to live up to Dhofari standards. When a neighbor decided to raise chickens and I was woken up at 5 am two days in a row by the rooster, I complained. The chickens stayed but the rooster disappeared. If it hadn't, I would have disappeared it myself.

16 Photos are never taken of preparations for condolence visits and there is a gender divide as to what is photographed. After the preparations are done but before guests arrive, women photograph their *salle*, *majlis* or kitchen counter to show that they are respectful women, i.e. they have filled their requirements as a host. The photos proclaim, "Look what I have done for others!" On the other hand, women who are being honored by a party will take photos to show that they are respected. The photos proclaim, "Look what someone has done for me!"

17 I have never seen a man share a photo of preparations but men will share photos of a special guest in their *majlis* to show who they are hosting or photos at wedding parties. Sometimes they will post picnic photos with a platter heaped with rice and meat; the implication being that the man is with a group of friends at a scenic location.

Although the places and objects shown are different, the house is never the focus.

References

For photos and a full bibliography, please see: *Come From Away*. https://mariellerisse.com

Al Mohannadi, Asmaa Saleh, Raffaelo Furlan and Mark David Major. 2019. "Socio-Cultural Factors Shaping the Spatial Form of Traditional and Contemporary Housing in Qatar: A Comparative Analysis based on Space Syntax." *Proceedings of the 12th Space Syntax Symposium*.

Al Thahab, Ali, Sabah Mushatat and Mohammed Abdelmonem. 2014. "Between Tradition and Modernity: Determining Spatial Systems of Privacy in the Domestic Architecture of Contemporary Iraq." *ArchNet - International Journal of Architectural Research* 8.3: 238–250.

Cazacova, Liudmila and Balkiz Yapicioglu. 2021. "Residential Architecture: Evaluation of Tenants' Satisfaction in Private Culture." *WIT Transactions on Ecology and the Environment* 253: 409–22.

Ghannam, Farah. 2011. "Mobility, Liminality, and Embodiment in Urban Egypt." *American Ethnologist* 38.4: 790–800.

Hegazy, Soheir. 2015. "Cultural Sustainability between Traditional and Contemporary Omani Residences: A Comparative Case Study." *European Journal of Sustainable Development* 42: 185–94.

Kotnik, Toni. 2005. "The Mirrored Public Architecture and Gender Relationship in Yemen." *Space and Culture* 8.4: 472–83.

Le Renard, Amélie. 2014. *A Society of Young Women: Opportunities of Place, Power and Reform in Saudi Arabia*. Stanford: Stanford University Press.

Maneval, Stefan. 2019. *New Islamic Urbanism: The Architecture of Public and Private Space in Jeddah, Saudi Arabia*. London: UCL Press.

Othman, Zulkeplee, Rosemary Aird and Laurie Buys. 2015. "Privacy, Modesty, Hospitality, and the Design of Muslim Homes: A Literature Review." *Frontiers of Architectural Research* 4: 12–23. https://doi.org/10.1016/j.foar.2014.12.001

Pyburn, Anne. 2003. "Worthless Women," in *Personal Encounters: A Reader in Cultural Anthropology*. Linda Walbridge and April Sievert, eds. Boston: McGraw Hill. 9–14.

Stephenson, Lindsey. 2011. "Women and the Malleability of the Kuwaiti Dīwāniyya." *Journal of Arabian Studies* 1.2: 183–99.

van Nes, Akkelies and Claudia Yamu. 2018. "Space Syntax: A Method to Measure Urban Space Related to Social, Economic and Cognative Factors," in *The Virtual And the Real in Planning and Urban Design: Perspectives, Practices and Applications*. C. Yamu, A. Poplin, O. Devisch and G. de Roo, eds. Routledge: New York. 136–150.

Vom Bruck, Gabriele. 1997. "A House Turned Inside Out: Inhabiting Space in a Yemeni City." *Journal of Material Culture* 2.2: 139–72.

Index